The Silver Coin

Art and lettering by
Michael Walsh

¹¹ "The Diner" written by
James Tynion IV

¹² "'Til Dawn" written by
Stephanie Phillips

¹³ "Threshold" written by
Johnnie Christmas

¹⁴ "The Bad Year" written by
Pornsak Pichetshote

¹⁵ "Into the Fire" written by
Michael Walsh

Colored by
Toni Marie Griffin
and Michael Walsh

Edited by
Chris Hampton

*Warning: Issue 13 contains graphic images
related to childbirth, including potential miscarriage,
which may be disturbing to some readers.*

The Silver Coin is created by
Michael Walsh, Ed Brisson, Jeff Lemire, Kelly Thompson, and Chip Zdarsky

AGE COMICS, INC. • Robert Kirkman: Chief Operating Officer • Erik Larsen: Chief Financial Officer • Todd McFarlane: President • Marc Silvestri: Chief Executive Officer • Valentino: Vice President • Eric Stephenson: Publisher / Chief Creative Officer • Nicole Lapalme: Vice President of Finance • Leanna Caunter: Accounting Analyst • Sue Korpela: counting & HR Manager • Matt Parkinson: Vice President of Sales & Publishing Planning • Lorelei Bunjes: Vice President of Digital Strategy • Dirk Wood: Vice President of International es & Licensing • Ryan Brewer: International Sales & Licensing Manager • Alex Cox: Director of Direct Market Sales • Chloe Ramos: Book Market & Library Sales Manager • Emilio atista: Digital Sales Coordinator • Jon Schlaffman: Specialty Sales Coordinator • Kat Salazar: Vice President of PR & Marketing • Deanna Phelps: Marketing Design Manager • Drew zgerald: Marketing Content Associate • Heather Doornink: Vice President of Production • Drew Gill: Art Director • Hilary DiLoreto: Print Manager • Tricia Ramos: Traffic Manager Melissa Gifford: Content Manager • Erika Schnatz: Senior Production Artist • Wesley Griffith: Production Artist • Rich Fowlks: Production Artist • IMAGECOMICS.COM

The Diner

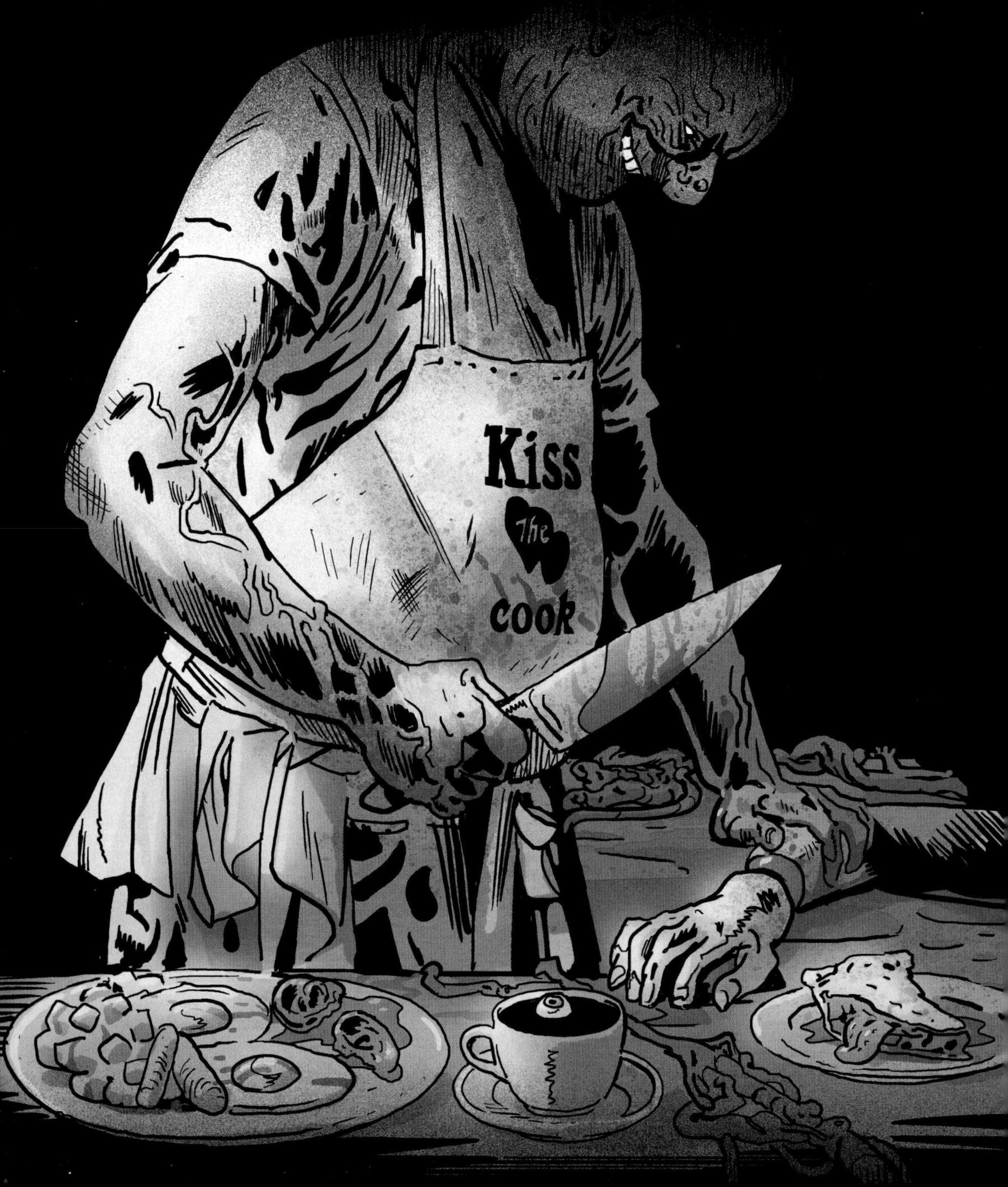
Kiss
The
cook

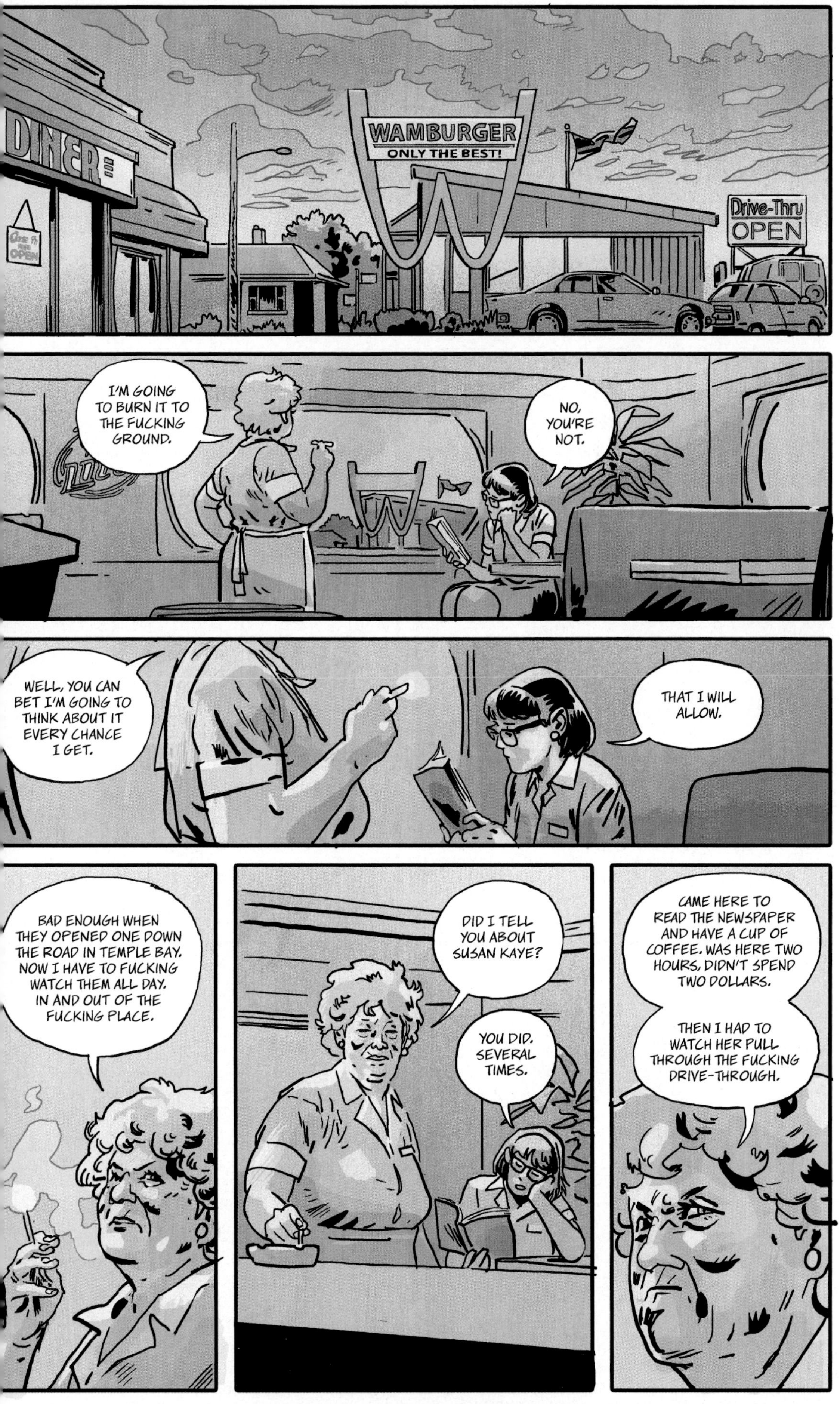
DINER
WAMBURGER
ONLY THE BEST!
Drive-Thru
OPEN
OPEN
I'M GOING TO BURN IT TO THE FUCKING GROUND.
NO, YOU'RE NOT.
WELL, YOU CAN BET I'M GOING TO THINK ABOUT IT EVERY CHANCE I GET.
THAT I WILL ALLOW.
BAD ENOUGH WHEN THEY OPENED ONE DOWN THE ROAD IN TEMPLE BAY. NOW I HAVE TO FUCKING WATCH THEM ALL DAY. IN AND OUT OF THE FUCKING PLACE.
DID I TELL YOU ABOUT SUSAN KAYE?
YOU DID. SEVERAL TIMES.
CAME HERE TO READ THE NEWSPAPER AND HAVE A CUP OF COFFEE. WAS HERE TWO HOURS, DIDN'T SPEND TWO DOLLARS.
THEN I HAD TO WATCH HER PULL THROUGH THE FUCKING DRIVE-THROUGH.

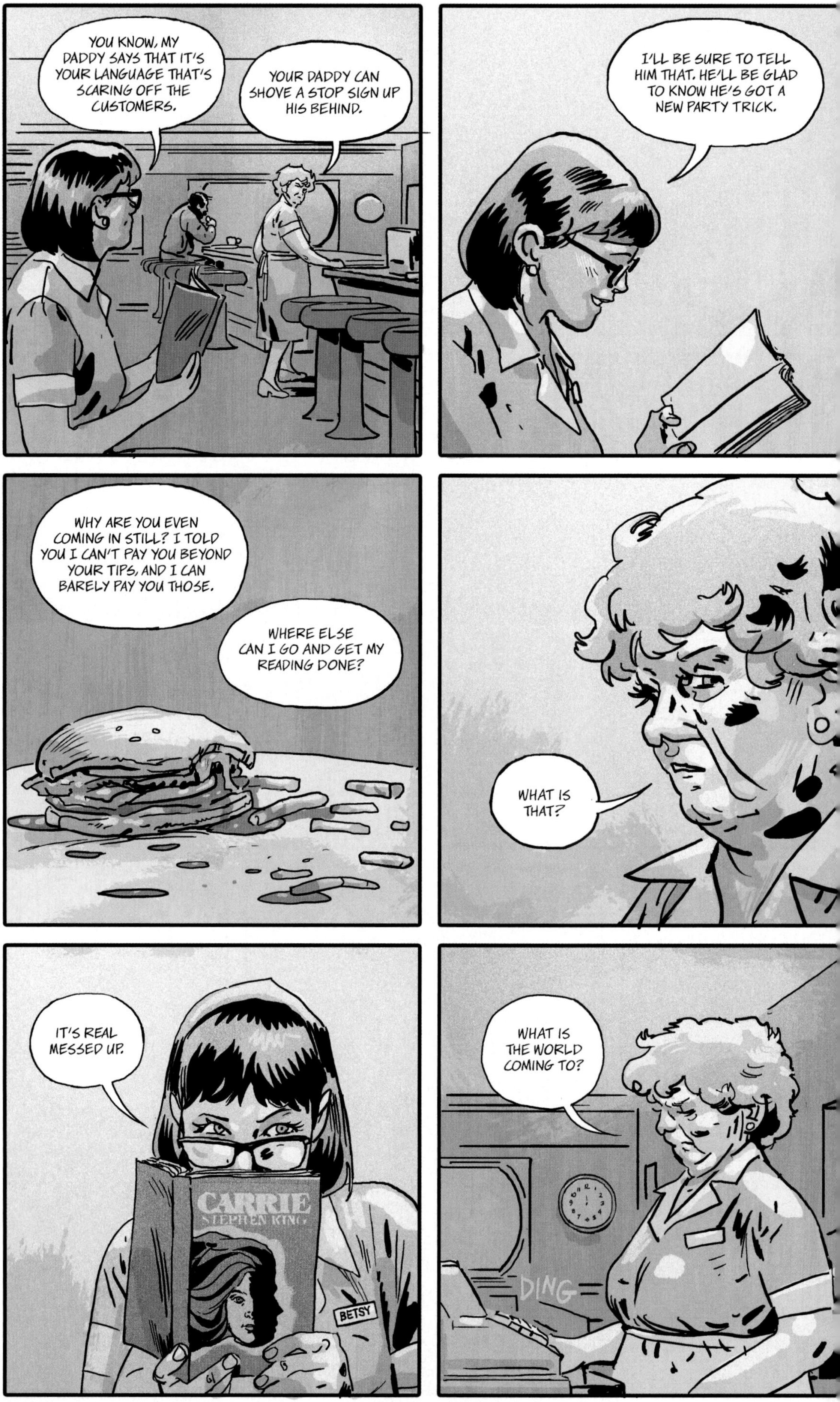
YOU KNOW, MY DADDY SAYS THAT IT'S YOUR LANGUAGE THAT'S SCARING OFF THE CUSTOMERS.
YOUR DADDY CAN SHOVE A STOP SIGN UP HIS BEHIND.
I'LL BE SURE TO TELL HIM THAT. HE'LL BE GLAD TO KNOW HE'S GOT A NEW PARTY TRICK.
WHY ARE YOU EVEN COMING IN STILL? I TOLD YOU I CAN'T PAY YOU BEYOND YOUR TIPS, AND I CAN BARELY PAY YOU THOSE.
WHERE ELSE CAN I GO AND GET MY READING DONE?
WHAT IS THAT?
IT'S REAL MESSED UP.
CARRIE
STEPHEN KING
BETSY
WHAT IS THE WORLD COMING TO?
DING

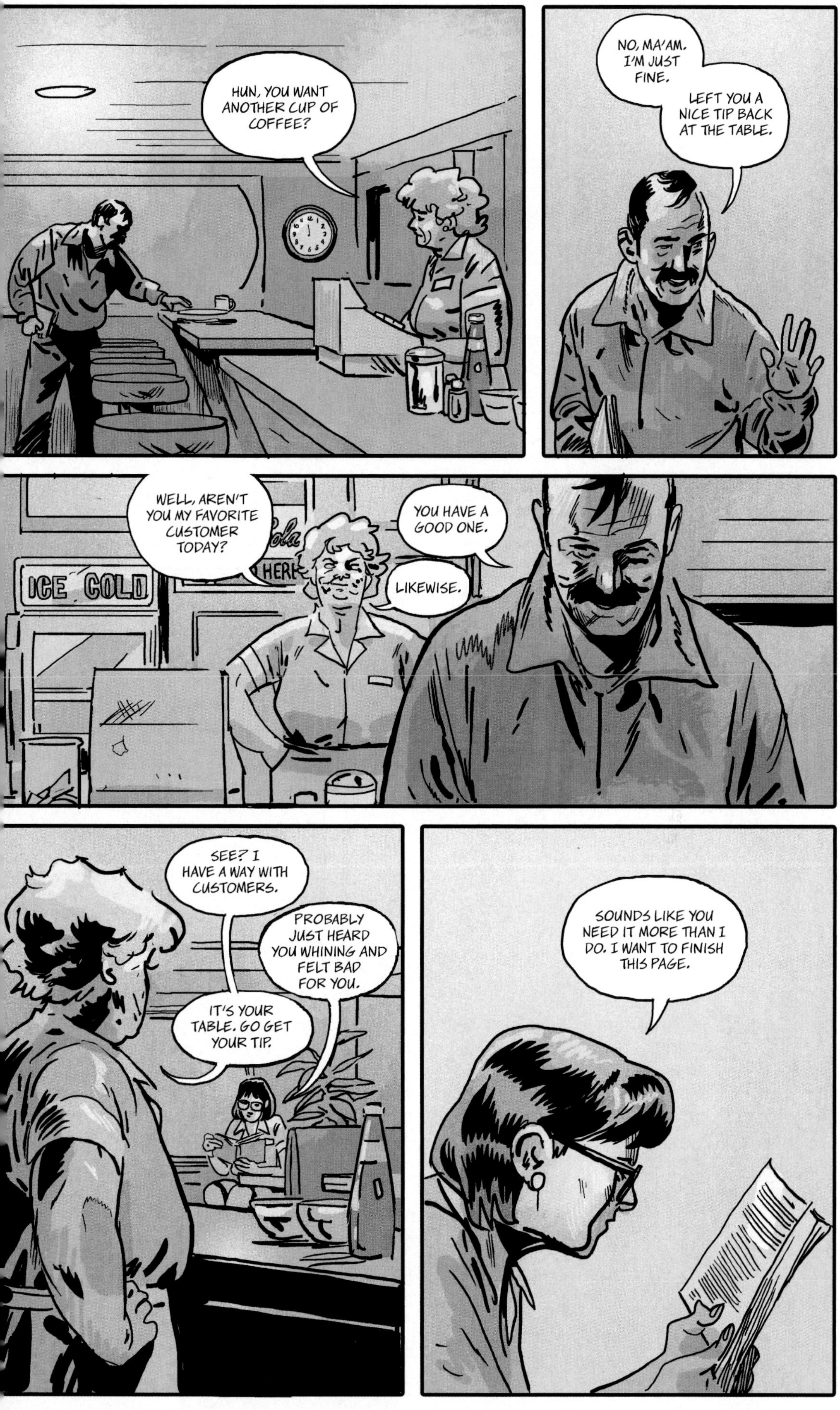
HUN, YOU WANT ANOTHER CUP OF COFFEE?
NO, MA'AM. I'M JUST FINE.
LEFT YOU A NICE TIP BACK AT THE TABLE.
ICE COLD
WELL, AREN'T YOU MY FAVORITE CUSTOMER TODAY?
YOU HAVE A GOOD ONE.
LIKEWISE.
SEE? I HAVE A WAY WITH CUSTOMERS.
PROBABLY JUST HEARD YOU WHINING AND FELT BAD FOR YOU.
IT'S YOUR TABLE. GO GET YOUR TIP.
SOUNDS LIKE YOU NEED IT MORE THAN I DO. I WANT TO FINISH THIS PAGE.

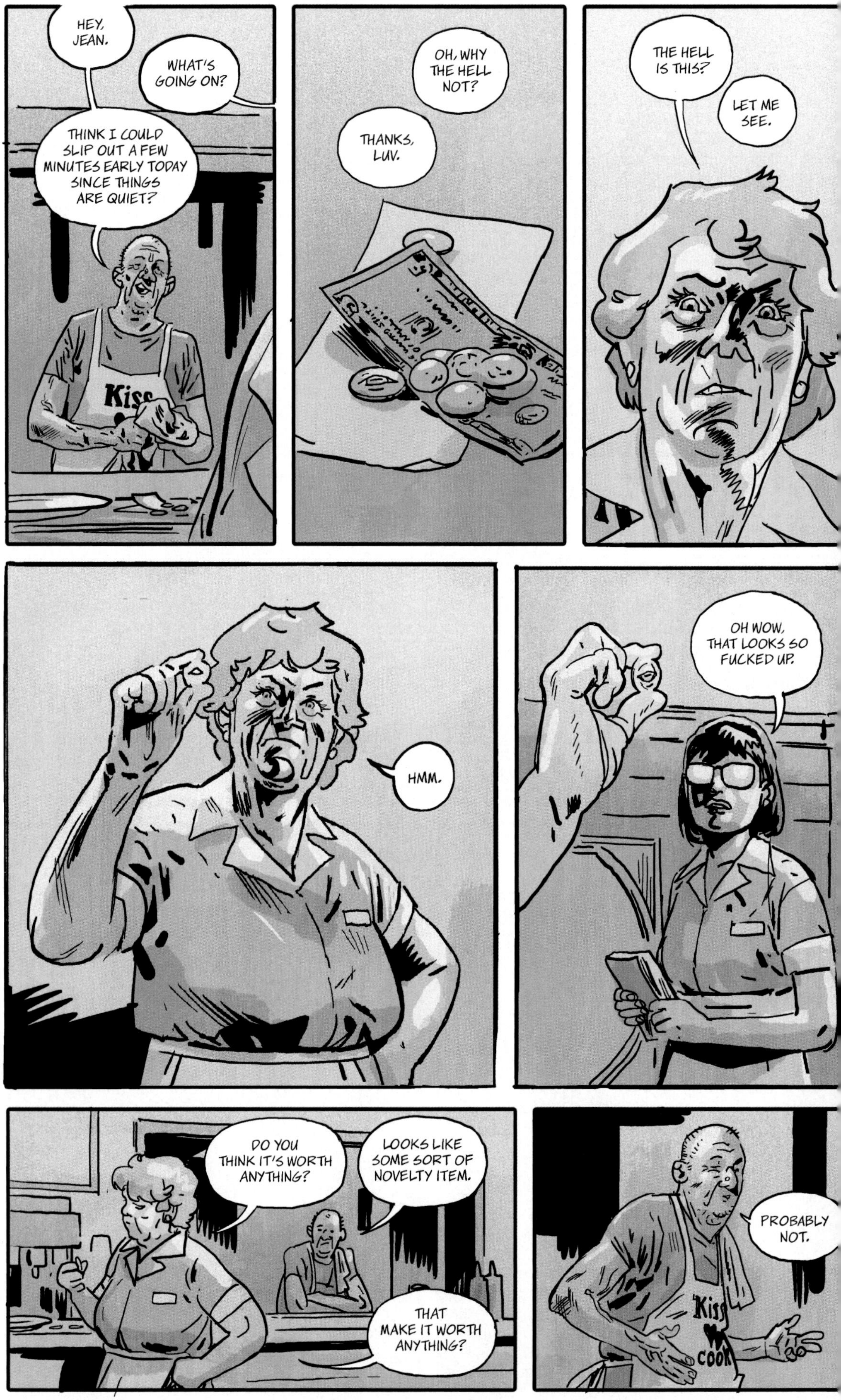

HEY, JEAN.
WHAT'S GOING ON?
THINK I COULD SLIP OUT A FEW MINUTES EARLY TODAY SINCE THINGS ARE QUIET?
OH, WHY THE HELL NOT?
THANKS, LUV.
THE HELL IS THIS?
LET ME SEE.
HMM.
OH WOW, THAT LOOKS SO FUCKED UP.
DO YOU THINK IT'S WORTH ANYTHING?
LOOKS LIKE SOME SORT OF NOVELTY ITEM.
THAT MAKE IT WORTH ANYTHING?
PROBABLY NOT.

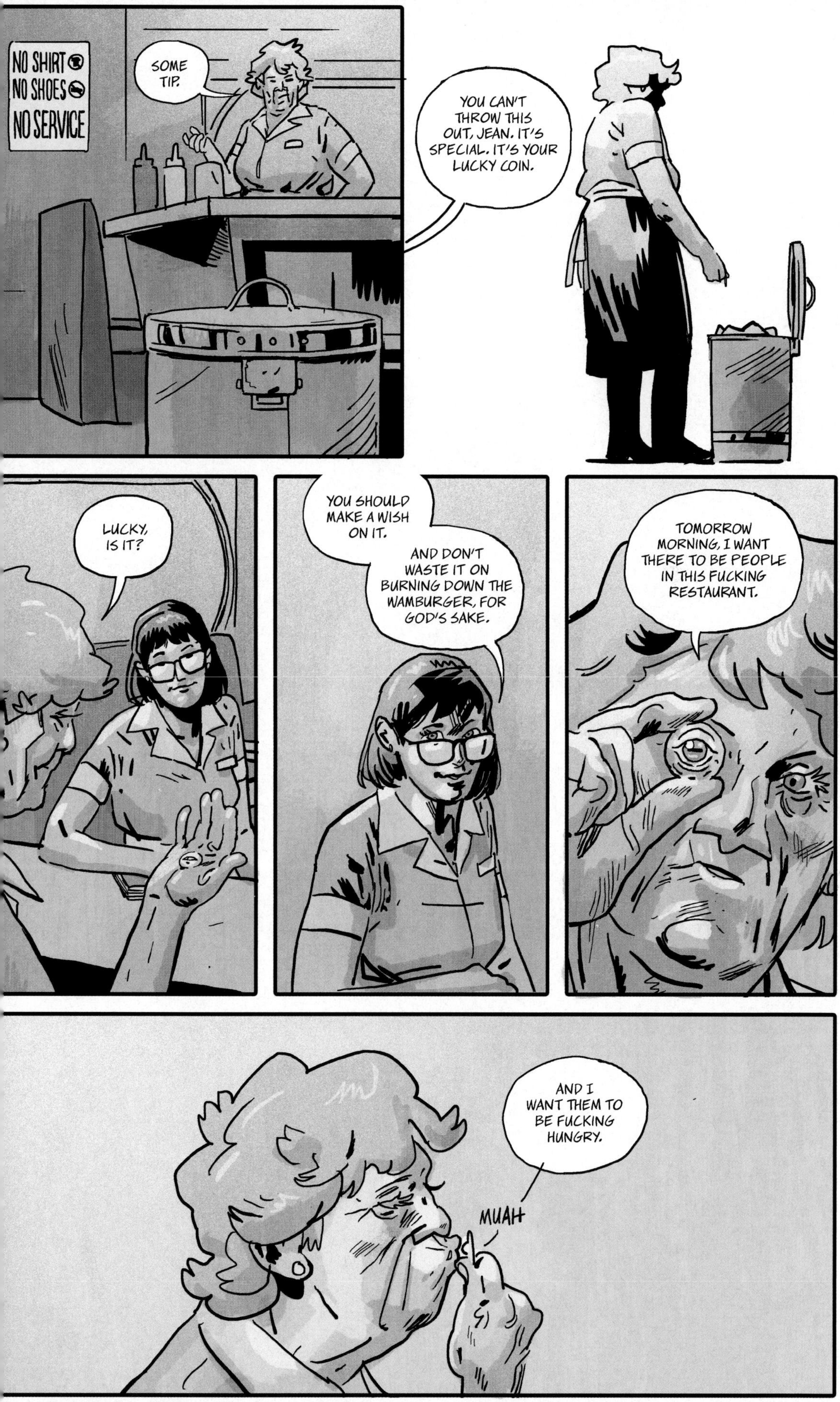
NO SHIRT
NO SHOES
NO SERVICE
SOME TIP.
YOU CAN'T THROW THIS OUT, JEAN. IT'S SPECIAL. IT'S YOUR LUCKY COIN.
LUCKY, IS IT?
YOU SHOULD MAKE A WISH ON IT.
AND DON'T WASTE IT ON BURNING DOWN THE WAMBURGER, FOR GOD'S SAKE.
TOMORROW MORNING, I WANT THERE TO BE PEOPLE IN THIS FUCKING RESTAURANT.
AND I WANT THEM TO BE FUCKING HUNGRY.
MUAH

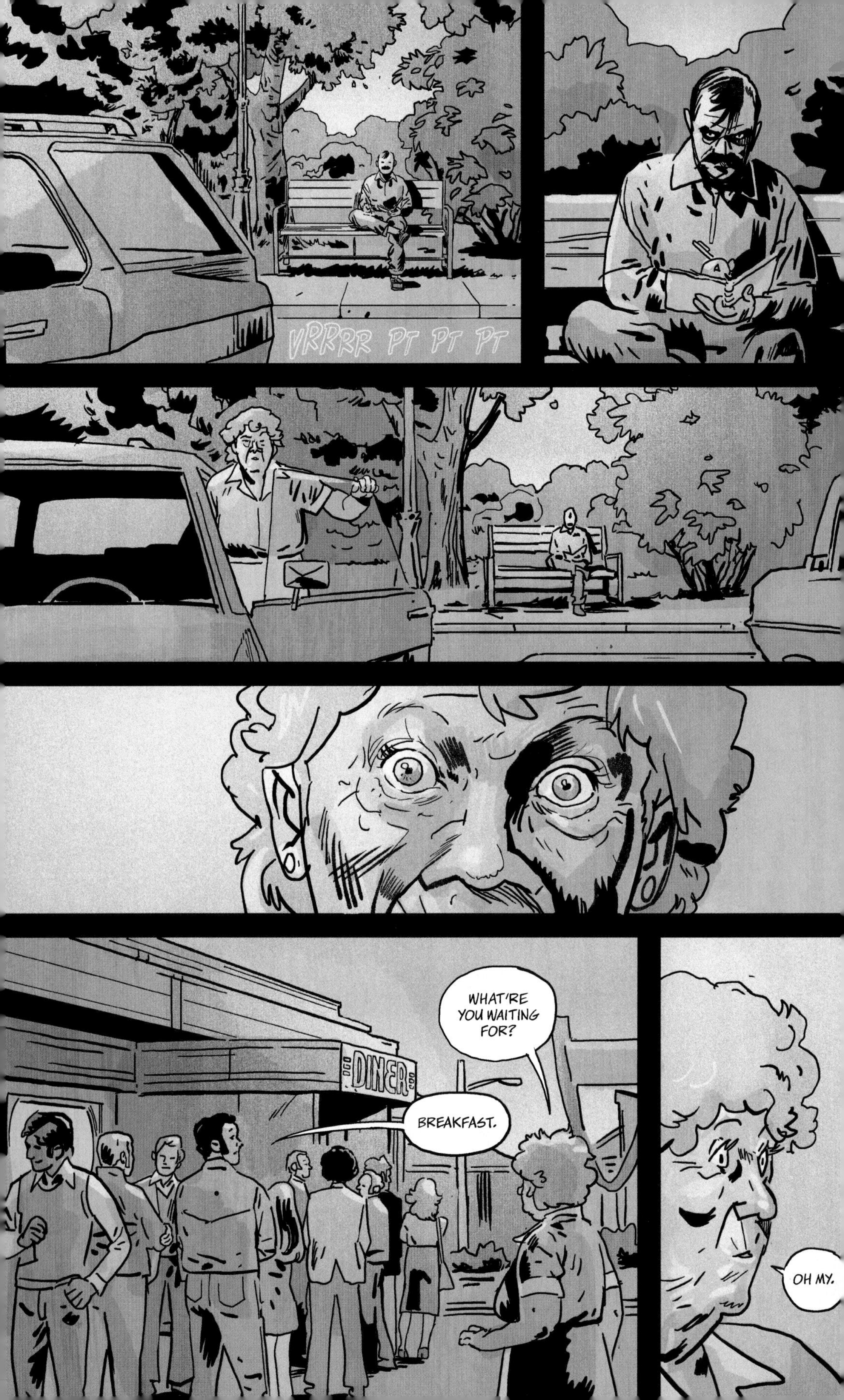
VRRRR PT PT PT
WHAT'RE YOU WAITING FOR?
BREAKFAST.
OH MY.

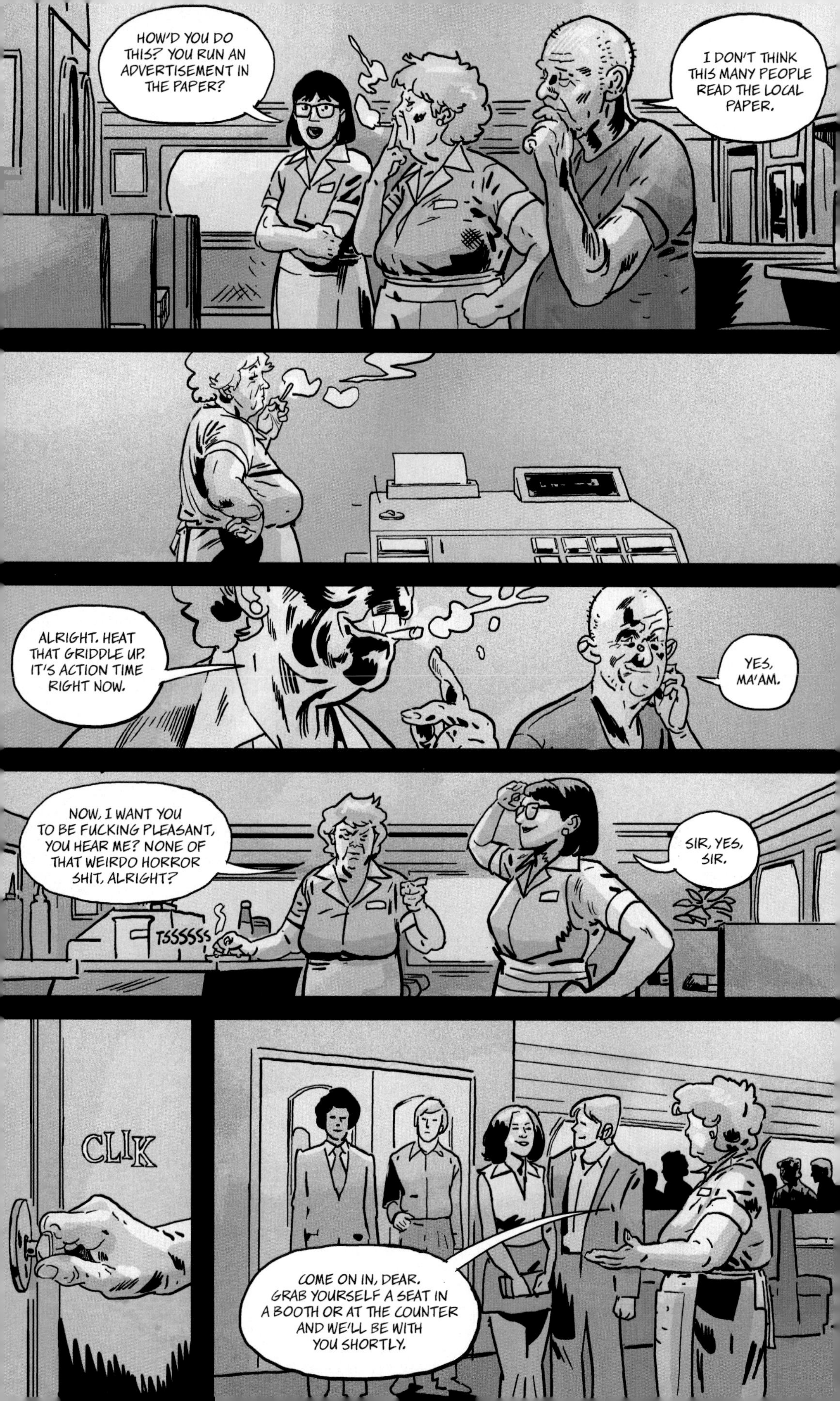
HOW'D YOU DO THIS? YOU RUN AN ADVERTISEMENT IN THE PAPER?
I DON'T THINK THIS MANY PEOPLE READ THE LOCAL PAPER.
ALRIGHT. HEAT THAT GRIDDLE UP. IT'S ACTION TIME RIGHT NOW.
YES, MA'AM.
NOW, I WANT YOU TO BE FUCKING PLEASANT, YOU HEAR ME? NONE OF THAT WEIRDO HORROR SHIT, ALRIGHT?
TSSSSSS
SIR, YES, SIR.
CLIK
COME ON IN, DEAR. GRAB YOURSELF A SEAT IN A BOOTH OR AT THE COUNTER AND WE'LL BE WITH YOU SHORTLY.

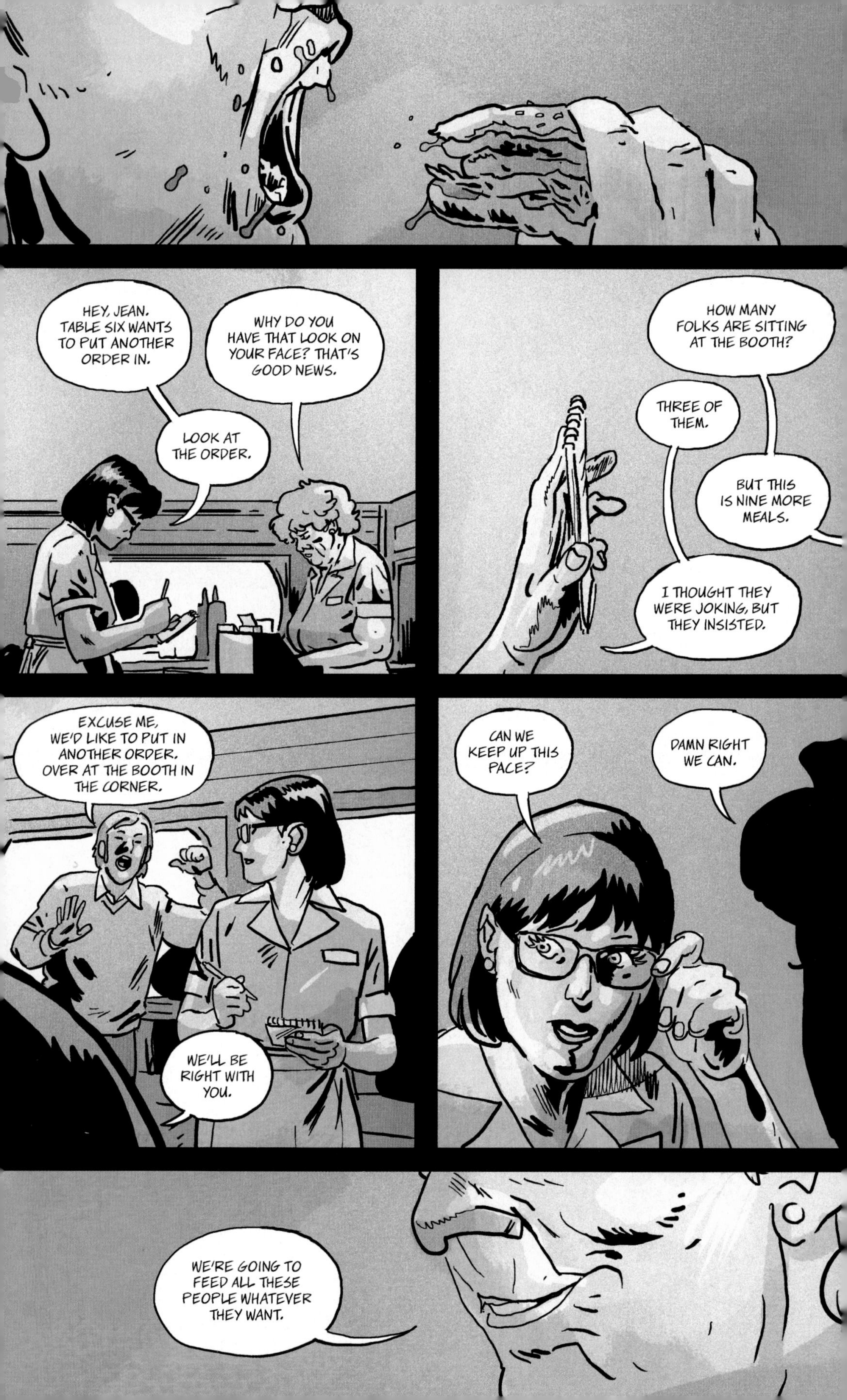
HEY, JEAN. TABLE SIX WANTS TO PUT ANOTHER ORDER IN.
WHY DO YOU HAVE THAT LOOK ON YOUR FACE? THAT'S GOOD NEWS.
LOOK AT THE ORDER.
HOW MANY FOLKS ARE SITTING AT THE BOOTH?
THREE OF THEM.
BUT THIS IS NINE MORE MEALS.
I THOUGHT THEY WERE JOKING, BUT THEY INSISTED.
EXCUSE ME, WE'D LIKE TO PUT IN ANOTHER ORDER. OVER AT THE BOOTH IN THE CORNER.
WE'LL BE RIGHT WITH YOU.
CAN WE KEEP UP THIS PACE?
DAMN RIGHT WE CAN.
WE'RE GOING TO FEED ALL THESE PEOPLE WHATEVER THEY WANT.

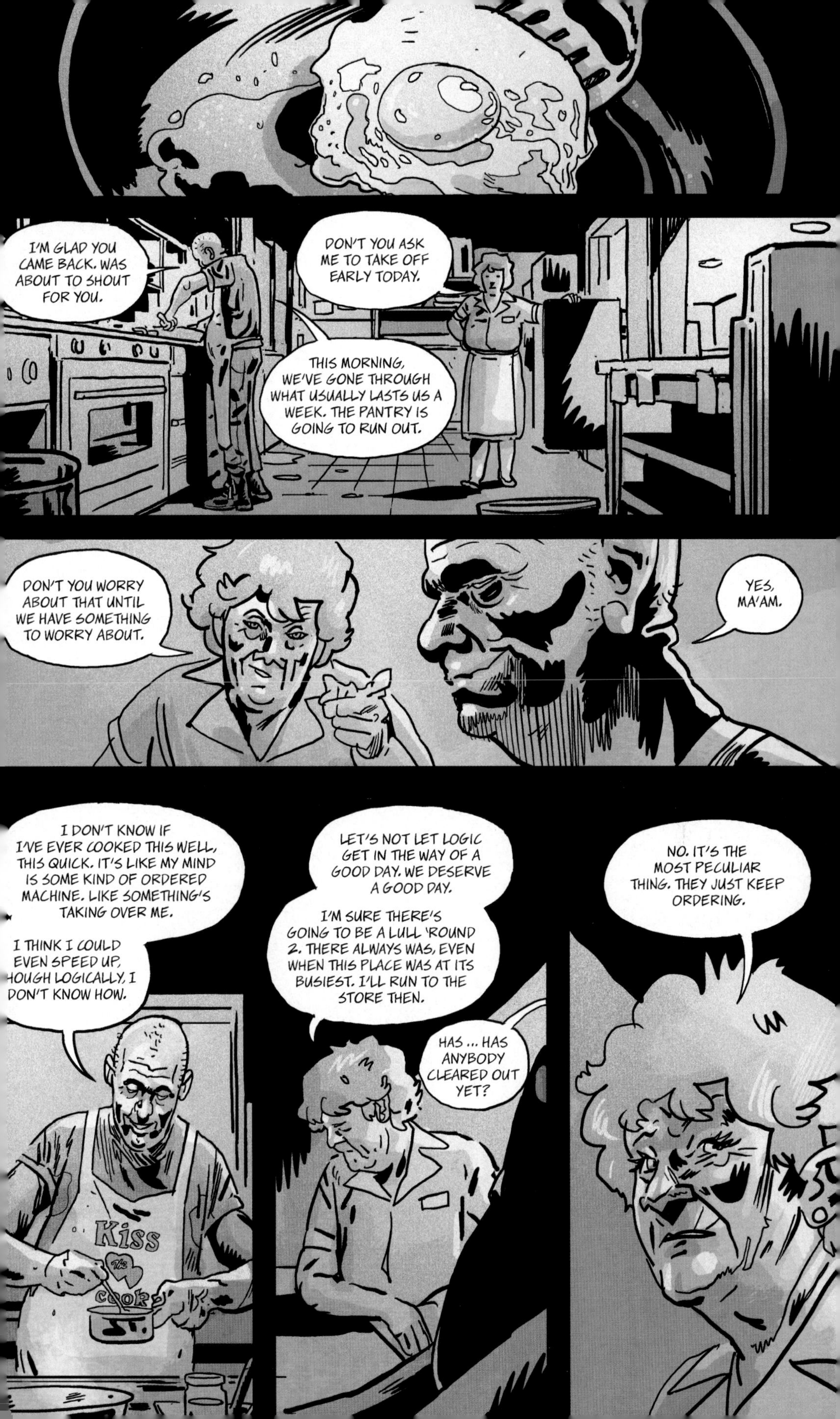
I'M GLAD YOU CAME BACK. WAS ABOUT TO SHOUT FOR YOU.
DON'T YOU ASK ME TO TAKE OFF EARLY TODAY.
THIS MORNING, WE'VE GONE THROUGH WHAT USUALLY LASTS US A WEEK. THE PANTRY IS GOING TO RUN OUT.
DON'T YOU WORRY ABOUT THAT UNTIL WE HAVE SOMETHING TO WORRY ABOUT.
YES, MA'AM.
I DON'T KNOW IF I'VE EVER COOKED THIS WELL, THIS QUICK. IT'S LIKE MY MIND IS SOME KIND OF ORDERED MACHINE. LIKE SOMETHING'S TAKING OVER ME.
I THINK I COULD EVEN SPEED UP, HOUGH LOGICALLY, I DON'T KNOW HOW.
LET'S NOT LET LOGIC GET IN THE WAY OF A GOOD DAY. WE DESERVE A GOOD DAY.
I'M SURE THERE'S GOING TO BE A LULL 'ROUND 2. THERE ALWAYS WAS, EVEN WHEN THIS PLACE WAS AT ITS BUSIEST. I'LL RUN TO THE STORE THEN.
HAS ... HAS ANYBODY CLEARED OUT YET?
NO. IT'S THE MOST PECULIAR THING. THEY JUST KEEP ORDERING.
Kiss the cook

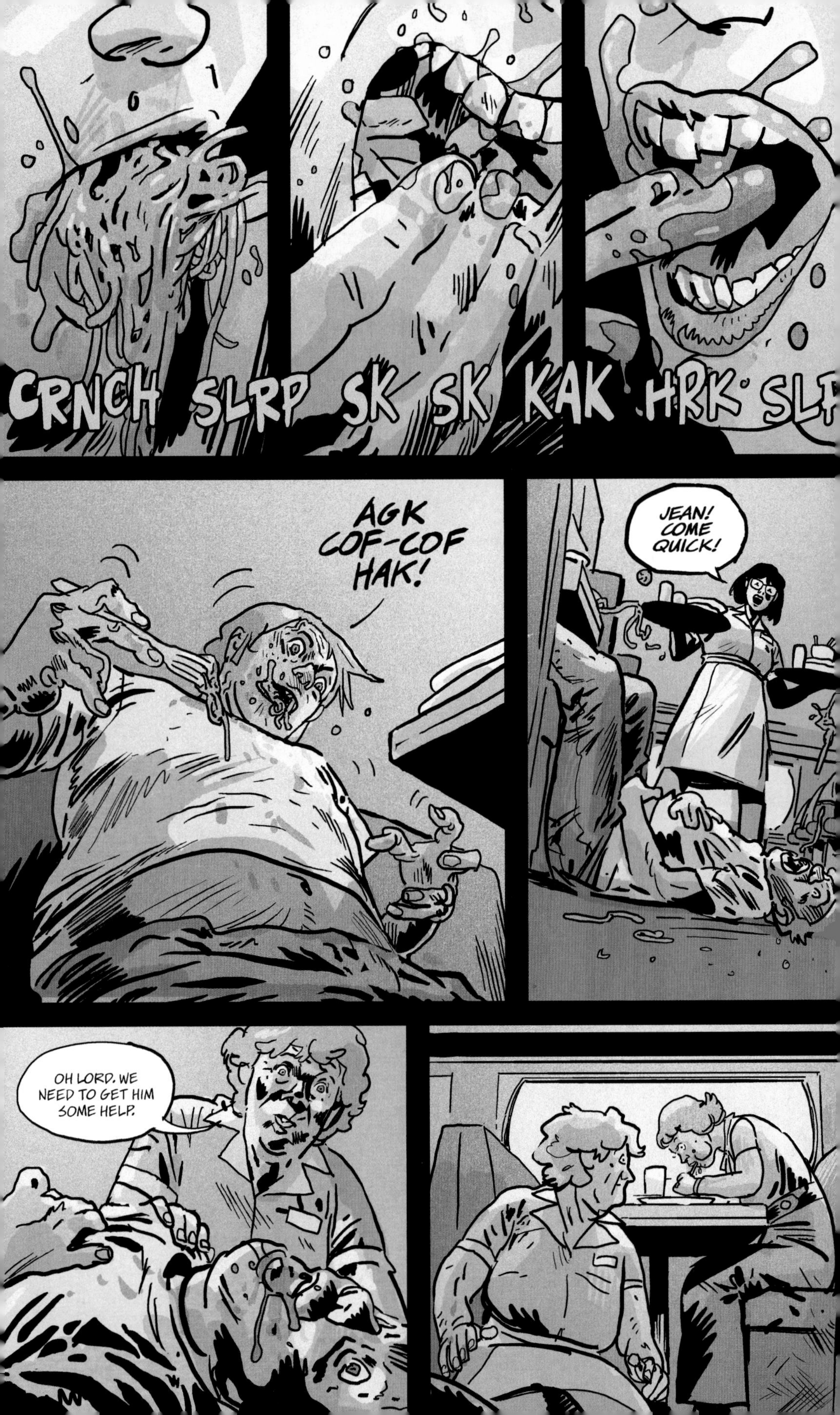
CRNCH SLRP SK SK KAK HRK SLF
AGK COF-COF HAK!
JEAN! COME QUICK!
OH LORD. WE NEED TO GET HIM SOME HELP.

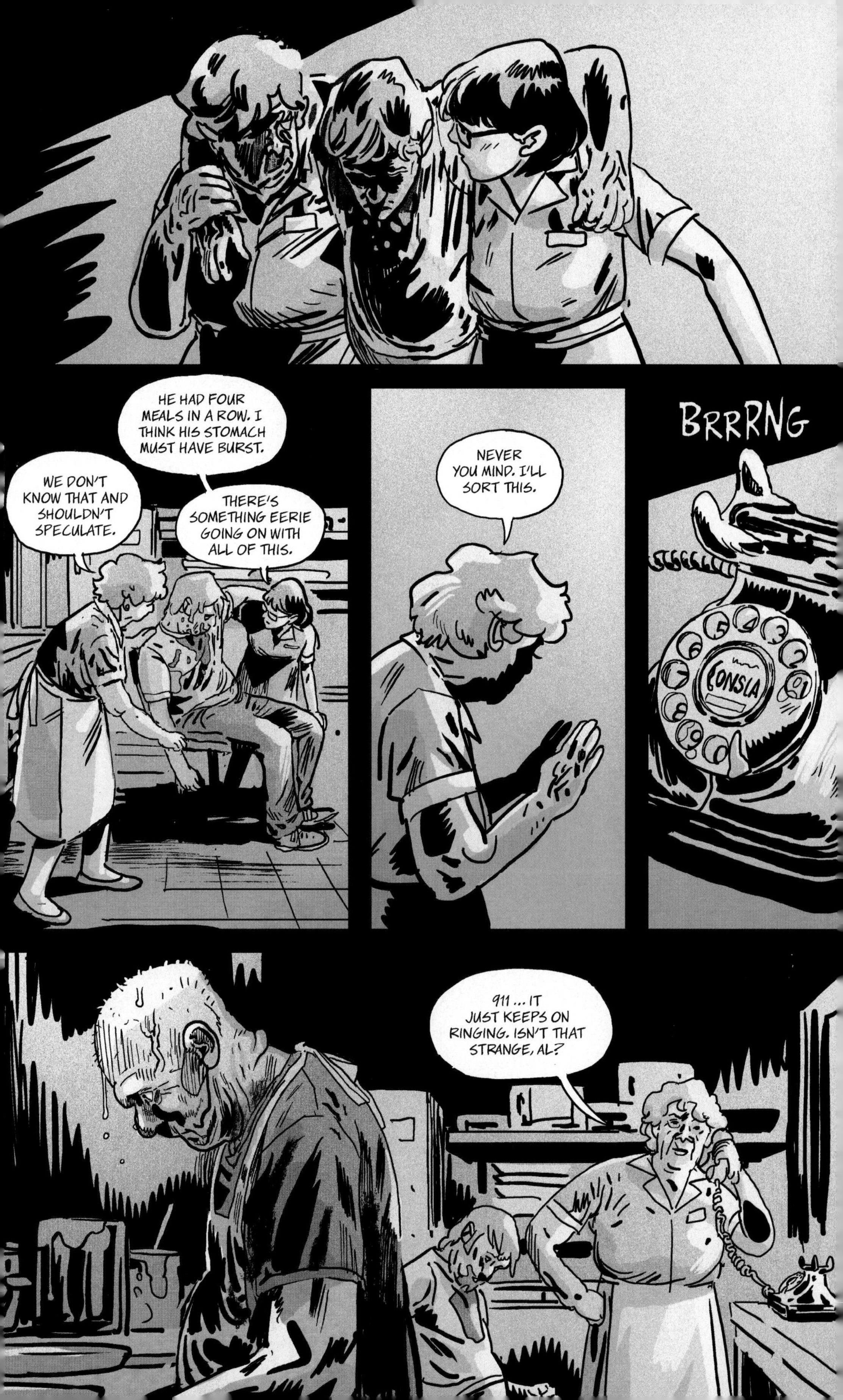
WE DON'T KNOW THAT AND SHOULDN'T SPECULATE.
HE HAD FOUR MEALS IN A ROW. I THINK HIS STOMACH MUST HAVE BURST.
THERE'S SOMETHING EERIE GOING ON WITH ALL OF THIS.
NEVER YOU MIND. I'LL SORT THIS.
BRRRNG
911 ... IT JUST KEEPS ON RINGING. ISN'T THAT STRANGE, AL?

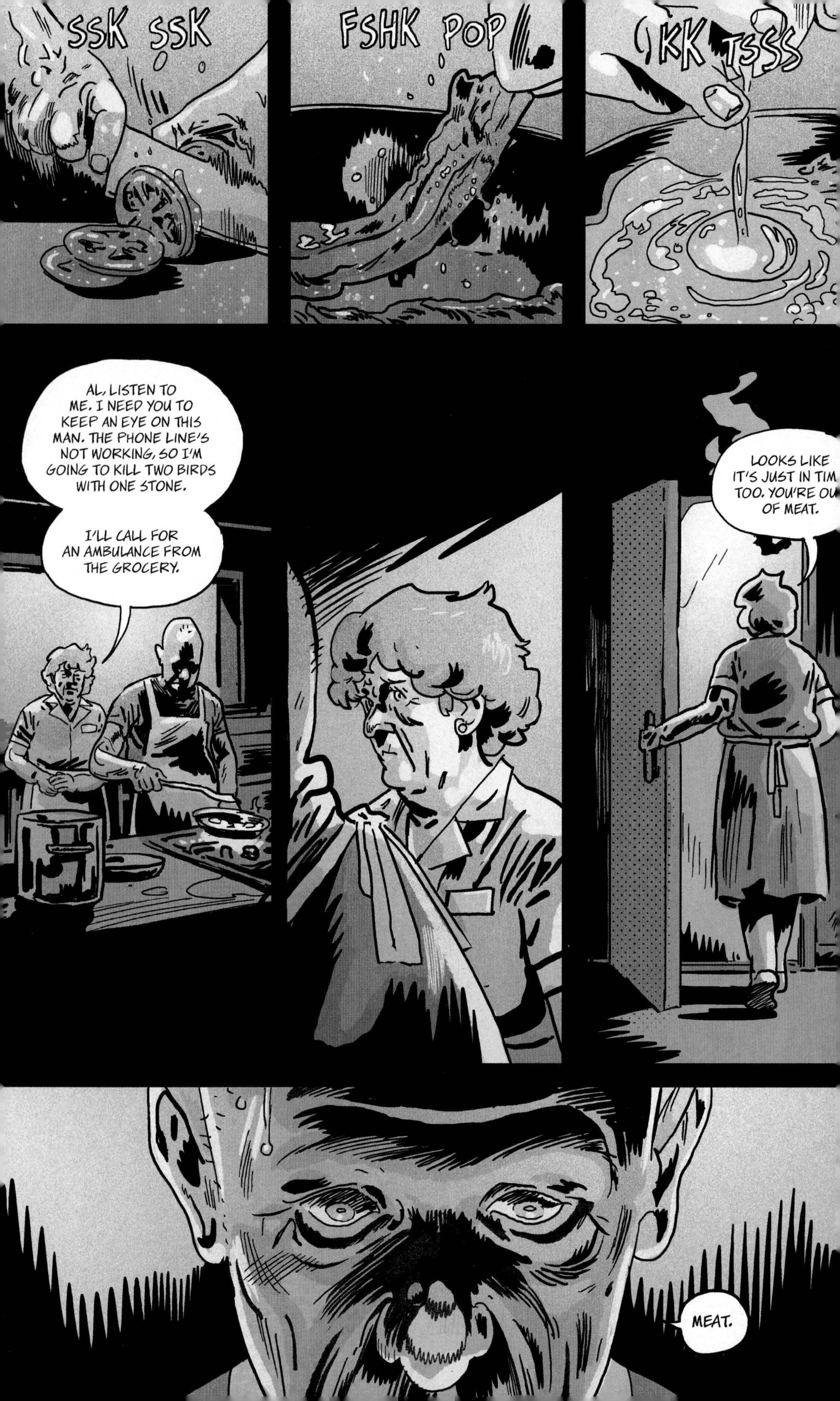
SSK SSK
FSHK POP
KK TSSS
AL, LISTEN TO ME. I NEED YOU TO KEEP AN EYE ON THIS MAN. THE PHONE LINE'S NOT WORKING, SO I'M GOING TO KILL TWO BIRDS WITH ONE STONE.
I'LL CALL FOR AN AMBULANCE FROM THE GROCERY.
LOOKS LIKE IT'S JUST IN TIM TOO. YOU'RE OU OF MEAT.
MEAT.

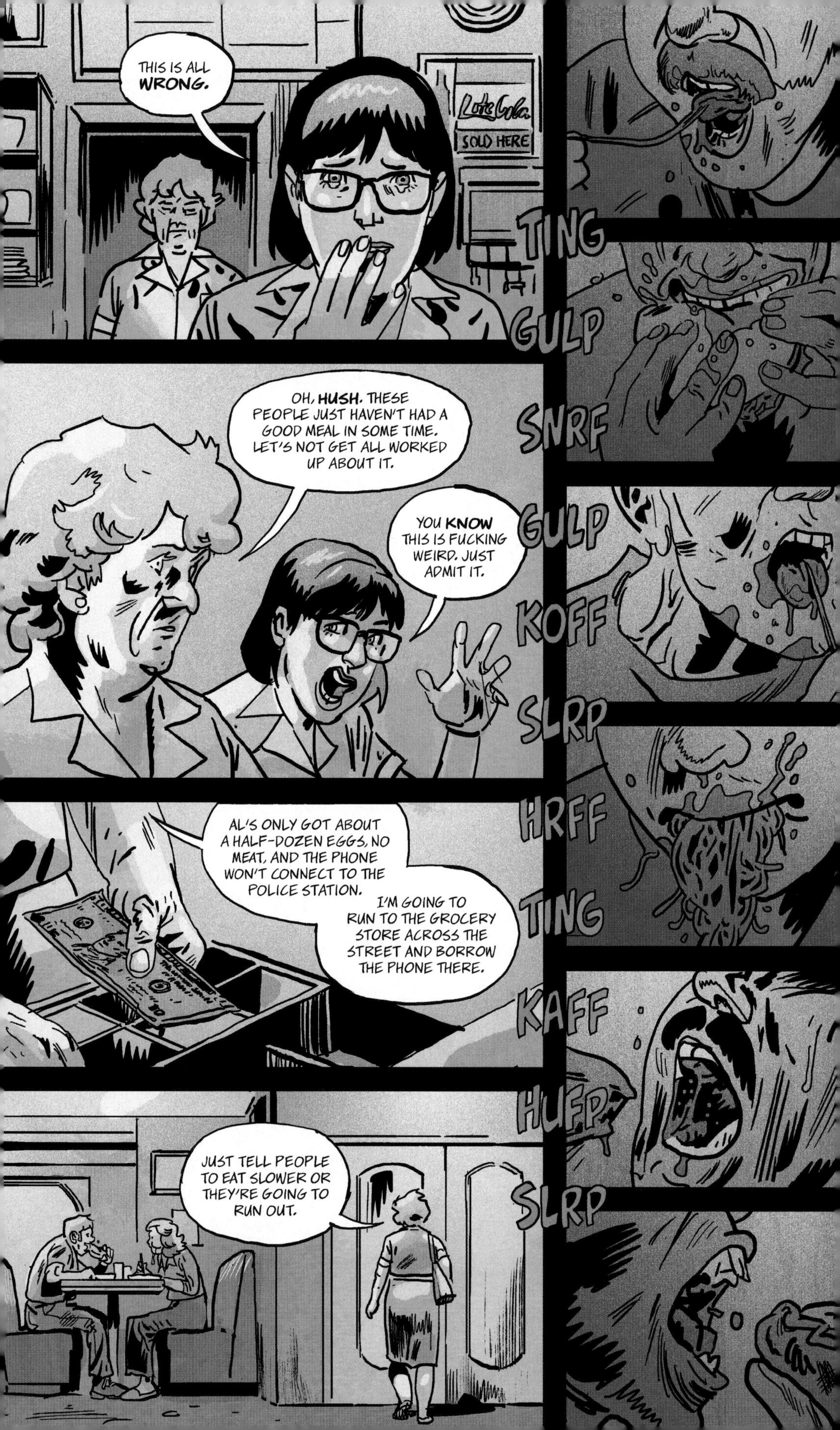
THIS IS ALL WRONG.
Loto Cola SOLD HERE
TING
GULP
OH, HUSH. THESE PEOPLE JUST HAVEN'T HAD A GOOD MEAL IN SOME TIME. LET'S NOT GET ALL WORKED UP ABOUT IT.
SNRF
YOU KNOW THIS IS FUCKING WEIRD. JUST ADMIT IT.
GULP
KOFF
SLRP
AL'S ONLY GOT ABOUT A HALF-DOZEN EGGS, NO MEAT, AND THE PHONE WON'T CONNECT TO THE POLICE STATION.
I'M GOING TO RUN TO THE GROCERY STORE ACROSS THE STREET AND BORROW THE PHONE THERE.
HRFF
TING
KAFF
HUFP
JUST TELL PEOPLE TO EAT SLOWER OR THEY'RE GOING TO RUN OUT.
SLRP

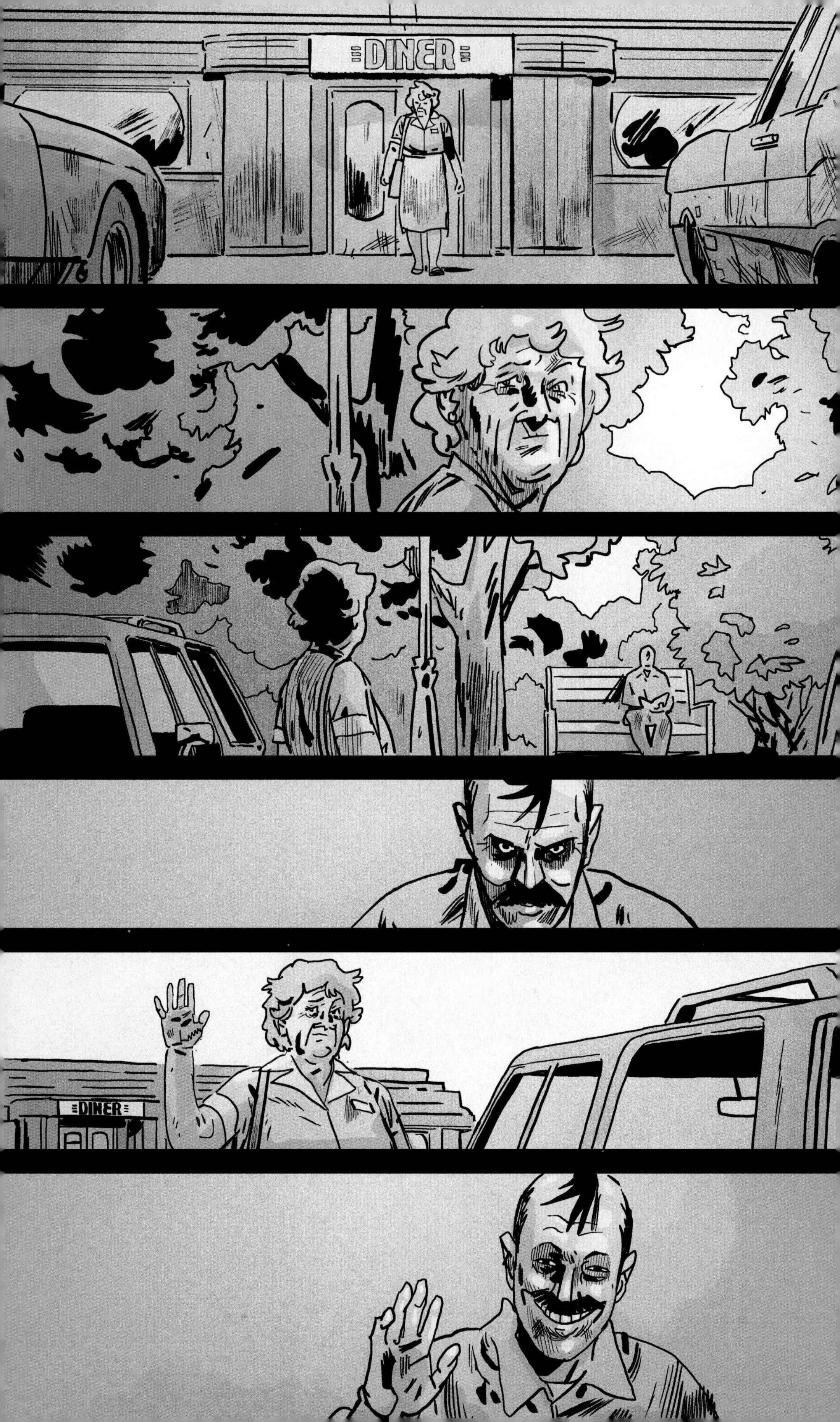
DINER
DINER

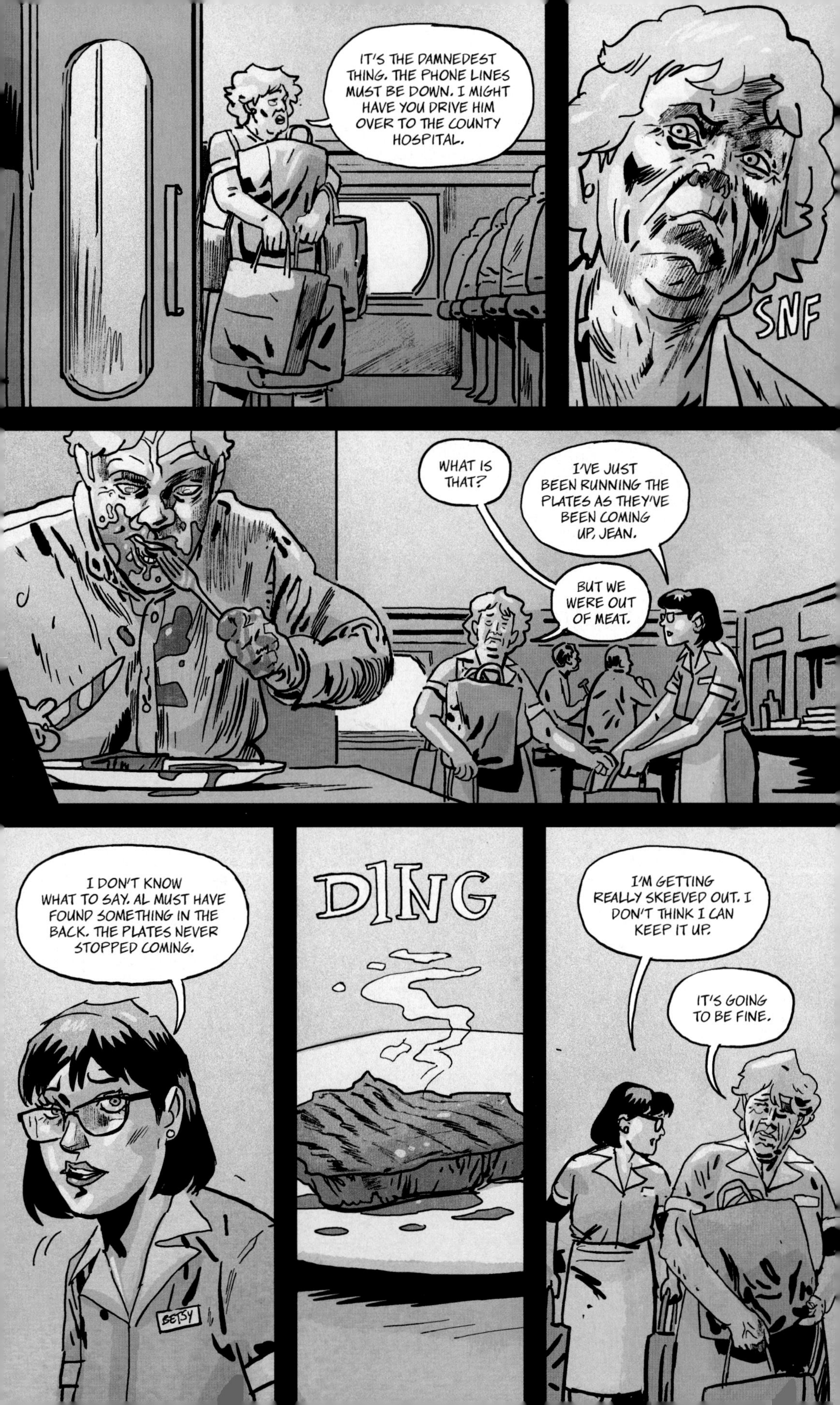
IT'S THE DAMNEDEST THING. THE PHONE LINES MUST BE DOWN. I MIGHT HAVE YOU DRIVE HIM OVER TO THE COUNTY HOSPITAL.
SNF
WHAT IS THAT?
I'VE JUST BEEN RUNNING THE PLATES AS THEY'VE BEEN COMING UP, JEAN.
BUT WE WERE OUT OF MEAT.
I DON'T KNOW WHAT TO SAY. AL MUST HAVE FOUND SOMETHING IN THE BACK. THE PLATES NEVER STOPPED COMING.
BETSY
DING
I'M GETTING REALLY SKEEVED OUT. I DON'T THINK I CAN KEEP IT UP.
IT'S GOING TO BE FINE.

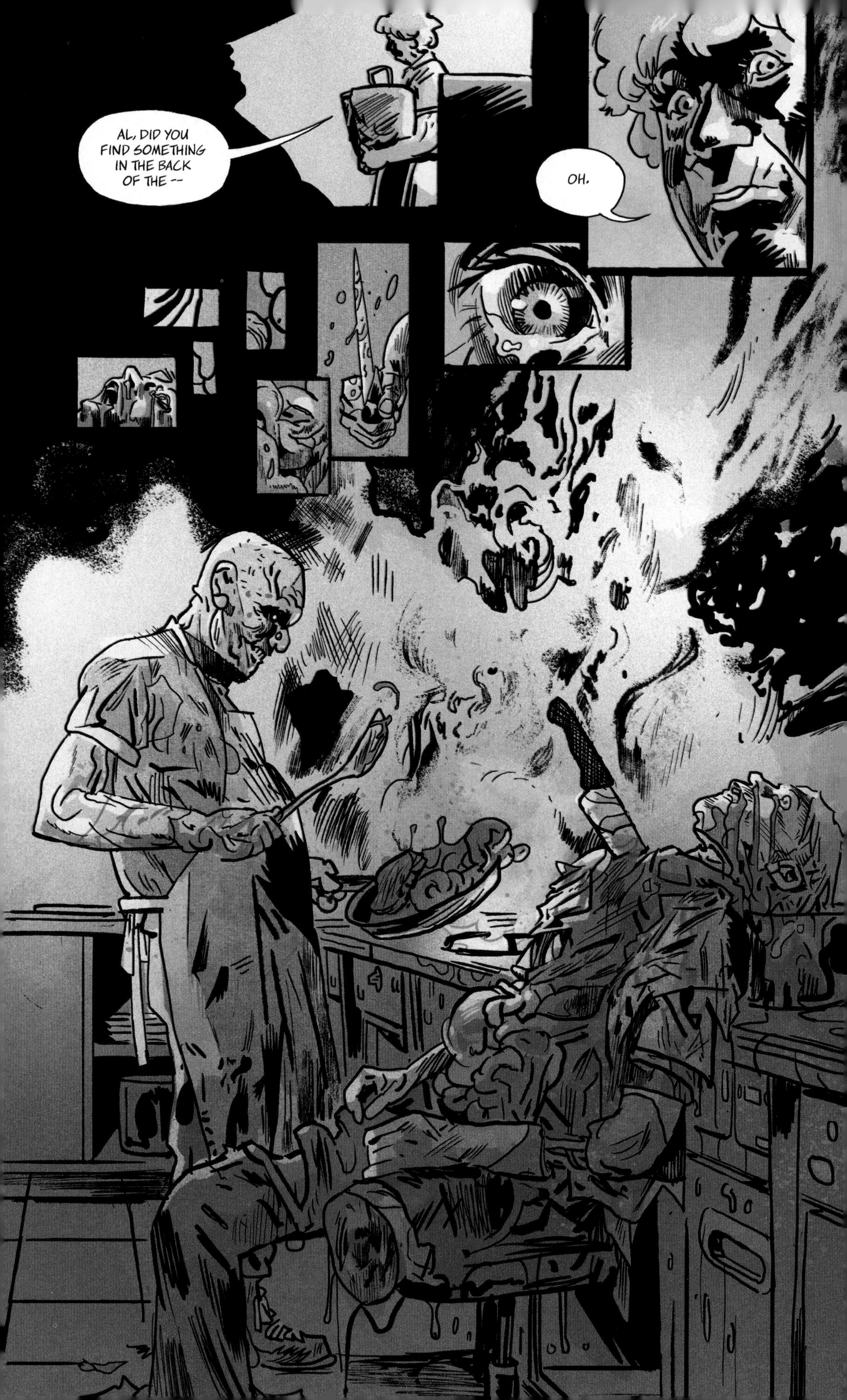
AL, DID YOU FIND SOMETHING IN THE BACK OF THE --
OH.

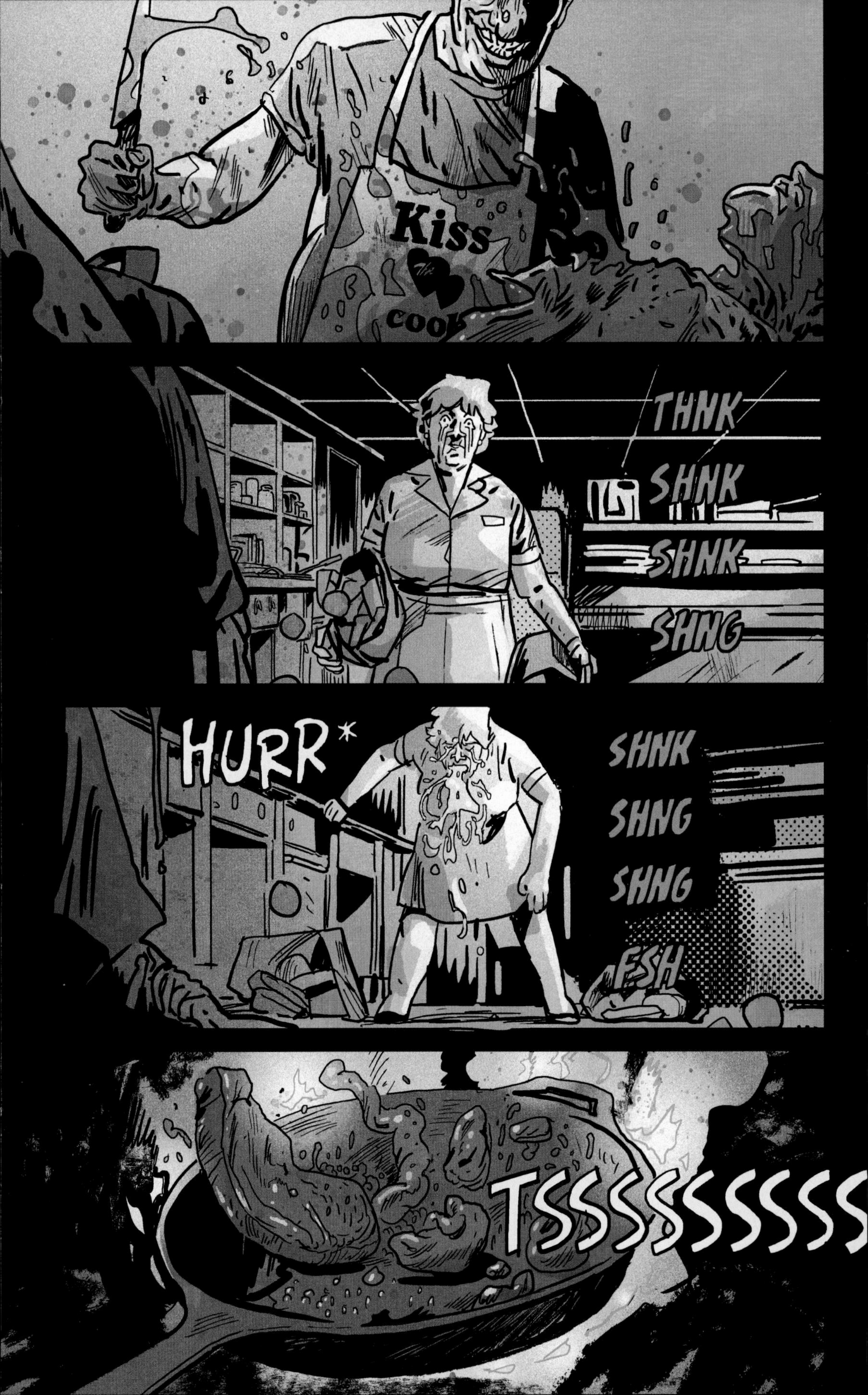
Kiss the cook
THNK
SHNK
SHNK
SHNG
HURR*
SHNK
SHNG
SHNG
FSH
TSSSSSSSSSS

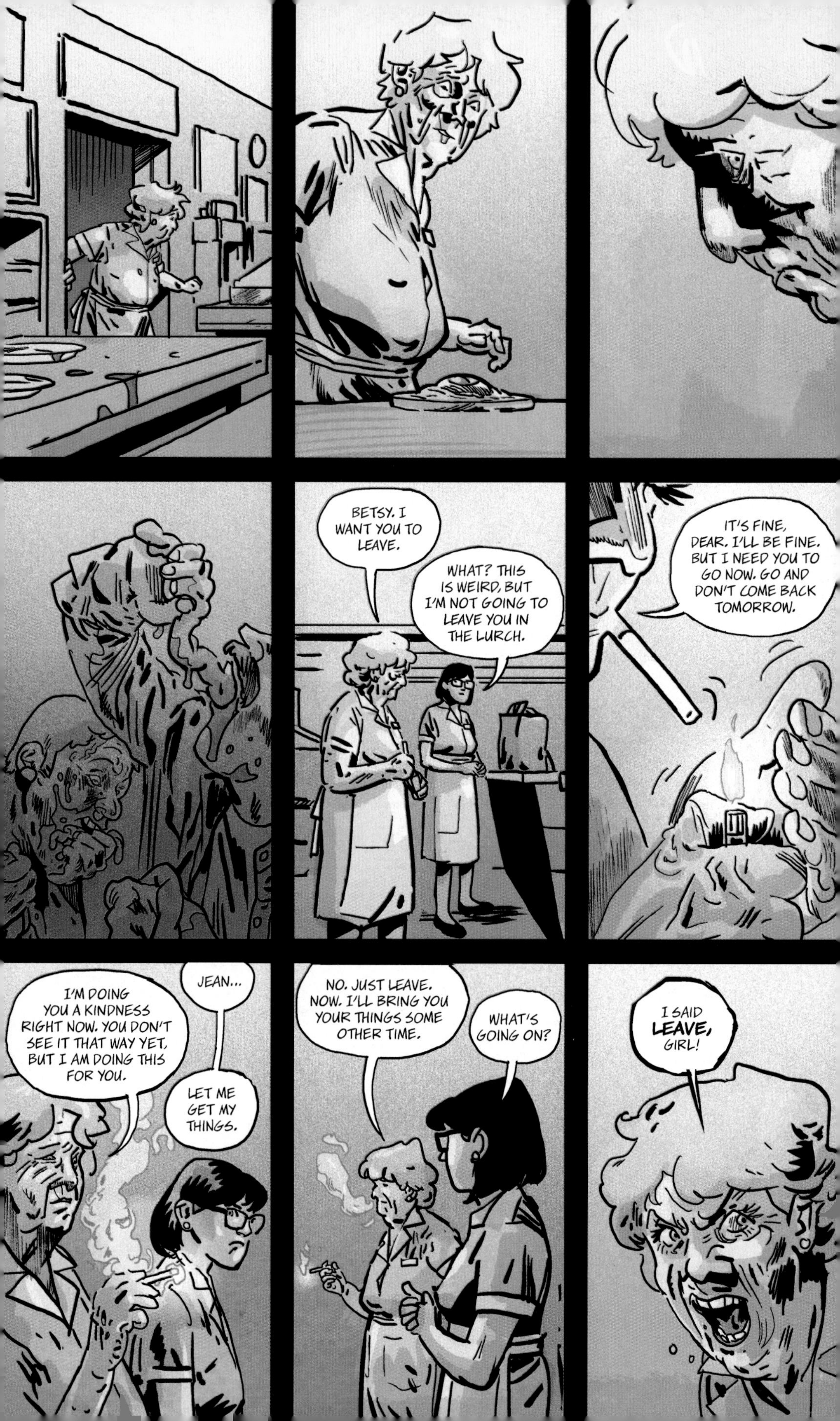
BETSY. I WANT YOU TO LEAVE.
WHAT? THIS IS WEIRD, BUT I'M NOT GOING TO LEAVE YOU IN THE LURCH.
IT'S FINE, DEAR. I'LL BE FINE. BUT I NEED YOU TO GO NOW. GO AND DON'T COME BACK TOMORROW.
JEAN...
I'M DOING YOU A KINDNESS RIGHT NOW. YOU DON'T SEE IT THAT WAY YET, BUT I AM DOING THIS FOR YOU.
LET ME GET MY THINGS.
NO. JUST LEAVE. NOW. I'LL BRING YOU YOUR THINGS SOME OTHER TIME.
WHAT'S GOING ON?
I SAID **LEAVE,** GIRL!

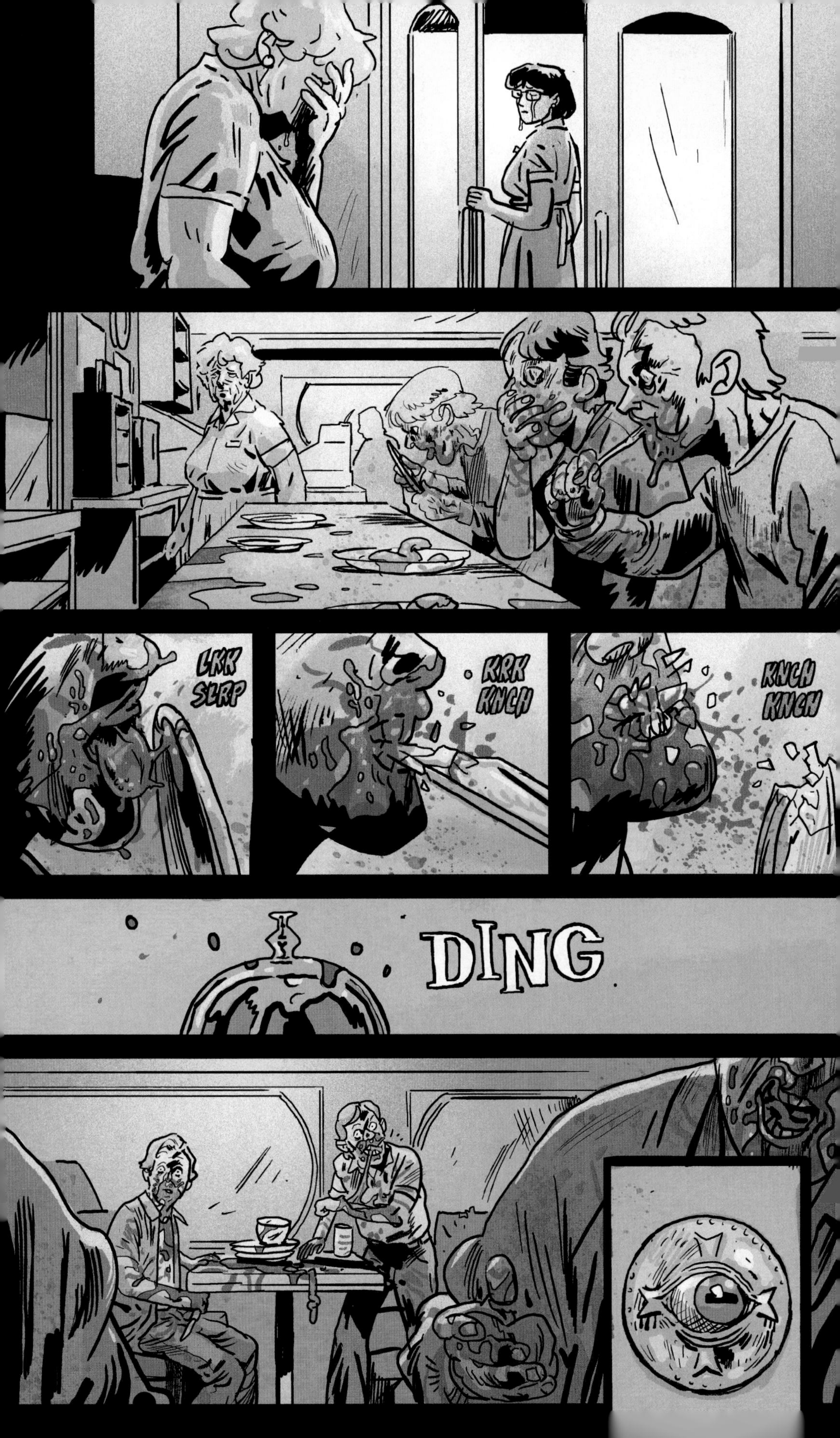
LKK
SLRP
KRK
KNCH
KNCH
KNCH
DING

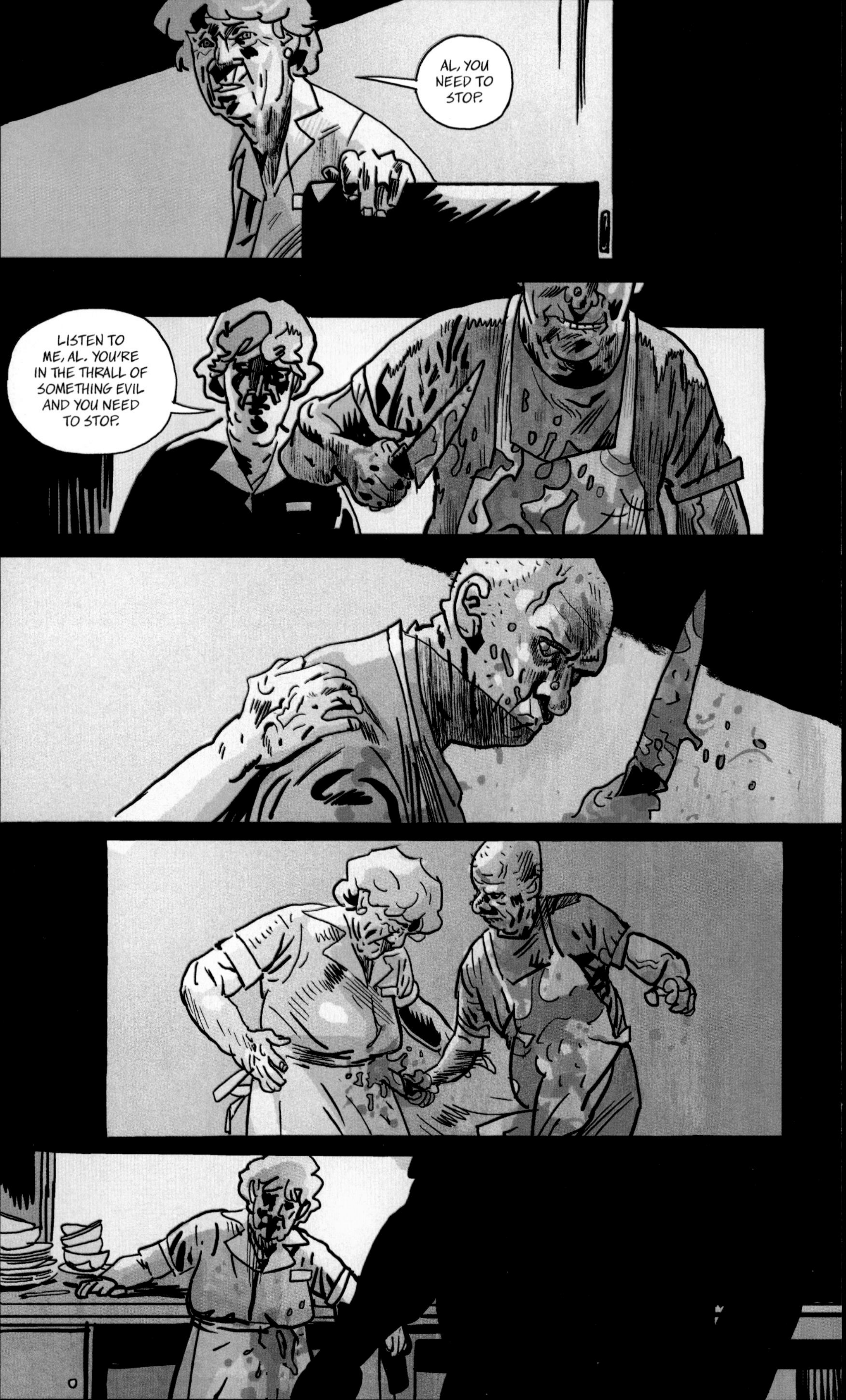
AL, YOU NEED TO STOP.
LISTEN TO ME, AL. YOU'RE IN THE THRALL OF SOMETHING EVIL AND YOU NEED TO STOP.

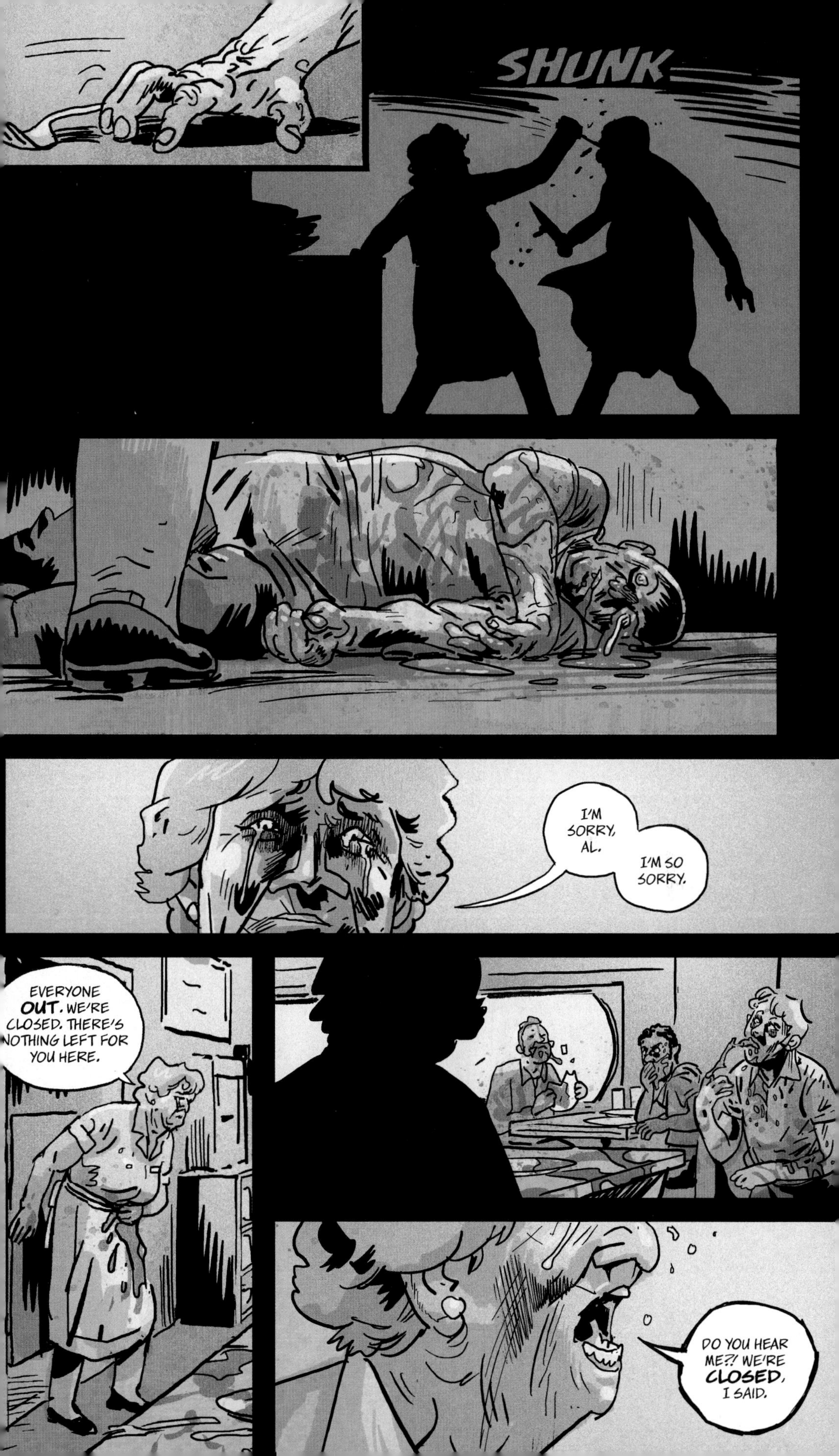
SHUNK
I'M SORRY, AL.
I'M SO SORRY.
EVERYONE OUT. WE'RE CLOSED. THERE'S NOTHING LEFT FOR YOU HERE.
DO YOU HEAR ME?! WE'RE CLOSED, I SAID.

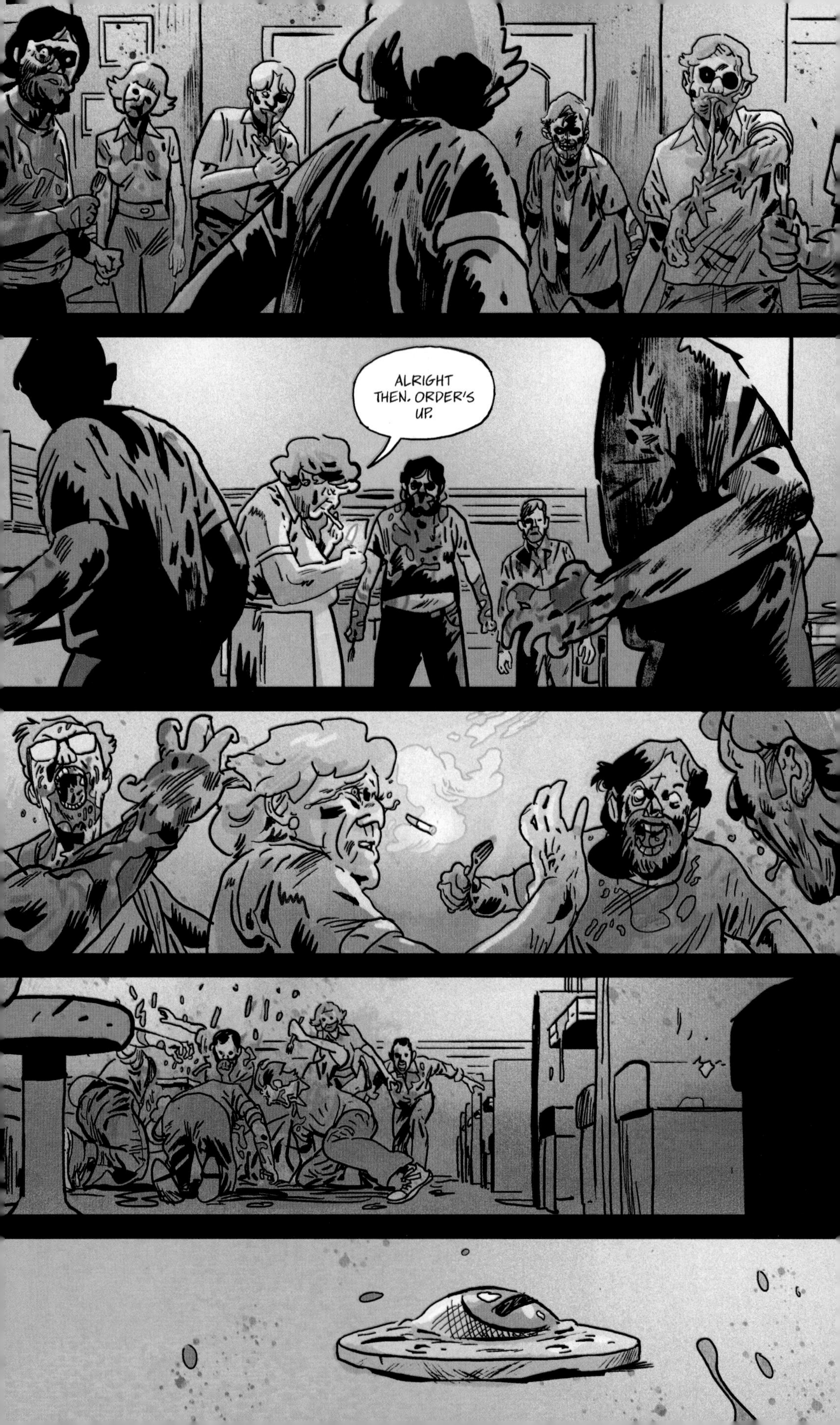
ALRIGHT THEN. ORDER'S UP.

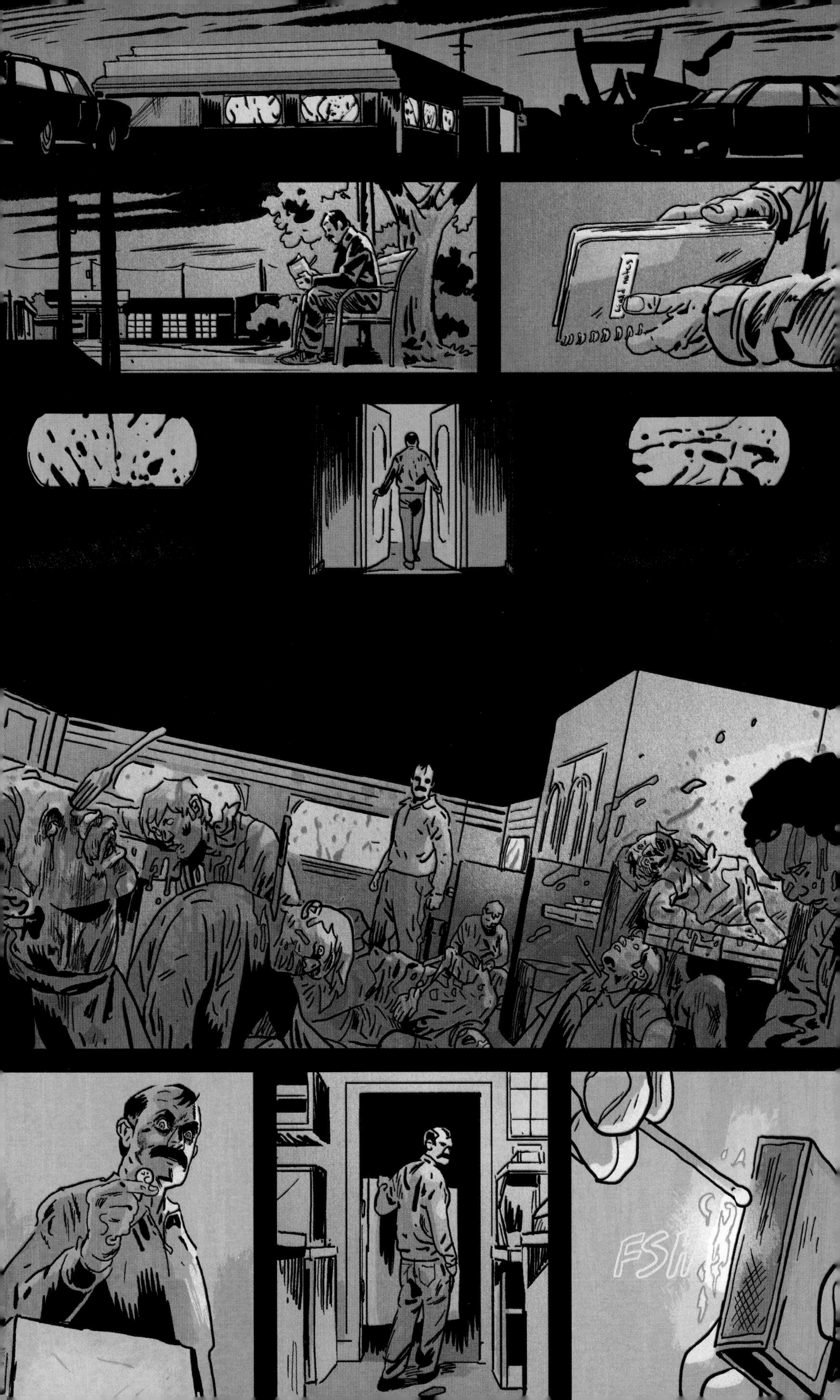
FSH

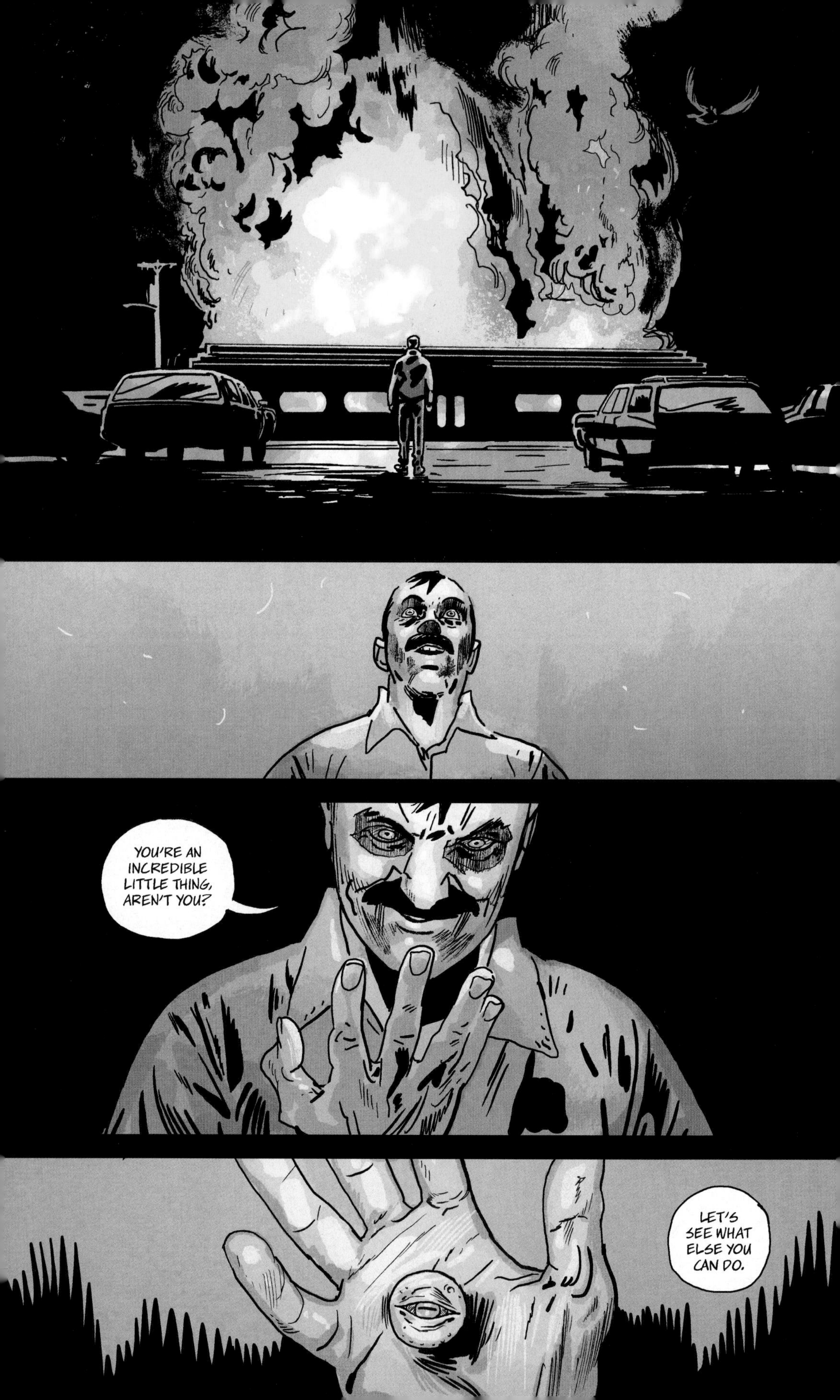
YOU'RE AN INCREDIBLE LITTLE THING, AREN'T YOU?
LET'S SEE WHAT ELSE YOU CAN DO.

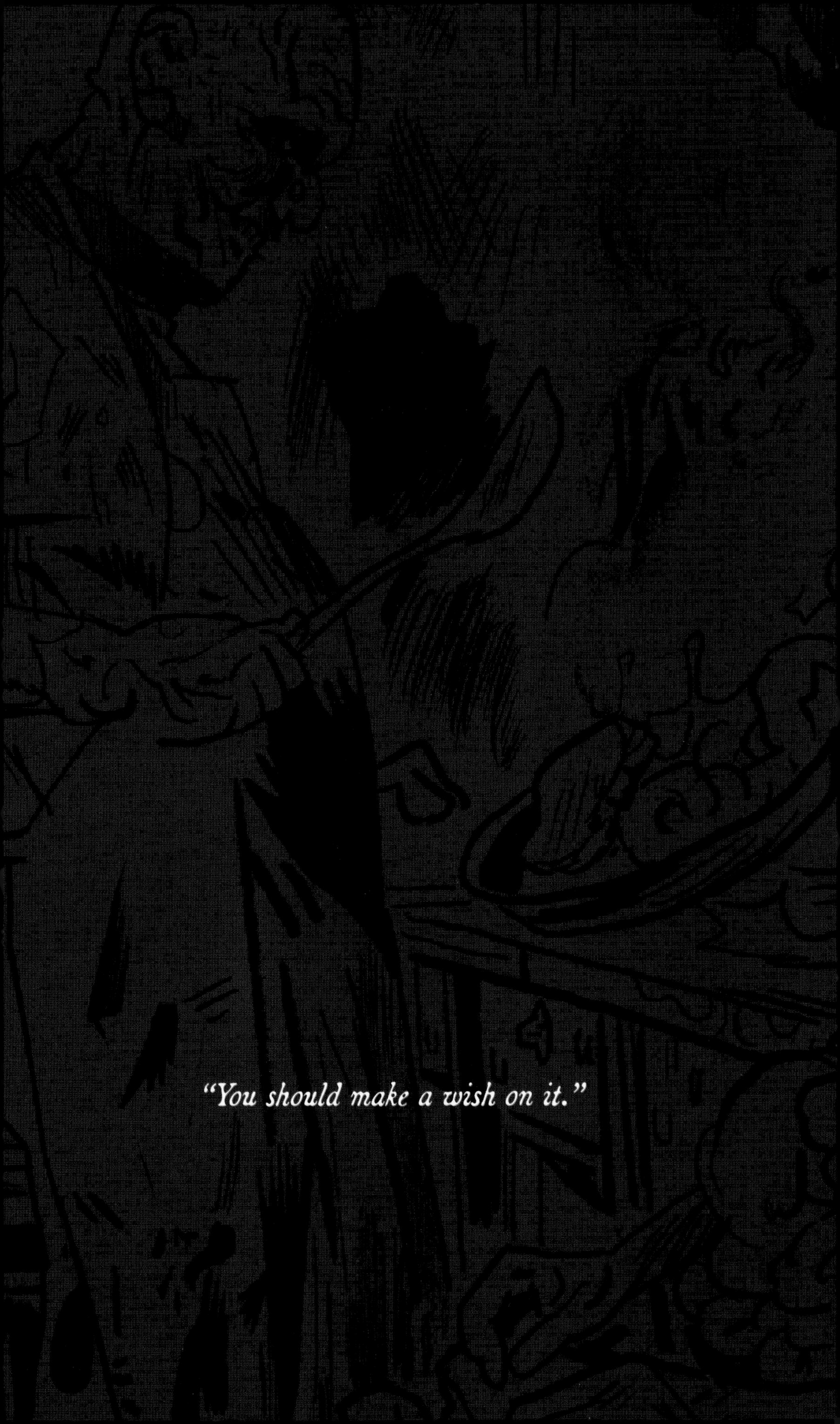

"You should make a wish on it."

'Til Dawn

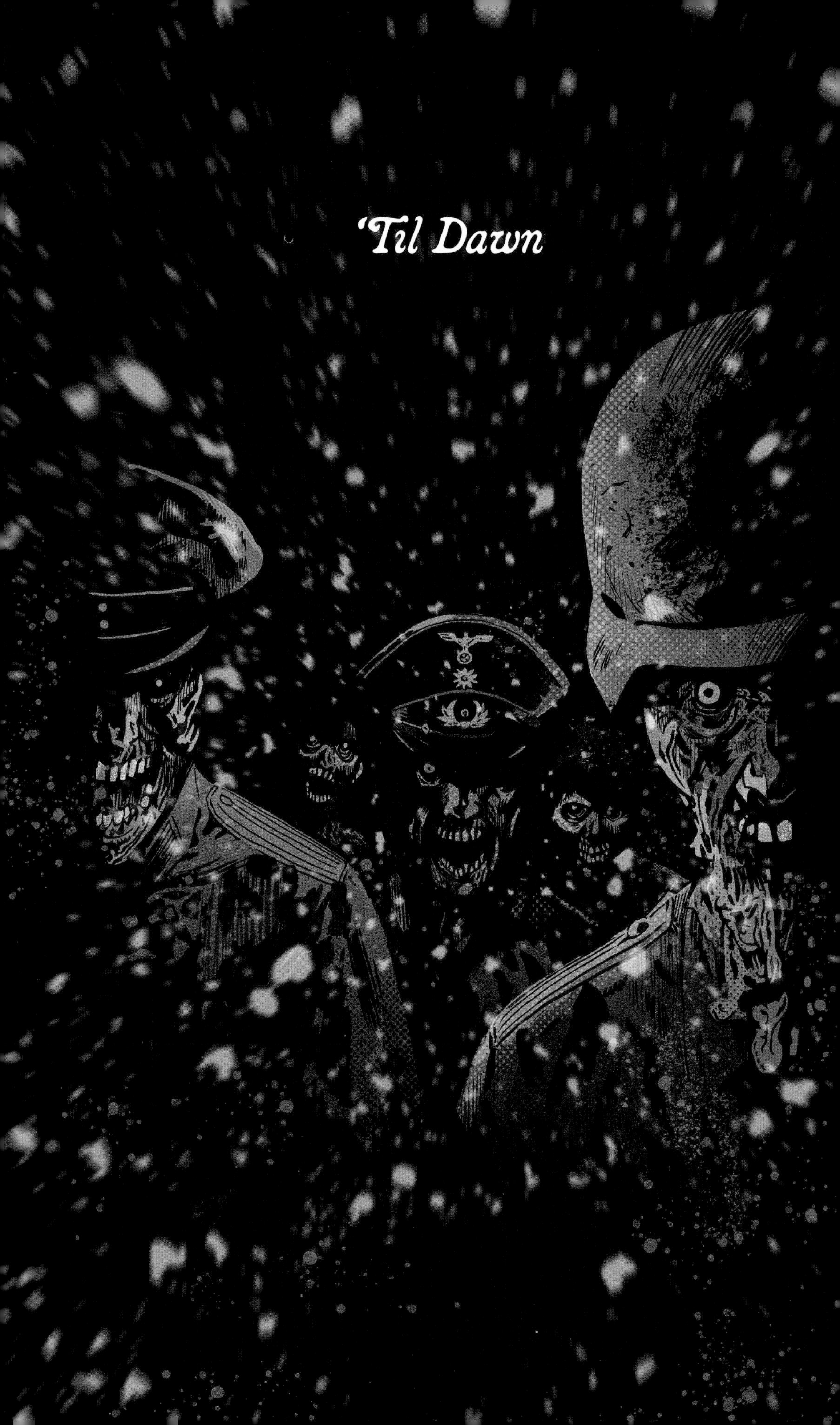

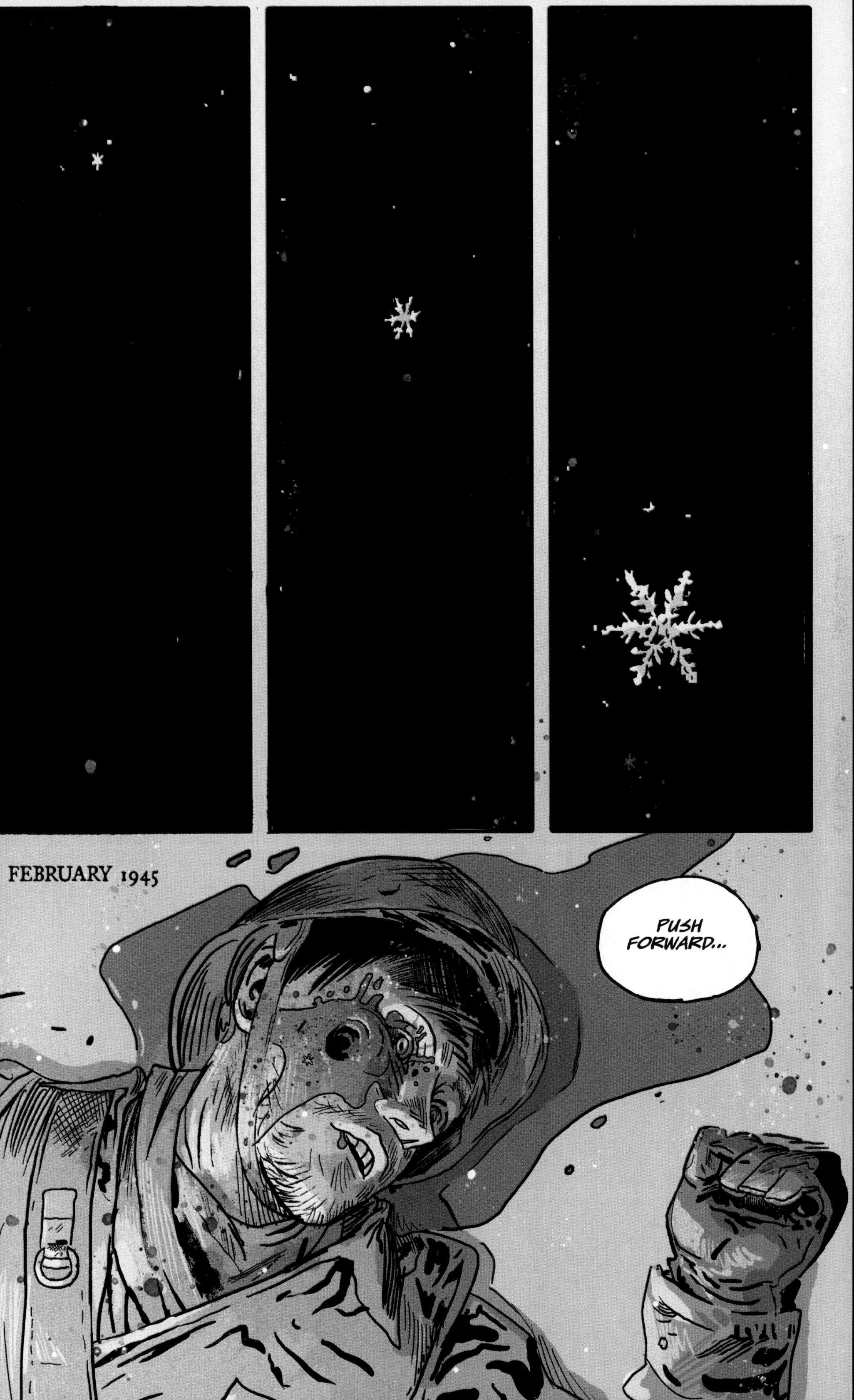
FEBRUARY 1945
PUSH FORWARD...

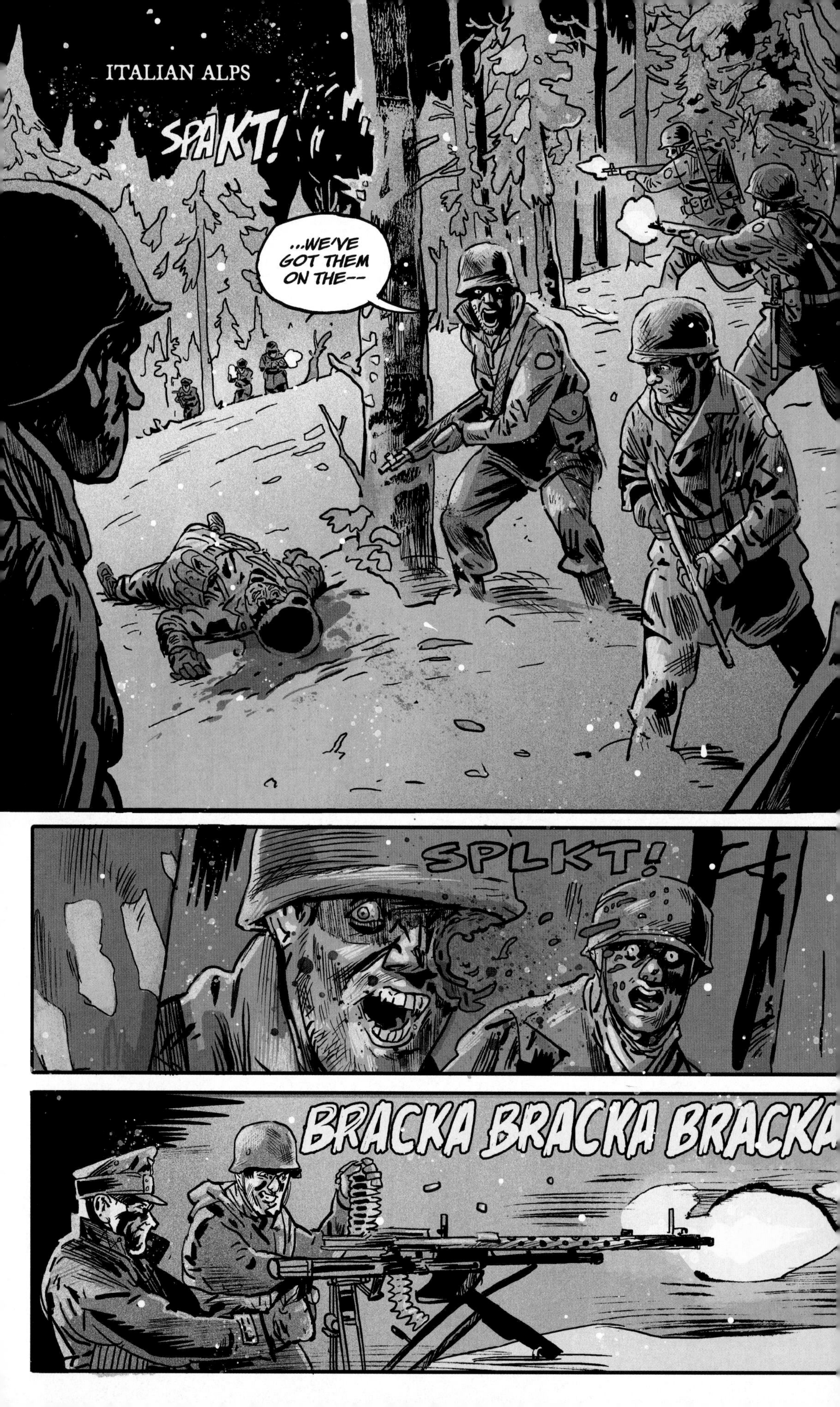
ITALIAN ALPS
SPAKT!
...WE'VE GOT THEM ON THE--
SPLKT!
BRACKA BRACKA BRACKA

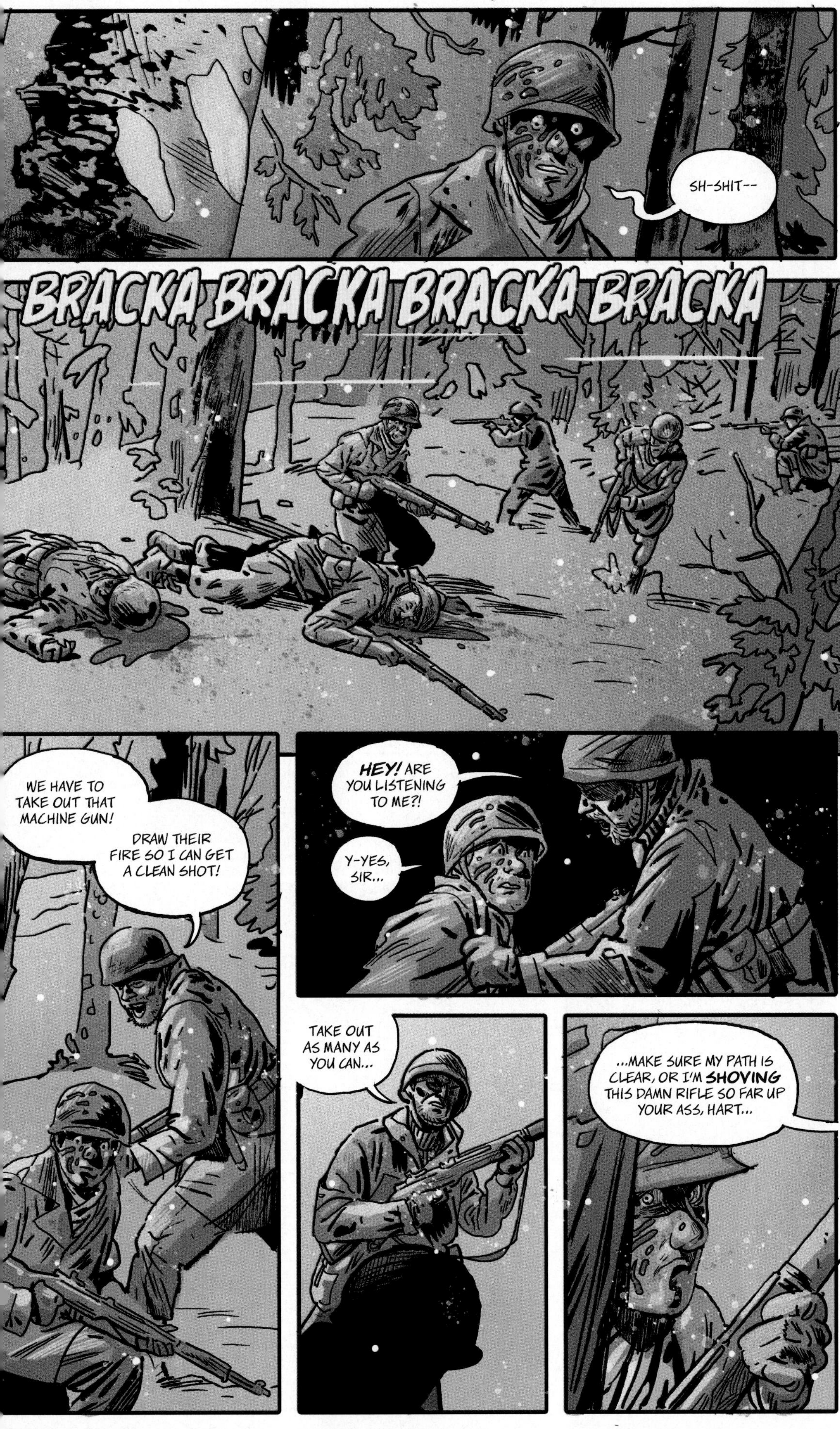

SH-SHIT--
BRACKA BRACKA BRACKA BRACKA
WE HAVE TO TAKE OUT THAT MACHINE GUN!
DRAW THEIR FIRE SO I CAN GET A CLEAN SHOT!
HEY! ARE YOU LISTENING TO ME?!
Y-YES, SIR...
TAKE OUT AS MANY AS YOU CAN...
...MAKE SURE MY PATH IS CLEAR, OR I'M SHOVING THIS DAMN RIFLE SO FAR UP YOUR ASS, HART...

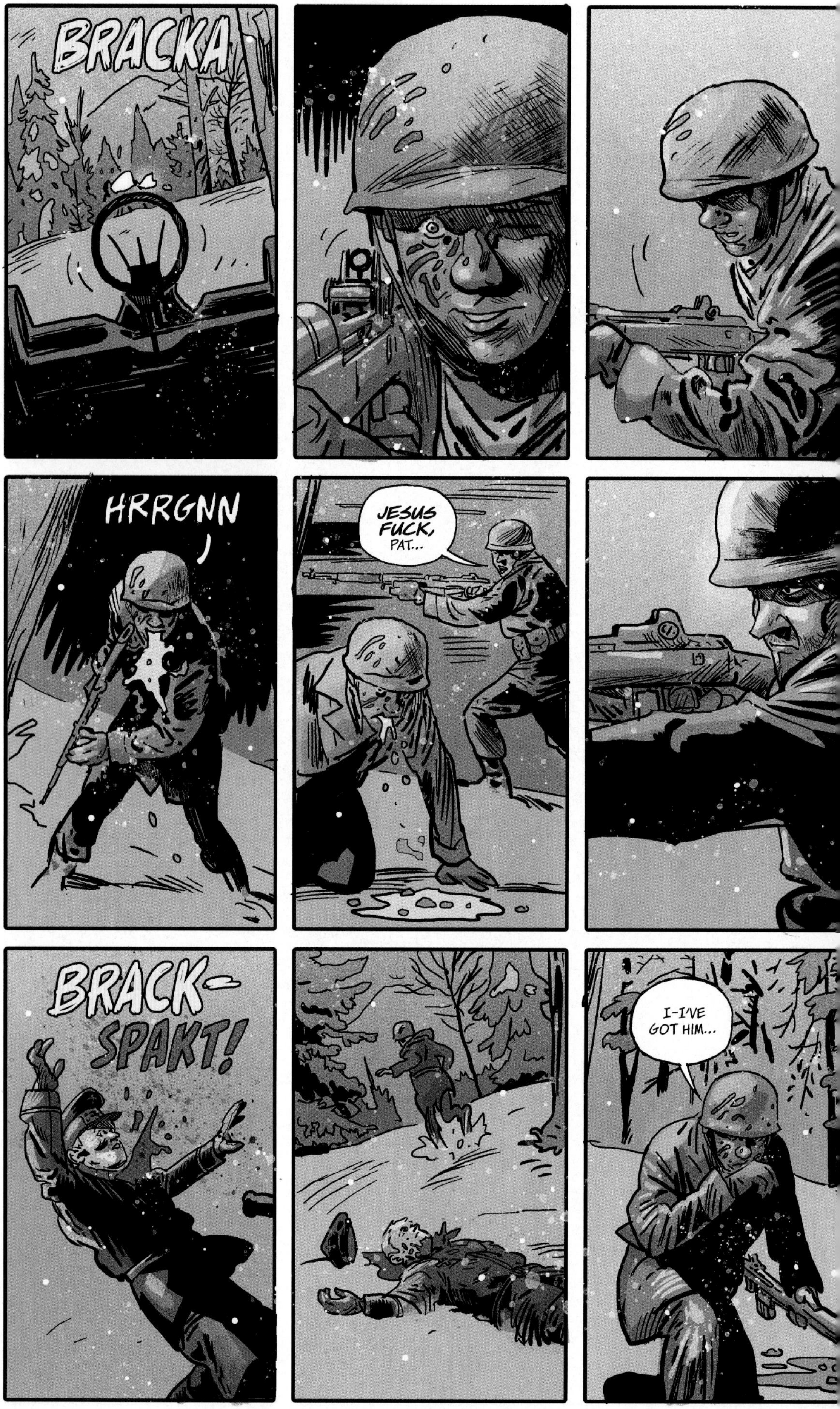
BRACKA
HRRGNN
JESUS FUCK, PAT...
BRACK-SPAKT!
I-I'VE GOT HIM...

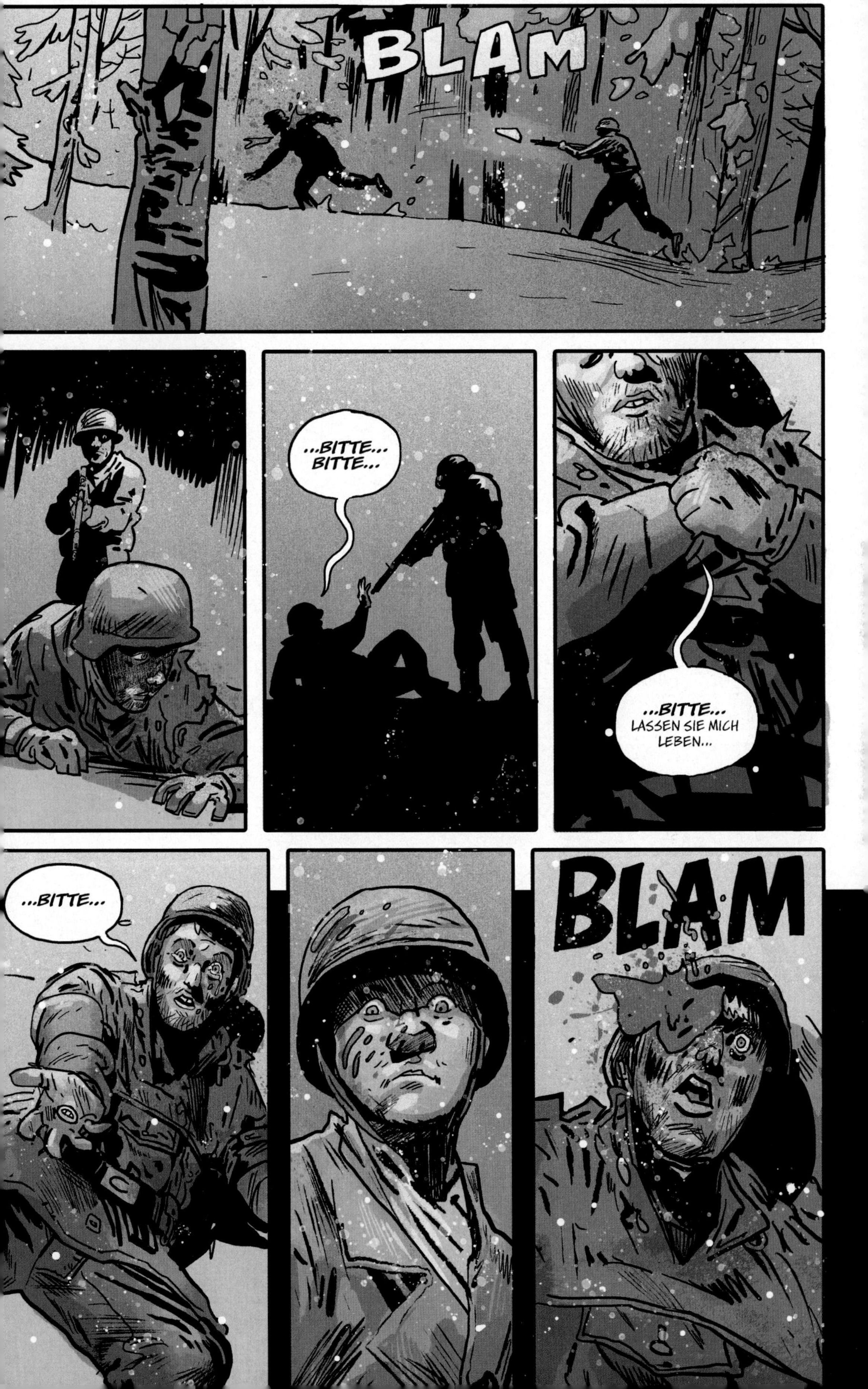
BLAM
...BITTE...
BITTE...
...BITTE...
LASSEN SIE MICH
LEBEN...
...BITTE...
BLAM

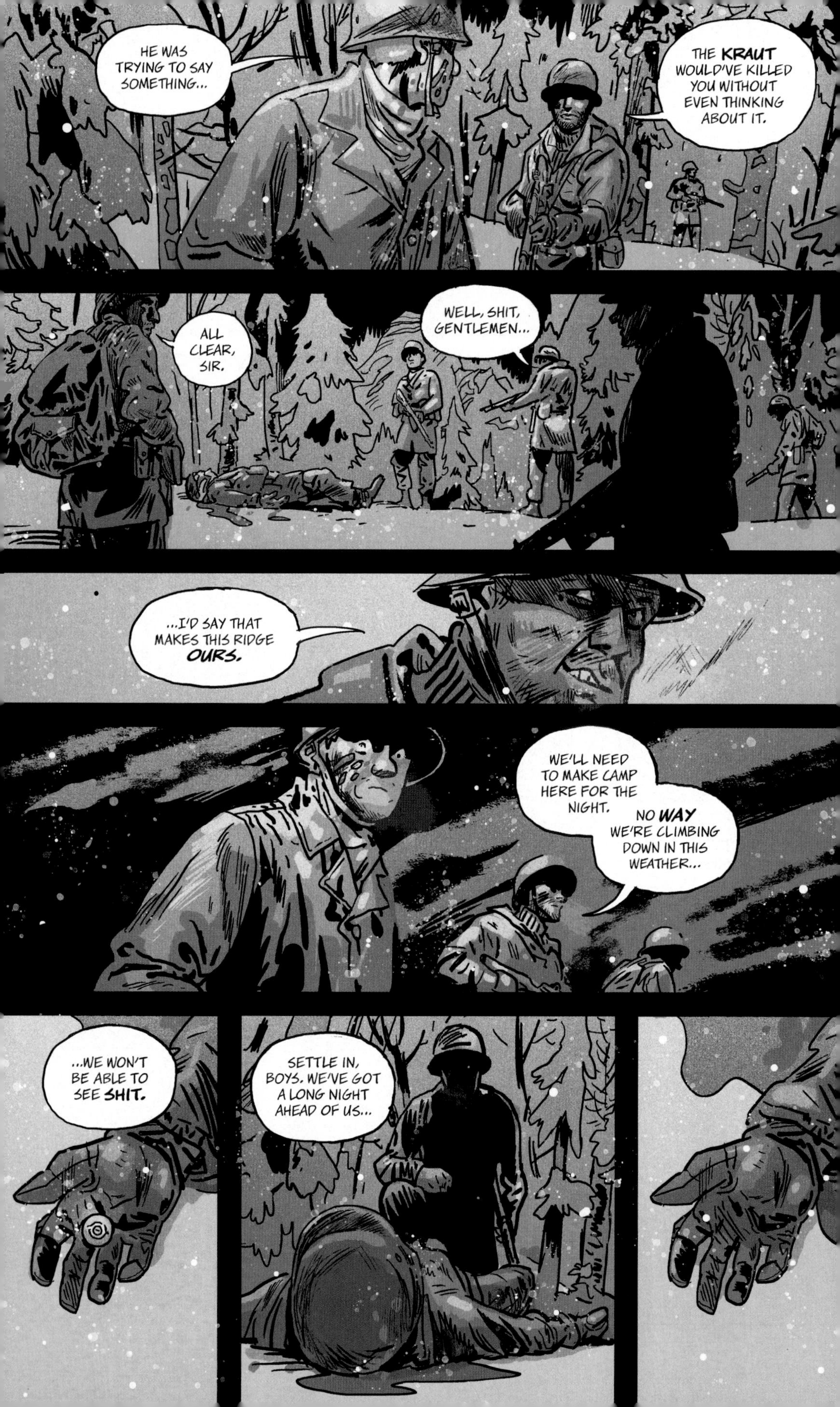
HE WAS TRYING TO SAY SOMETHING...
THE KRAUT WOULD'VE KILLED YOU WITHOUT EVEN THINKING ABOUT IT.
ALL CLEAR, SIR.
WELL, SHIT, GENTLEMEN...
...I'D SAY THAT MAKES THIS RIDGE OURS.
WE'LL NEED TO MAKE CAMP HERE FOR THE NIGHT.
NO WAY WE'RE CLIMBING DOWN IN THIS WEATHER...
...WE WON'T BE ABLE TO SEE SHIT.
SETTLE IN, BOYS. WE'VE GOT A LONG NIGHT AHEAD OF US...

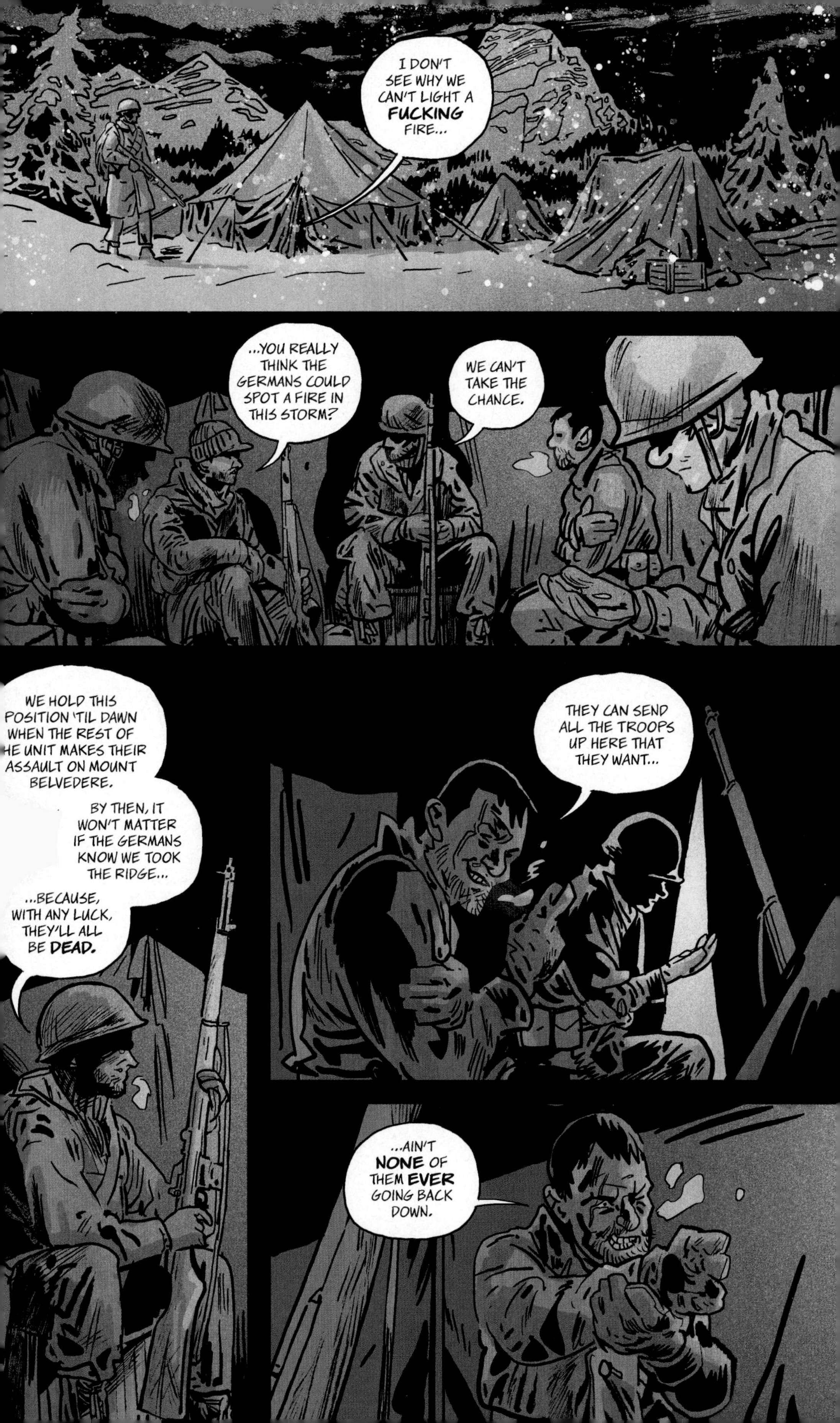
I DON'T SEE WHY WE CAN'T LIGHT A **FUCKING** FIRE...
...YOU REALLY THINK THE GERMANS COULD SPOT A FIRE IN THIS STORM?
WE CAN'T TAKE THE CHANCE.
WE HOLD THIS POSITION 'TIL DAWN WHEN THE REST OF HE UNIT MAKES THEIR ASSAULT ON MOUNT BELVEDERE.
BY THEN, IT WON'T MATTER IF THE GERMANS KNOW WE TOOK THE RIDGE...
...BECAUSE, WITH ANY LUCK, THEY'LL ALL BE **DEAD.**
THEY CAN SEND ALL THE TROOPS UP HERE THAT THEY WANT...
...AIN'T **NONE** OF THEM **EVER** GOING BACK DOWN.

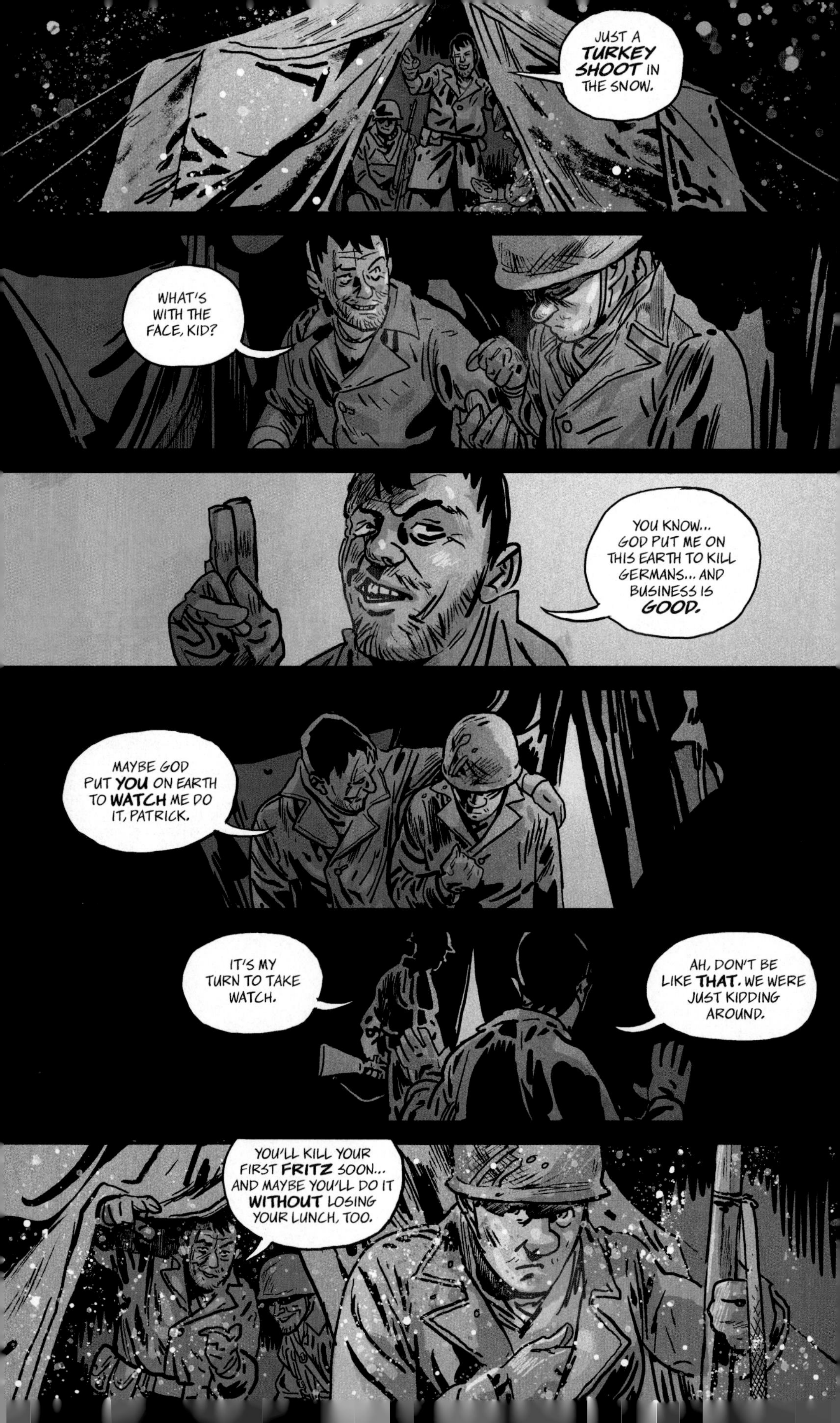
JUST A TURKEY SHOOT IN THE SNOW.
WHAT'S WITH THE FACE, KID?
YOU KNOW... GOD PUT ME ON THIS EARTH TO KILL GERMANS... AND BUSINESS IS GOOD.
MAYBE GOD PUT YOU ON EARTH TO WATCH ME DO IT, PATRICK.
IT'S MY TURN TO TAKE WATCH.
AH, DON'T BE LIKE THAT. WE WERE JUST KIDDING AROUND.
YOU'LL KILL YOUR FIRST FRITZ SOON... AND MAYBE YOU'LL DO IT WITHOUT LOSING YOUR LUNCH, TOO.

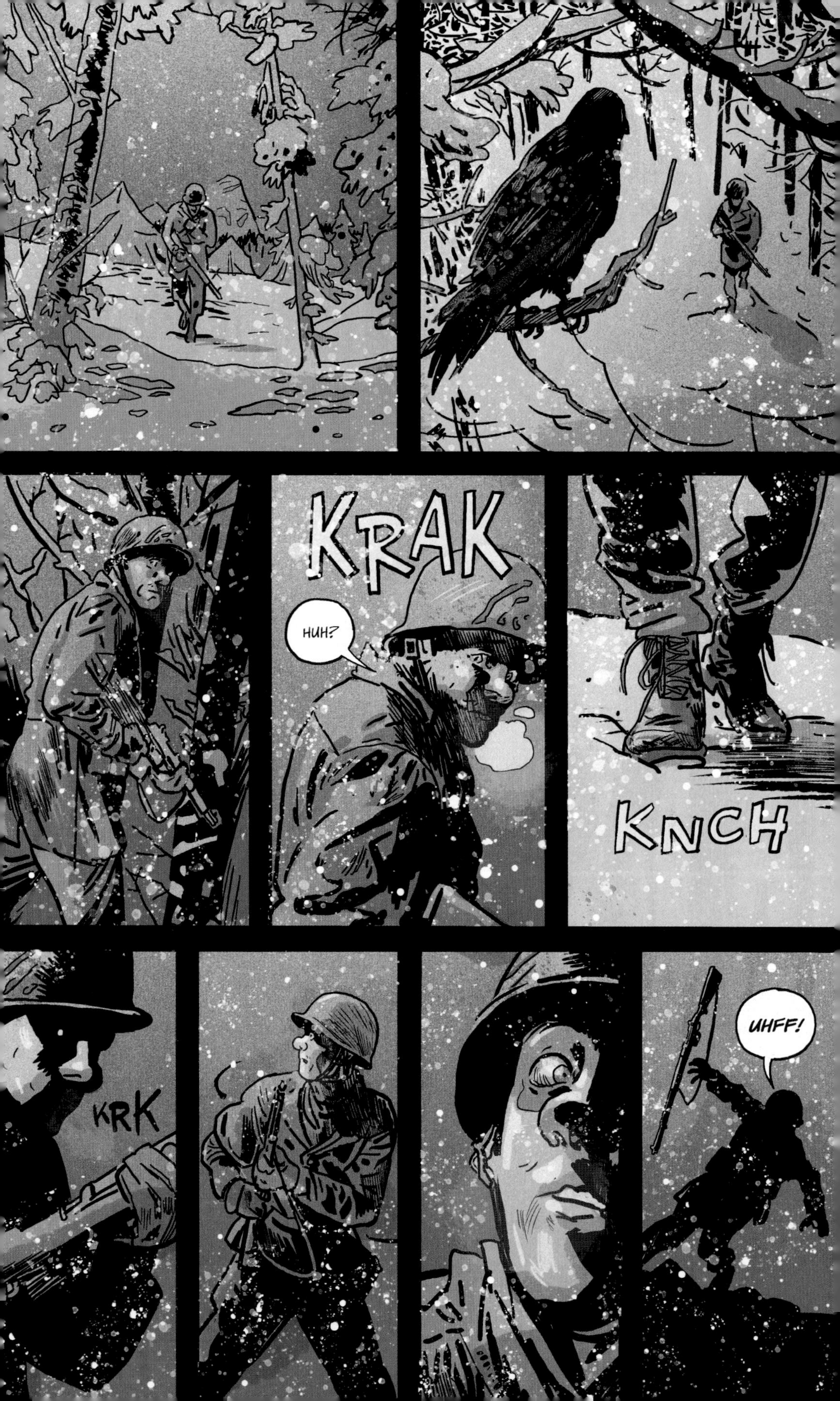
KRAK
HUH?
KNCH
KRK
UHFF!

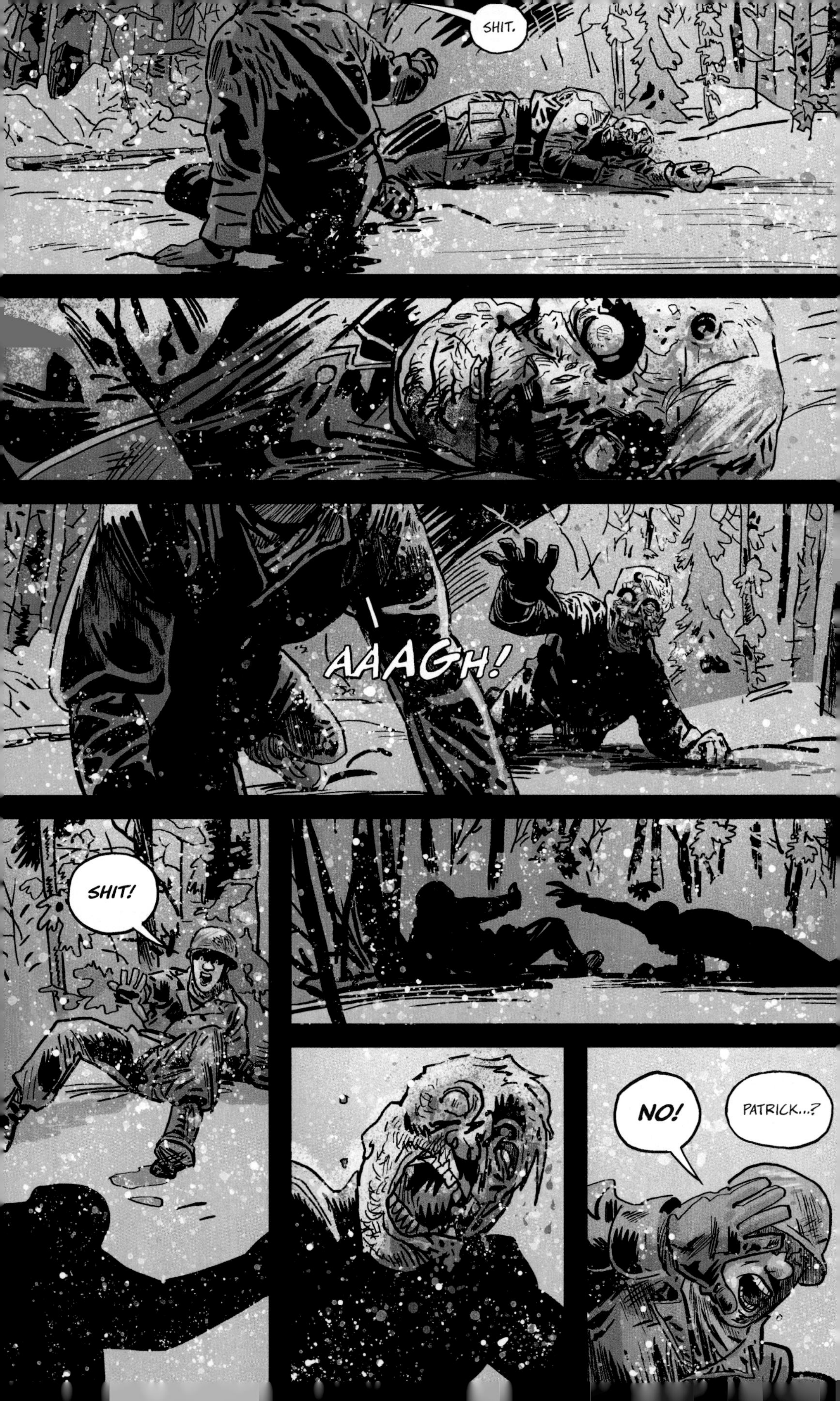
SHIT.
AAAGH!
SHIT!
NO!
PATRICK...?

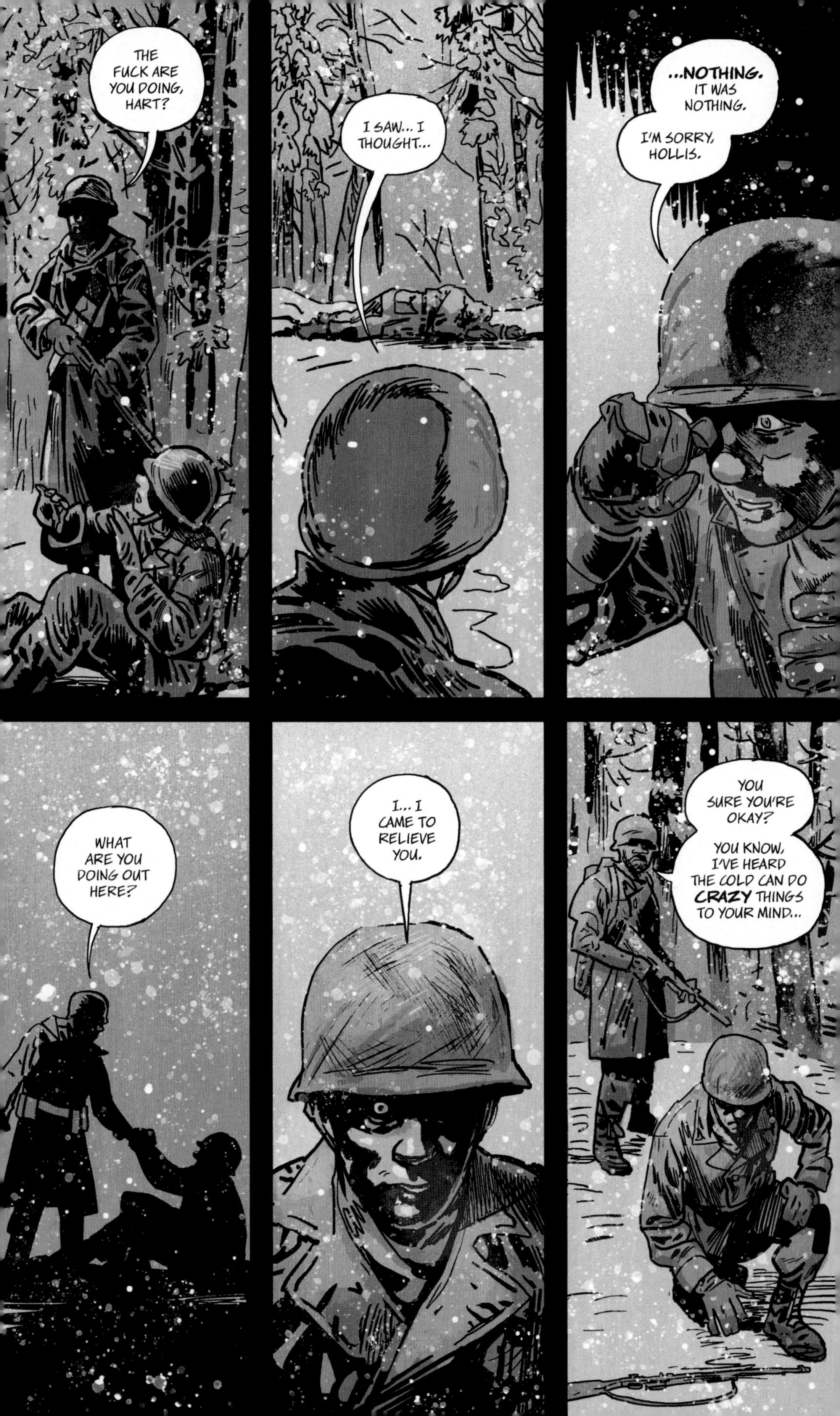
THE FUCK ARE YOU DOING, HART?
I SAW... I THOUGHT...
...NOTHING. IT WAS NOTHING.
I'M SORRY, HOLLIS.
WHAT ARE YOU DOING OUT HERE?
I... I CAME TO RELIEVE YOU.
YOU SURE YOU'RE OKAY?
YOU KNOW, I'VE HEARD THE COLD CAN DO CRAZY THINGS TO YOUR MIND...

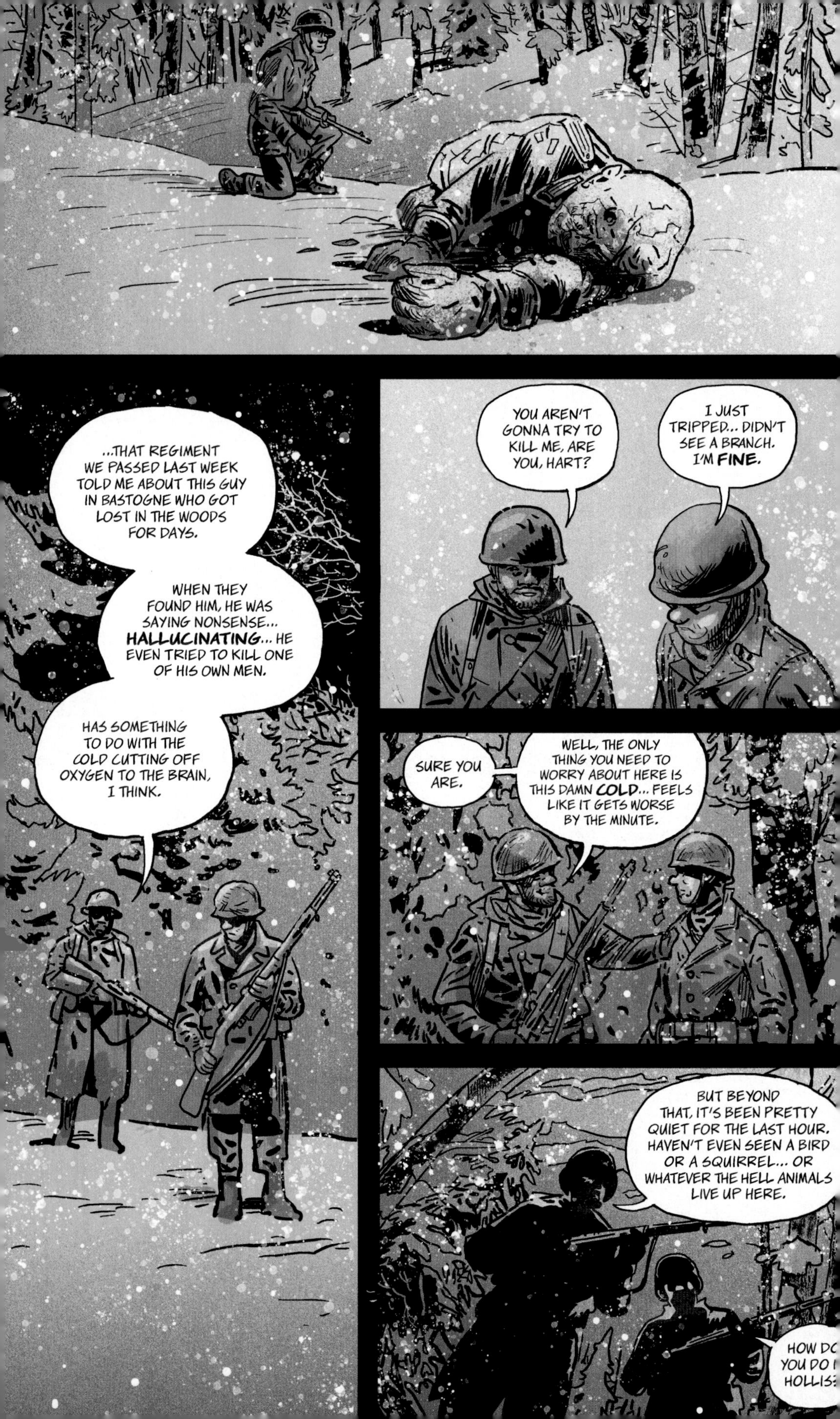
...THAT REGIMENT WE PASSED LAST WEEK TOLD ME ABOUT THIS GUY IN BASTOGNE WHO GOT LOST IN THE WOODS FOR DAYS.
WHEN THEY FOUND HIM, HE WAS SAYING NONSENSE... **HALLUCINATING**... HE EVEN TRIED TO KILL ONE OF HIS OWN MEN.
HAS SOMETHING TO DO WITH THE COLD CUTTING OFF OXYGEN TO THE BRAIN, I THINK.
YOU AREN'T GONNA TRY TO KILL ME, ARE YOU, HART?
I JUST TRIPPED... DIDN'T SEE A BRANCH. I'M **FINE**.
SURE YOU ARE.
WELL, THE ONLY THING YOU NEED TO WORRY ABOUT HERE IS THIS DAMN **COLD**... FEELS LIKE IT GETS WORSE BY THE MINUTE.
BUT BEYOND THAT, IT'S BEEN PRETTY QUIET FOR THE LAST HOUR. HAVEN'T EVEN SEEN A BIRD OR A SQUIRREL... OR WHATEVER THE HELL ANIMALS LIVE UP HERE.

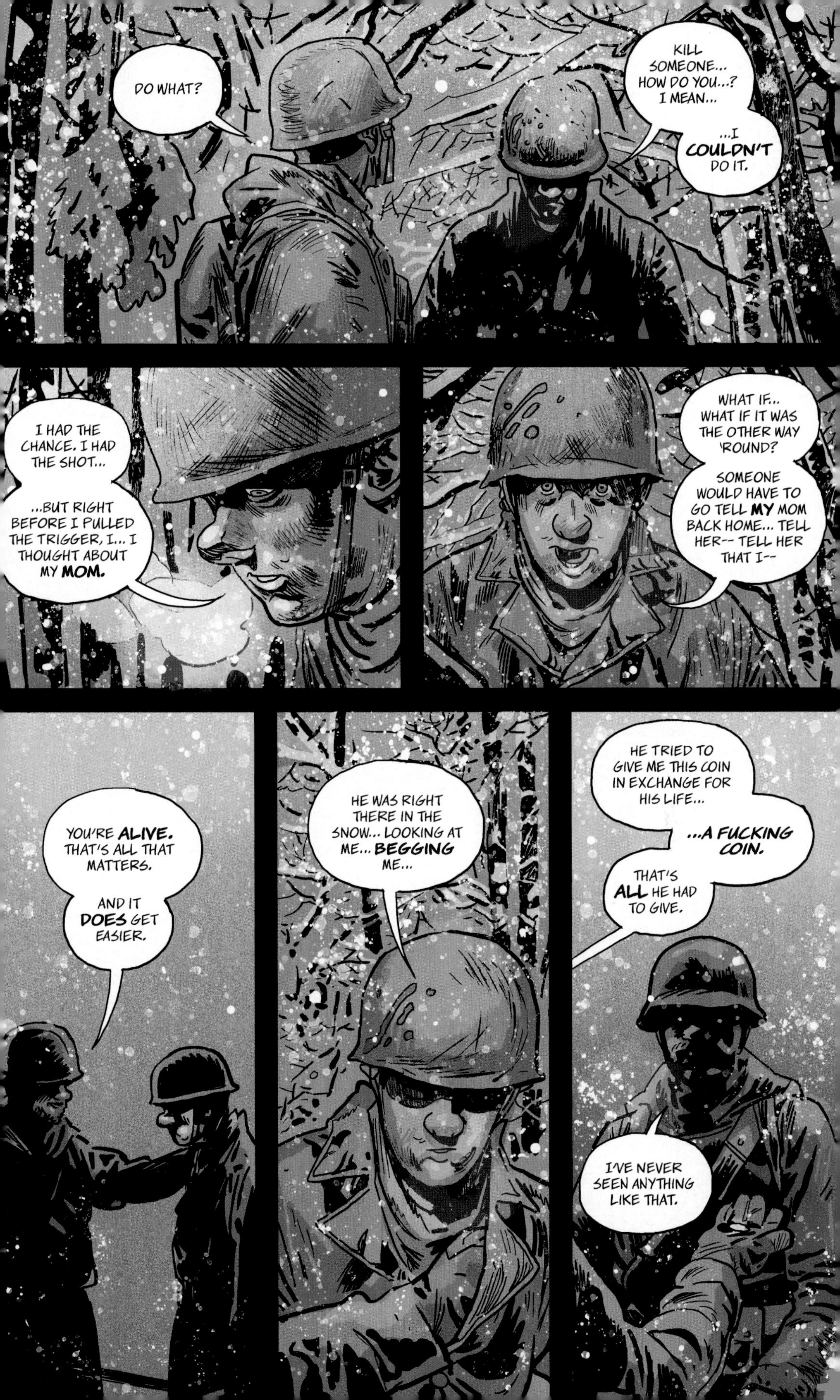
DO WHAT?
KILL SOMEONE... HOW DO YOU...? I MEAN...
...I COULDN'T DO IT.
I HAD THE CHANCE. I HAD THE SHOT...
...BUT RIGHT BEFORE I PULLED THE TRIGGER, I... I THOUGHT ABOUT MY MOM.
WHAT IF... WHAT IF IT WAS THE OTHER WAY 'ROUND?
SOMEONE WOULD HAVE TO GO TELL MY MOM BACK HOME... TELL HER-- TELL HER THAT I--
YOU'RE ALIVE. THAT'S ALL THAT MATTERS.
AND IT DOES GET EASIER.
HE WAS RIGHT THERE IN THE SNOW... LOOKING AT ME... BEGGING ME...
HE TRIED TO GIVE ME THIS COIN IN EXCHANGE FOR HIS LIFE...
...A FUCKING COIN.
THAT'S ALL HE HAD TO GIVE.
I'VE NEVER SEEN ANYTHING LIKE THAT.

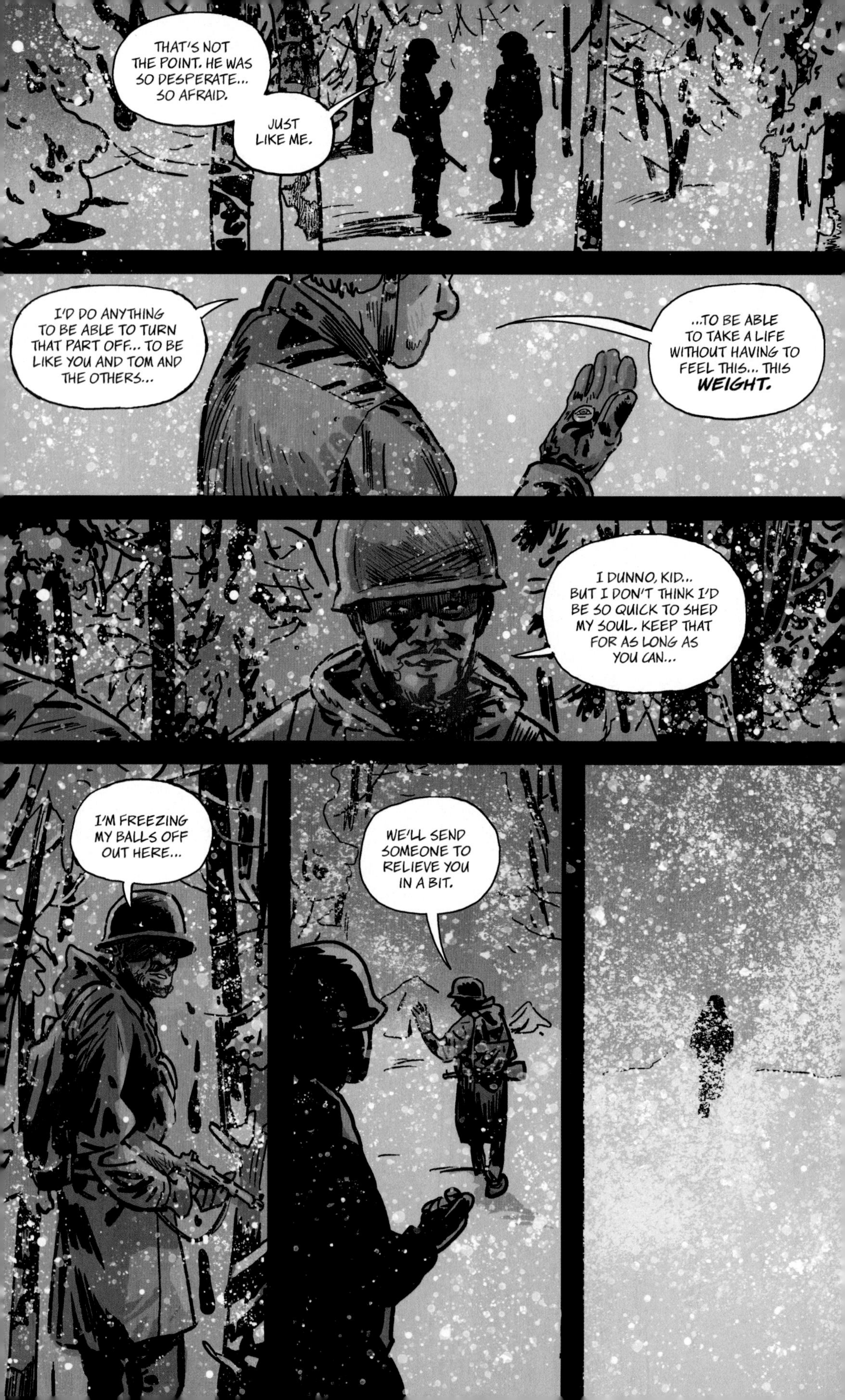
THAT'S NOT THE POINT. HE WAS SO DESPERATE... SO AFRAID.
JUST LIKE ME.
I'D DO ANYTHING TO BE ABLE TO TURN THAT PART OFF... TO BE LIKE YOU AND TOM AND THE OTHERS...
...TO BE ABLE TO TAKE A LIFE WITHOUT HAVING TO FEEL THIS... THIS WEIGHT.
I DUNNO, KID... BUT I DON'T THINK I'D BE SO QUICK TO SHED MY SOUL. KEEP THAT FOR AS LONG AS YOU CAN...
I'M FREEZING MY BALLS OFF OUT HERE...
WE'LL SEND SOMEONE TO RELIEVE YOU IN A BIT.

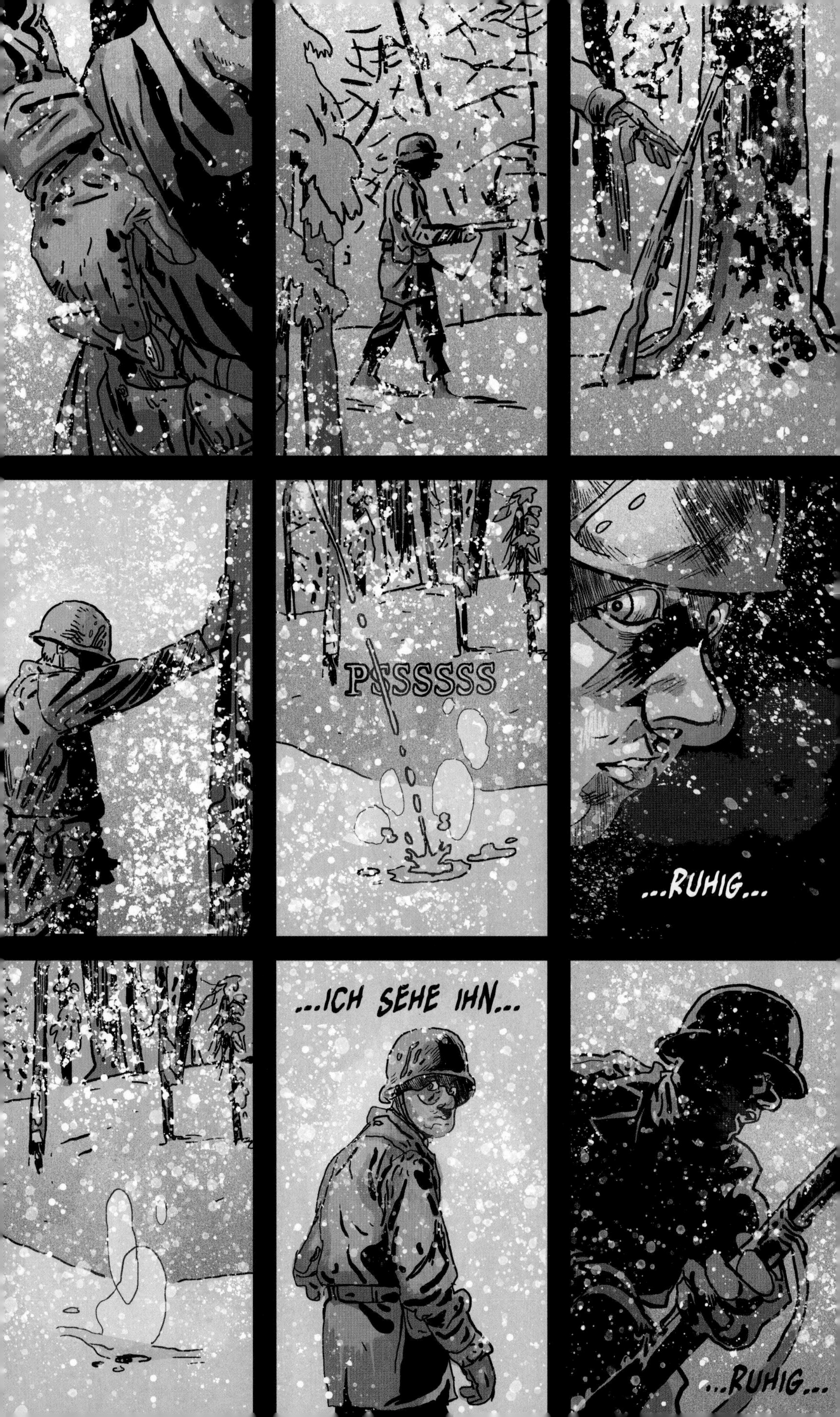
PSSSSSS
...RUHIG...
...ICH SEHE IHN...
...RUHIG...

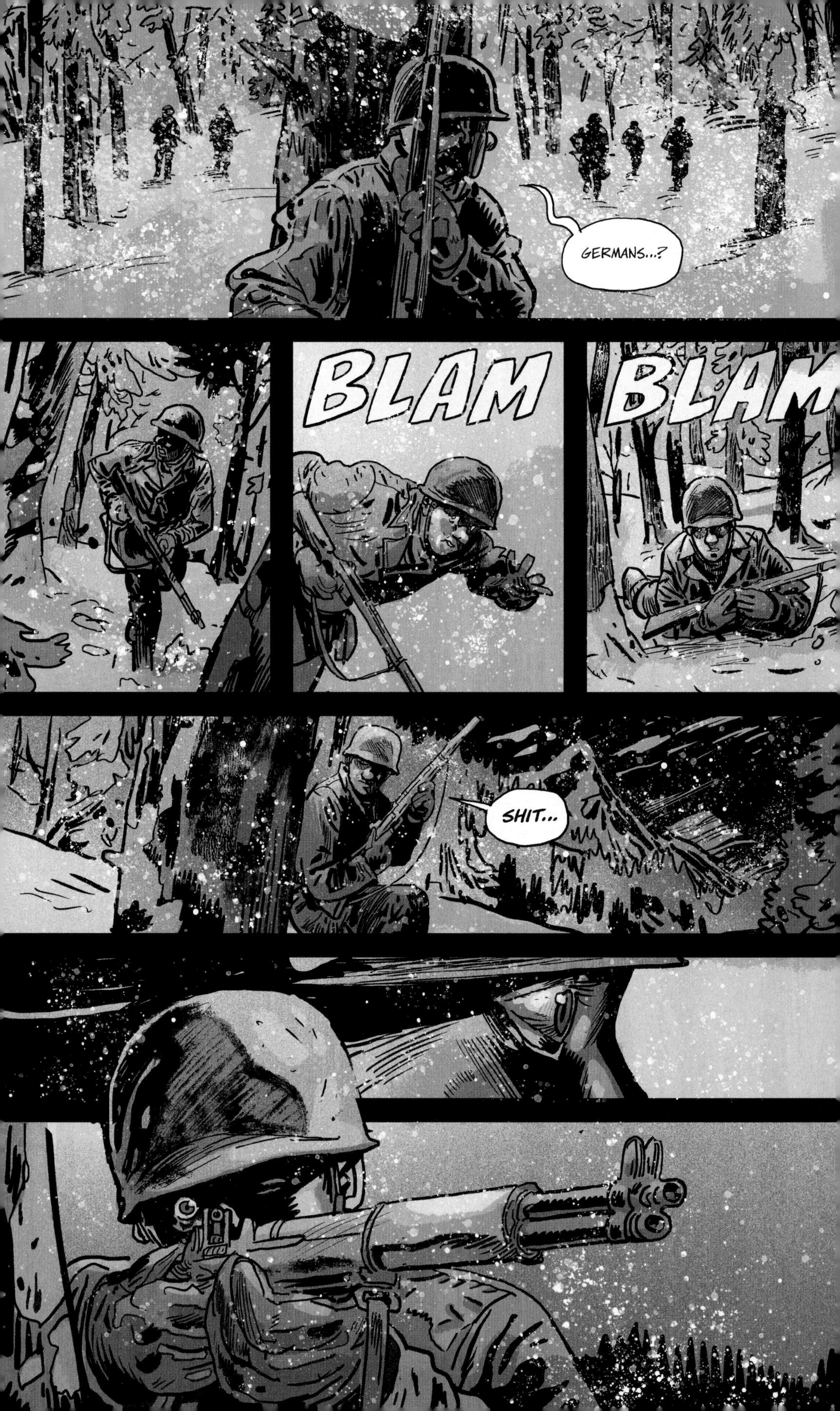
GERMANS...?
BLAM
BLAM
SHIT...

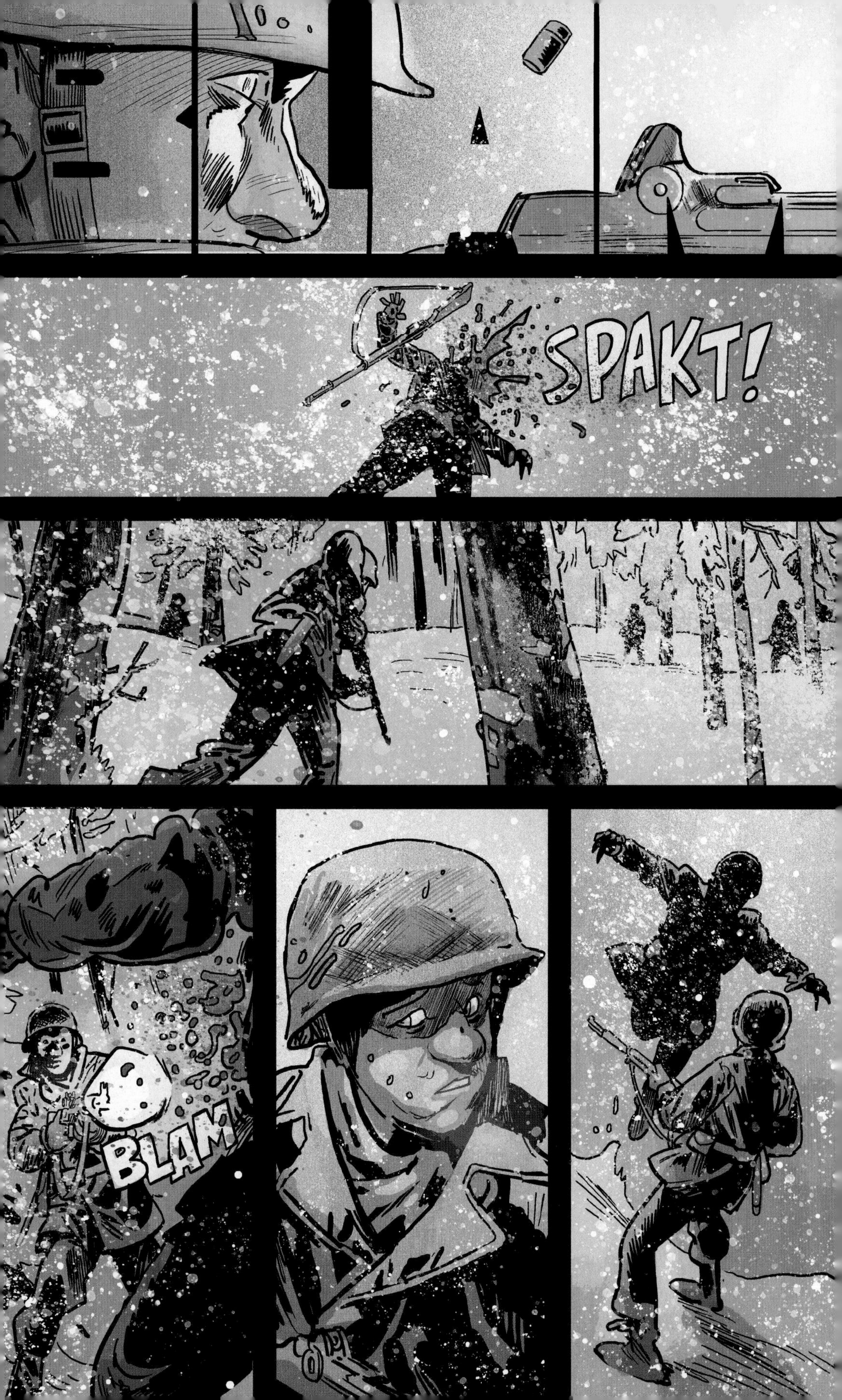
SPAKT!
BLAM

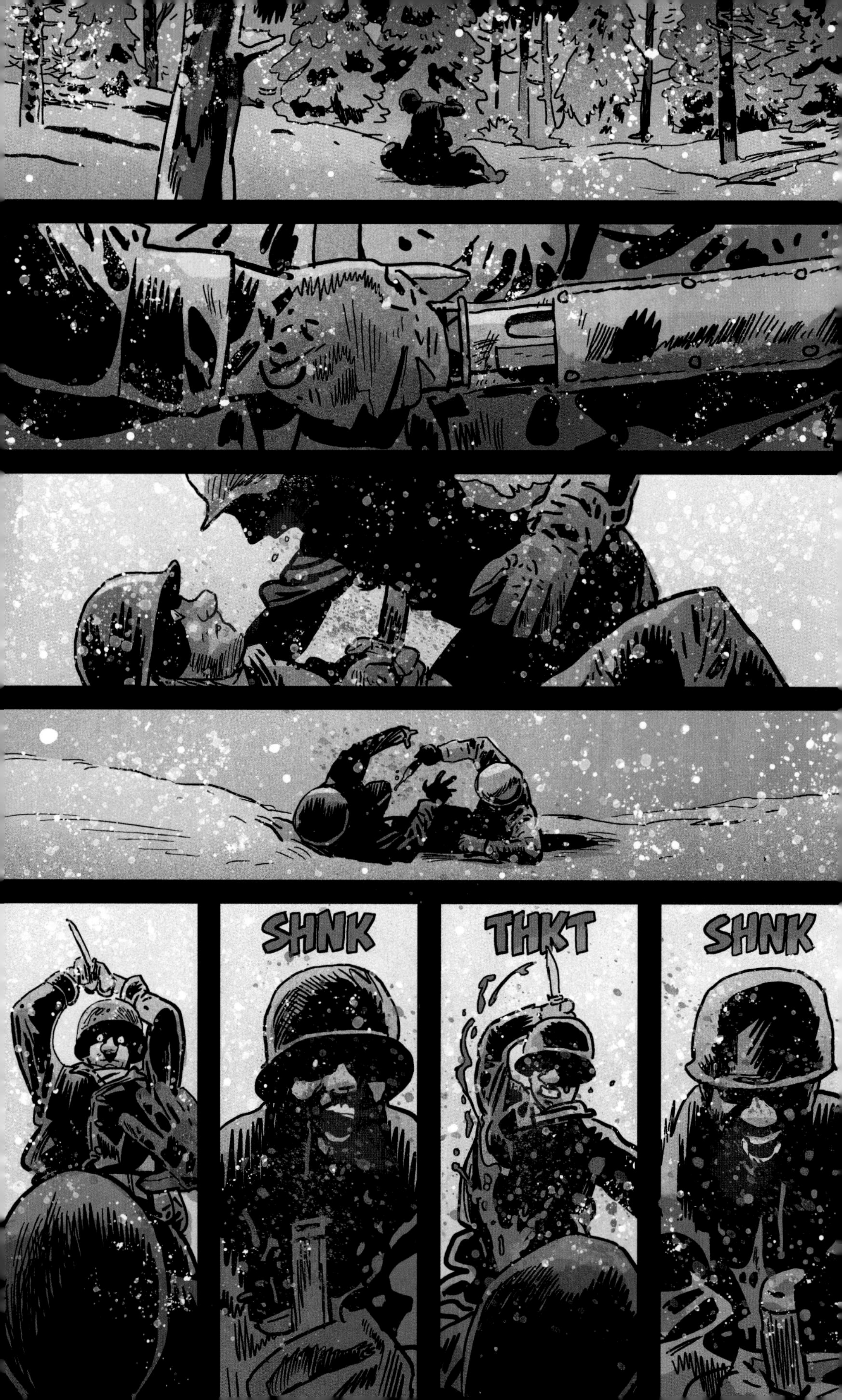
SHNK
THKT
SHNK

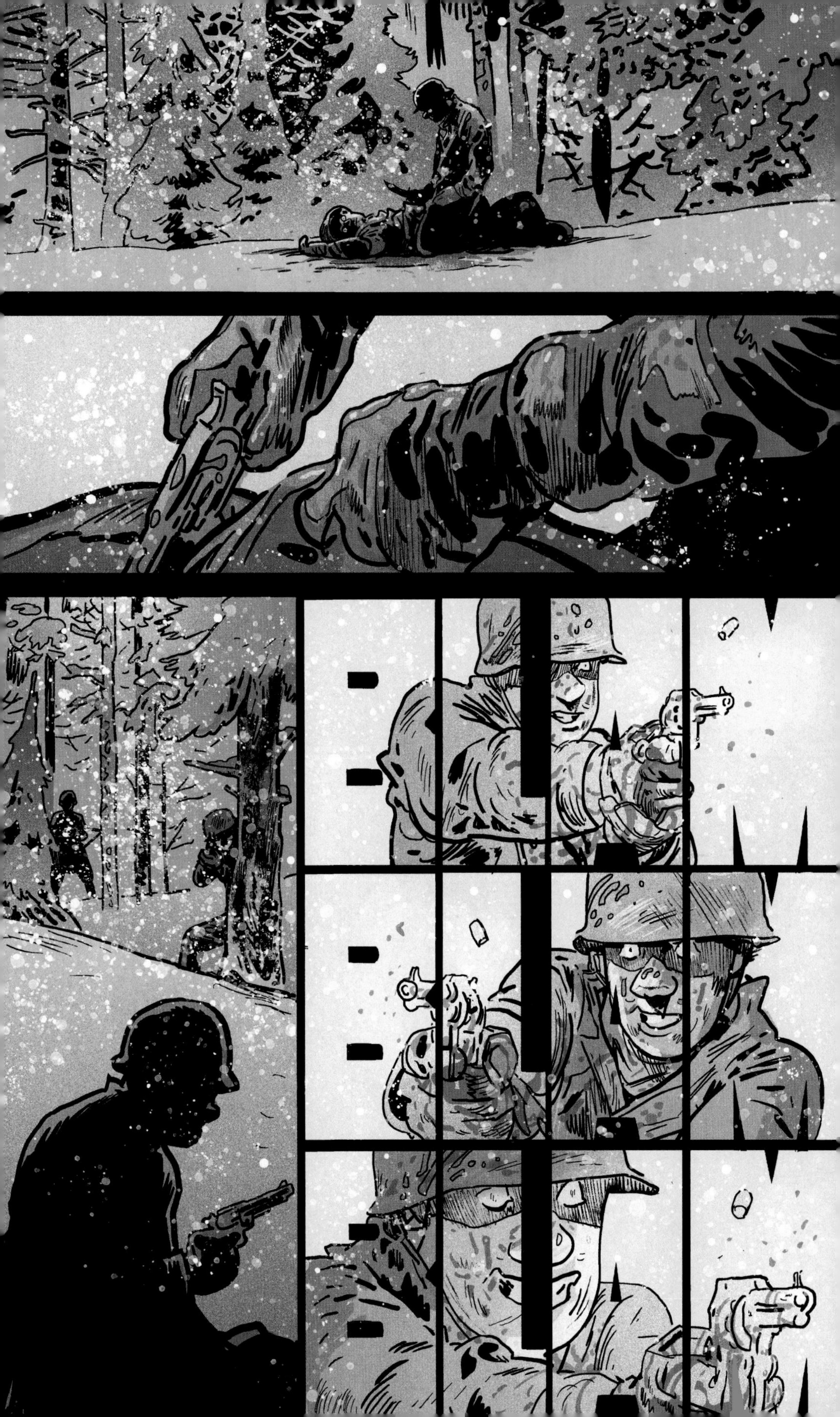

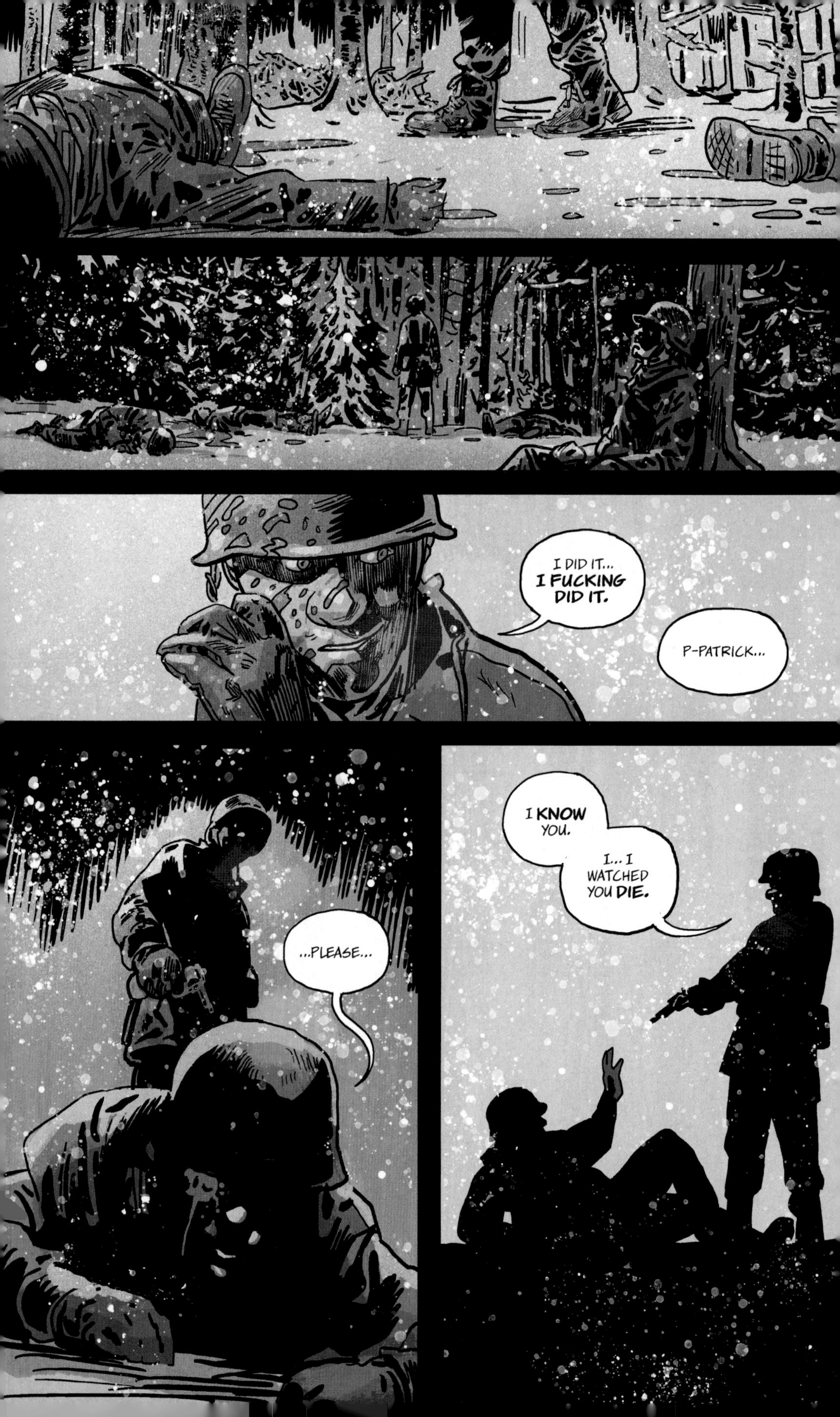
I DID IT... I FUCKING DID IT.
P-PATRICK...
...PLEASE...
I KNOW YOU.
I... I WATCHED YOU DIE.

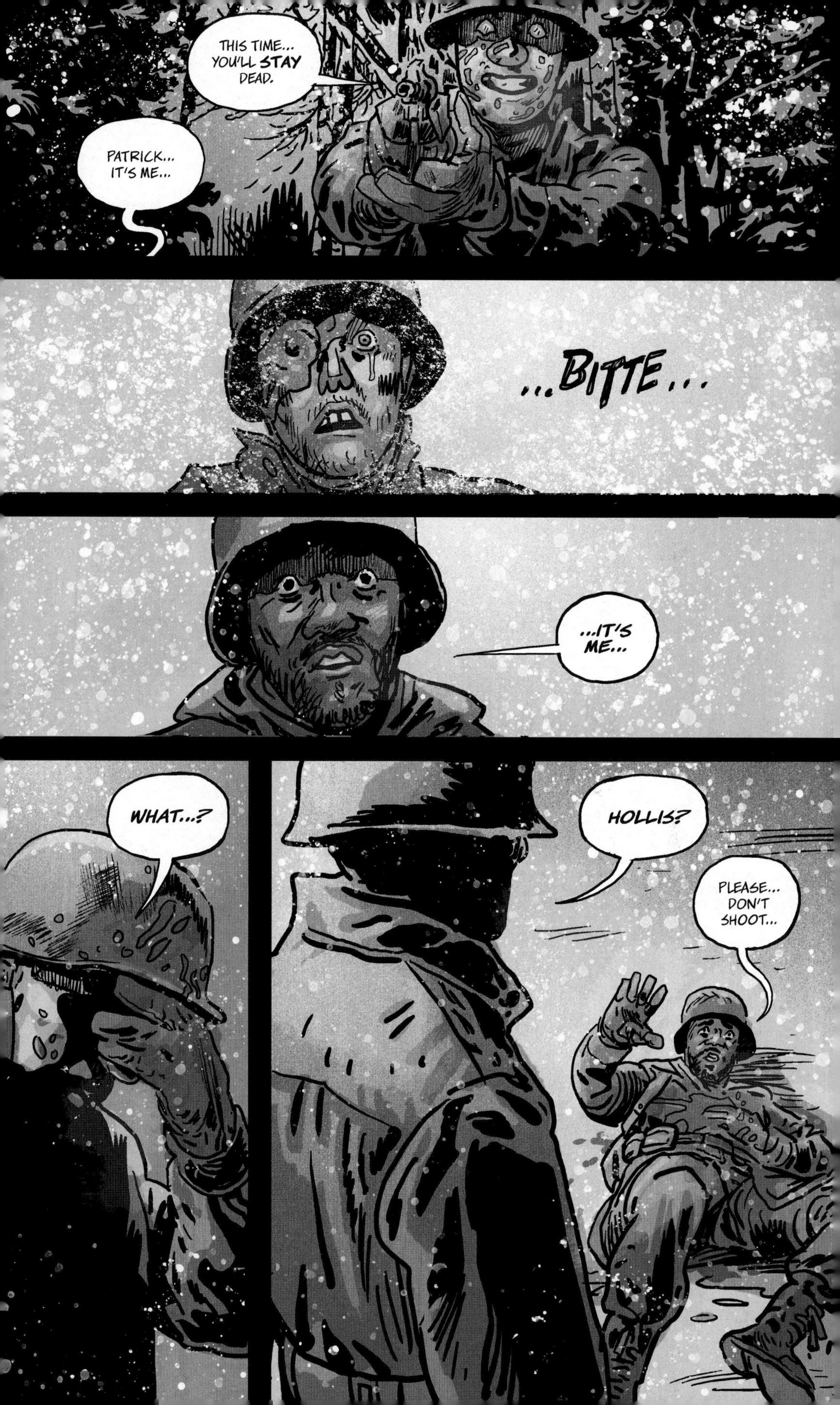
PATRICK... IT'S ME...
THIS TIME... YOU'LL STAY DEAD.
...BITTE...
...IT'S ME...
WHAT...?
HOLLIS?
PLEASE... DON'T SHOOT...

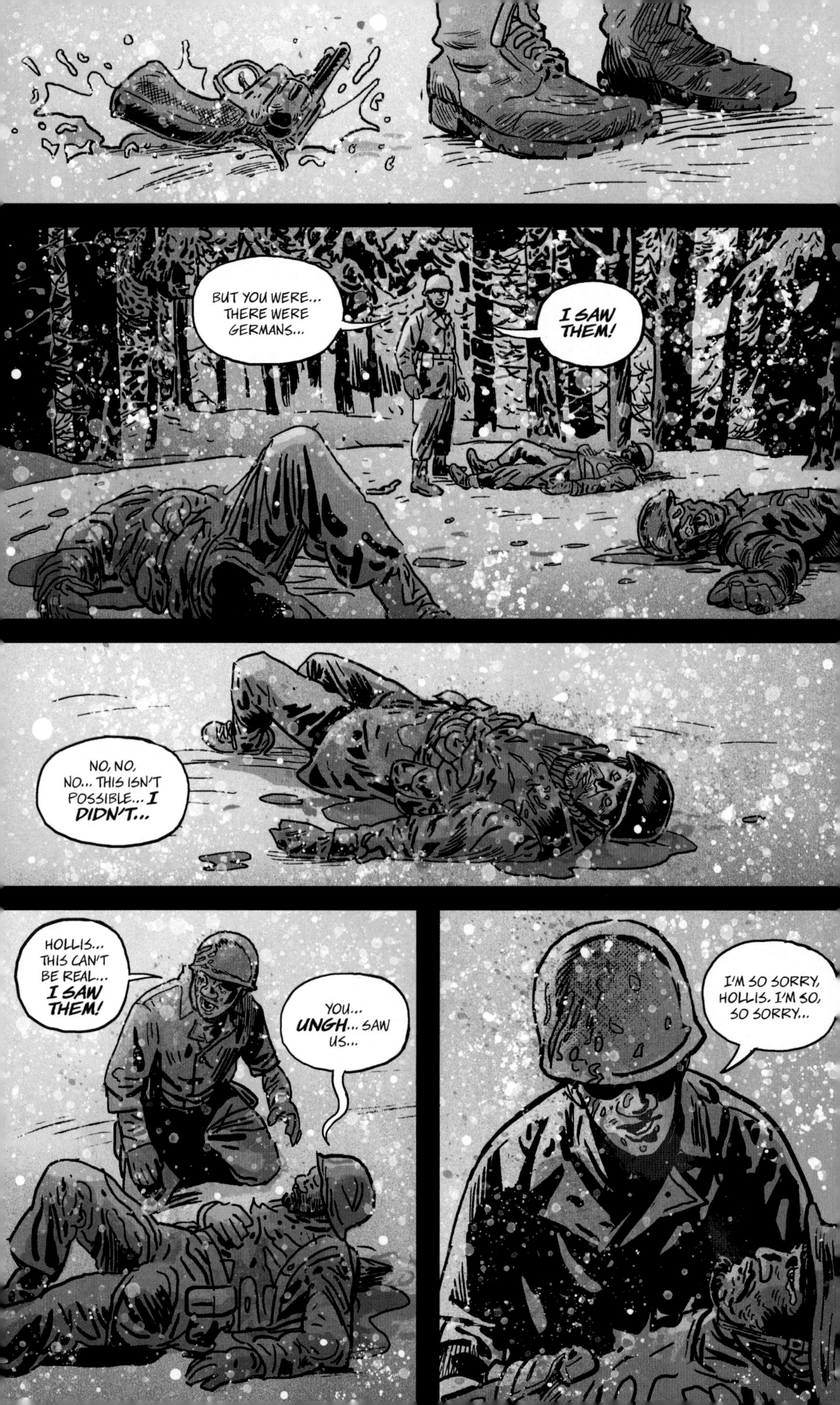
BUT YOU WERE... THERE WERE GERMANS...
I SAW THEM!
NO, NO, NO... THIS ISN'T POSSIBLE... I DIDN'T...
HOLLIS... THIS CAN'T BE REAL... I SAW THEM!
YOU... UNGH... SAW US...
I'M SO SORRY, HOLLIS. I'M SO, SO SORRY...

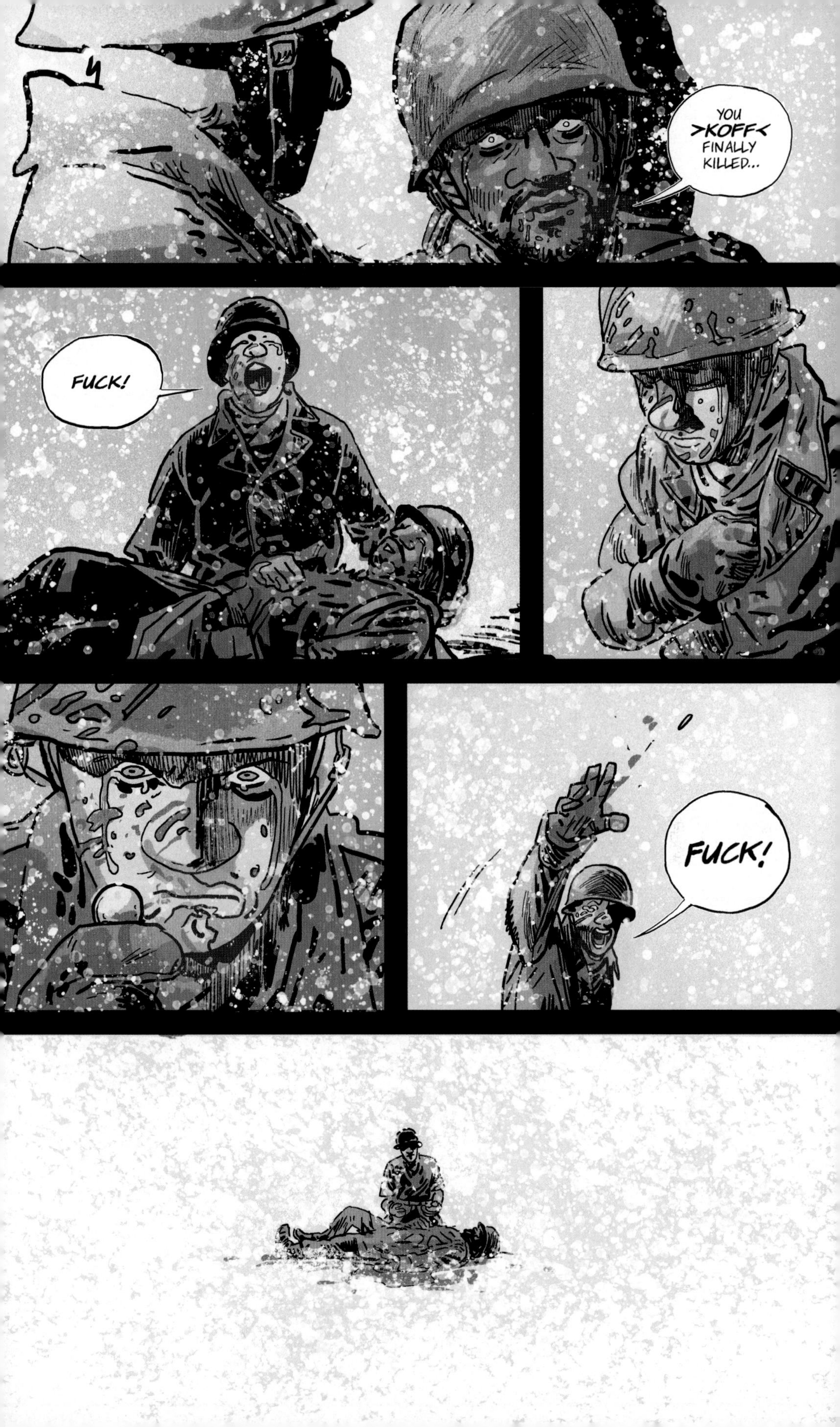
YOU >KOFF< FINALLY KILLED...
FUCK!
FUCK!

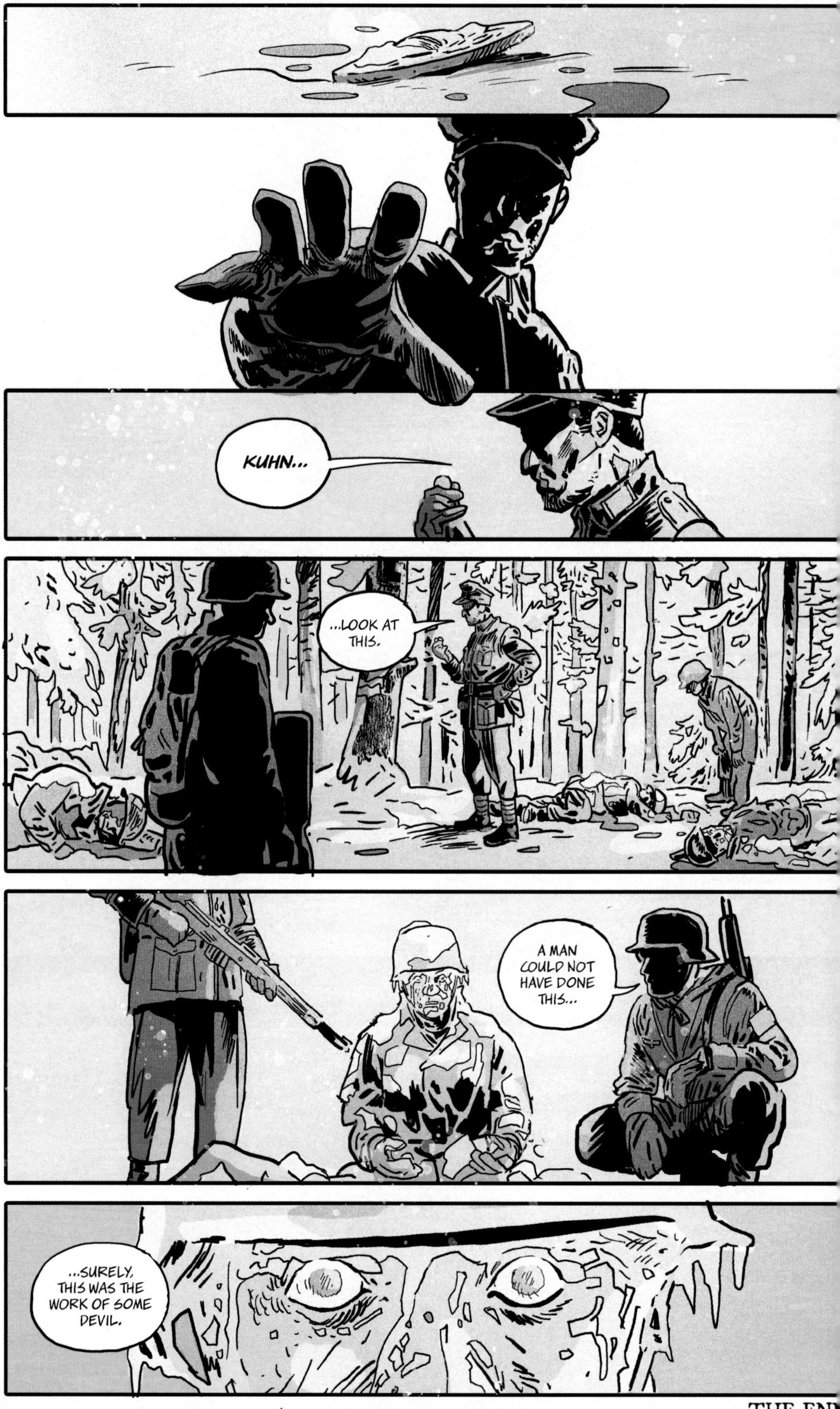
KUHN...
...LOOK AT THIS.
A MAN COULD NOT HAVE DONE THIS...
...SURELY, THIS WAS THE WORK OF SOME DEVIL.

THE END

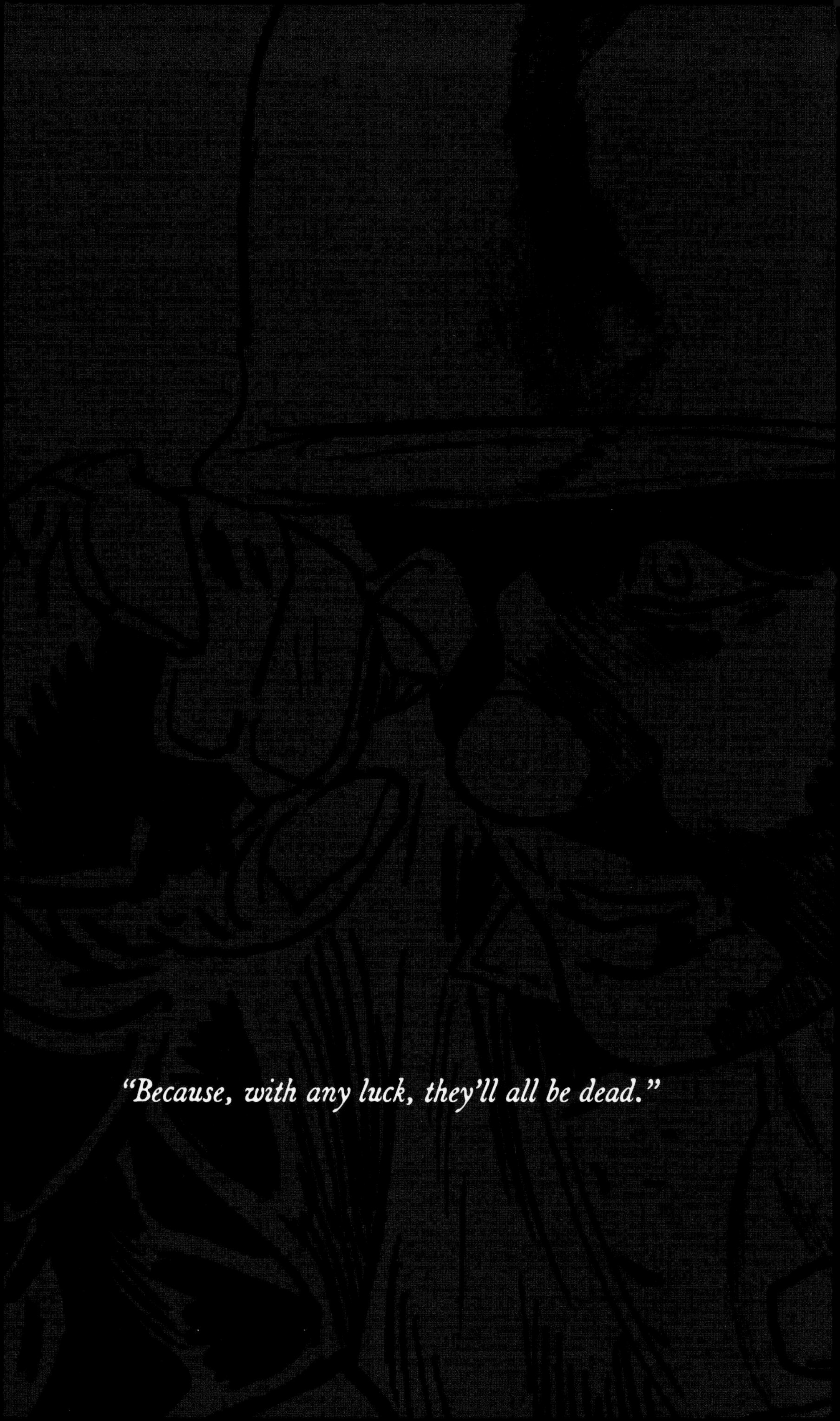

"Because, with any luck, they'll all be dead."

Threshold

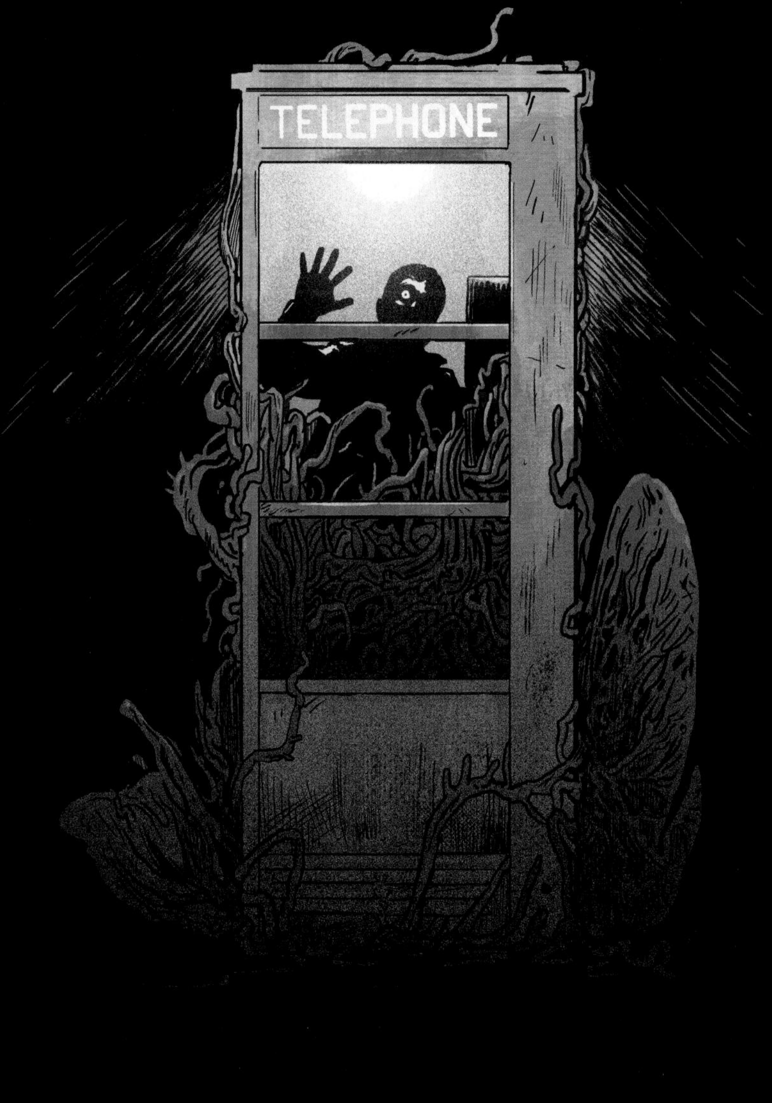
TELEPHONE

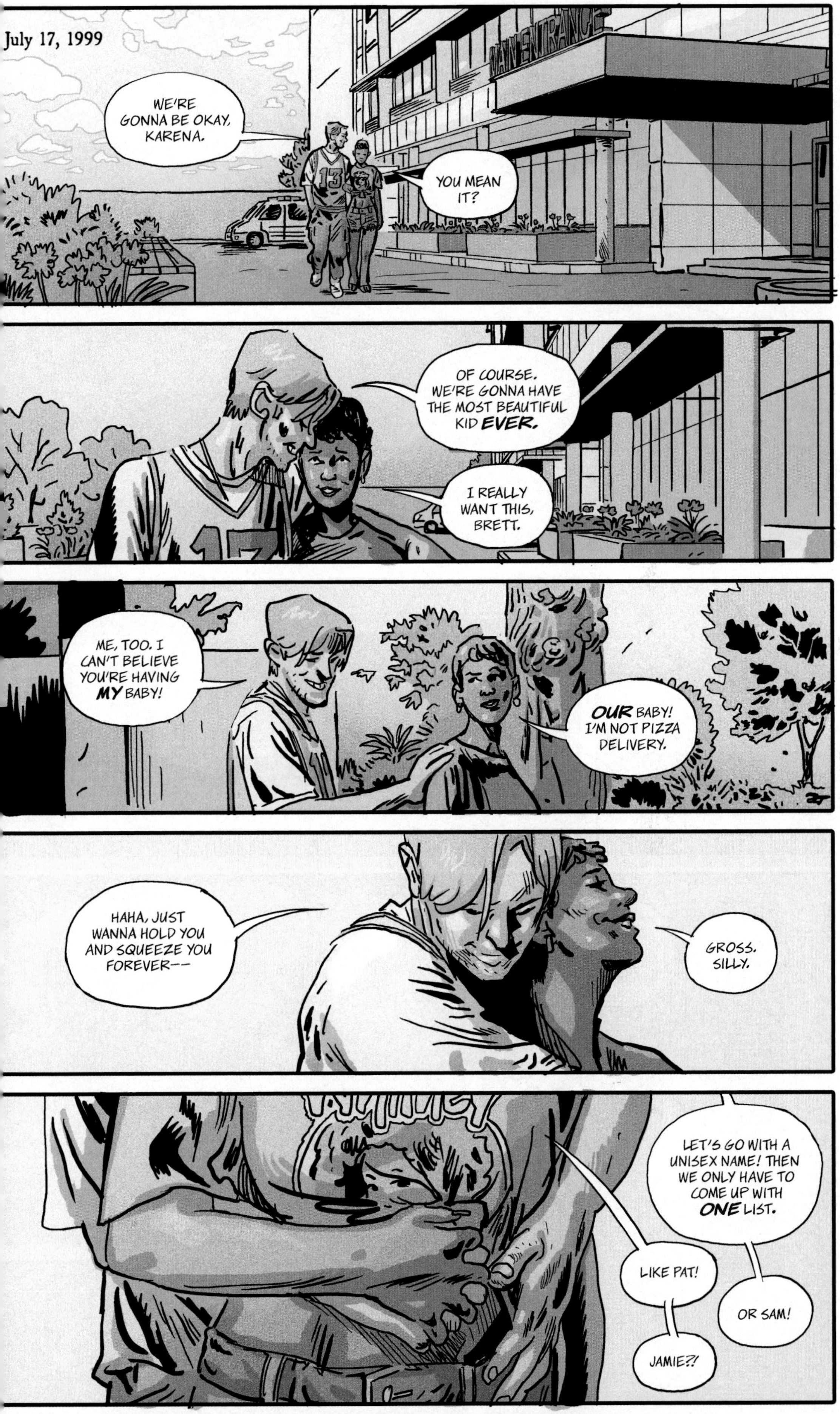
July 17, 1999
WE'RE GONNA BE OKAY, KARENA.
YOU MEAN IT?
MAIN ENTRANCE
OF COURSE. WE'RE GONNA HAVE THE MOST BEAUTIFUL KID EVER.
I REALLY WANT THIS, BRETT.
ME, TOO. I CAN'T BELIEVE YOU'RE HAVING MY BABY!
OUR BABY! I'M NOT PIZZA DELIVERY.
HAHA, JUST WANNA HOLD YOU AND SQUEEZE YOU FOREVER--
GROSS. SILLY.
LET'S GO WITH A UNISEX NAME! THEN WE ONLY HAVE TO COME UP WITH ONE LIST.
LIKE PAT!
OR SAM!
JAMIE?!

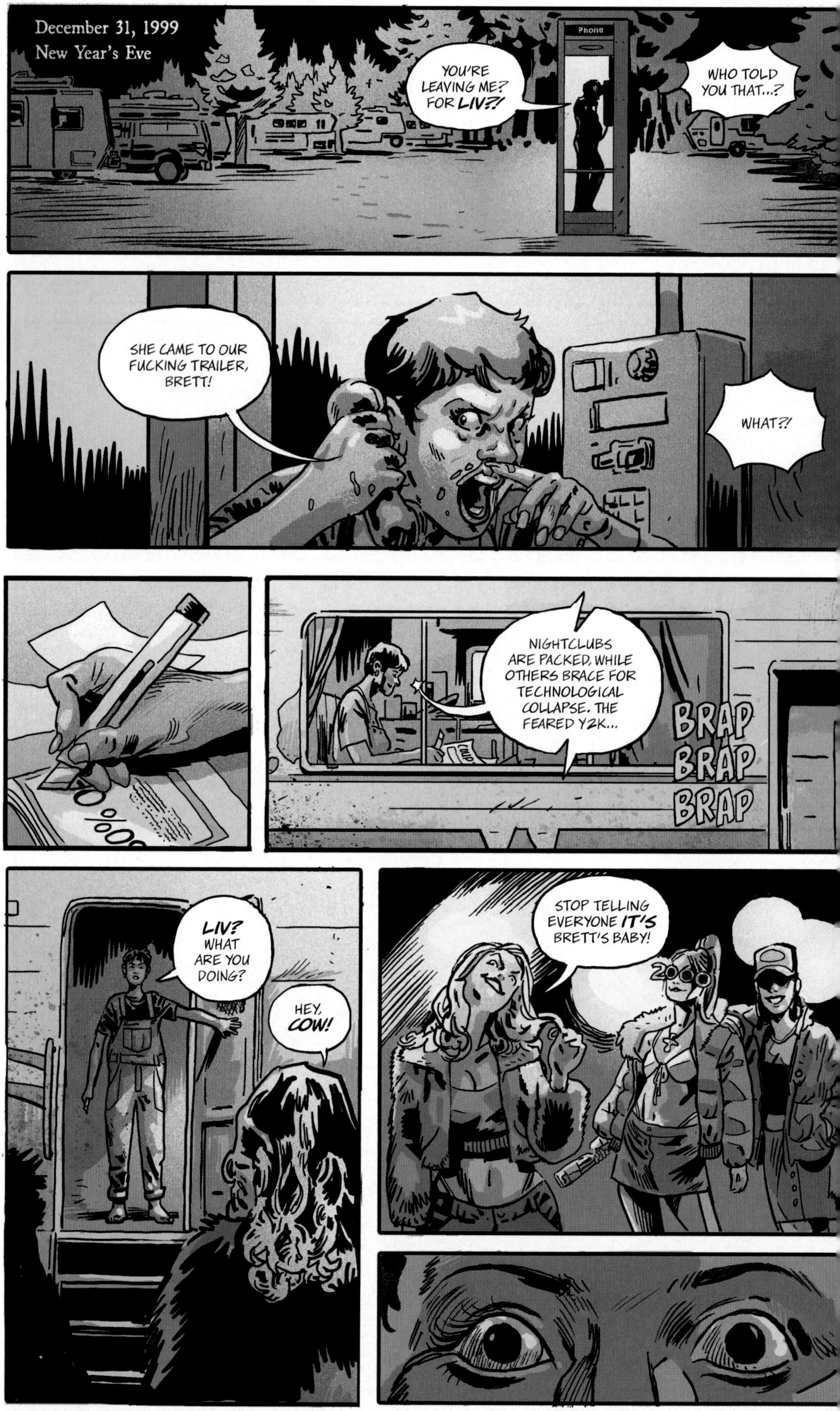
December 31, 1999
New Year's Eve
YOU'RE LEAVING ME? FOR LIV?!
WHO TOLD YOU THAT...?
SHE CAME TO OUR FUCKING TRAILER, BRETT!
WHAT?!
NIGHTCLUBS ARE PACKED, WHILE OTHERS BRACE FOR TECHNOLOGICAL COLLAPSE. THE FEARED Y2K...
BRAP
BRAP
BRAP
LIV? WHAT ARE YOU DOING?
HEY, COW!
STOP TELLING EVERYONE IT'S BRETT'S BABY!

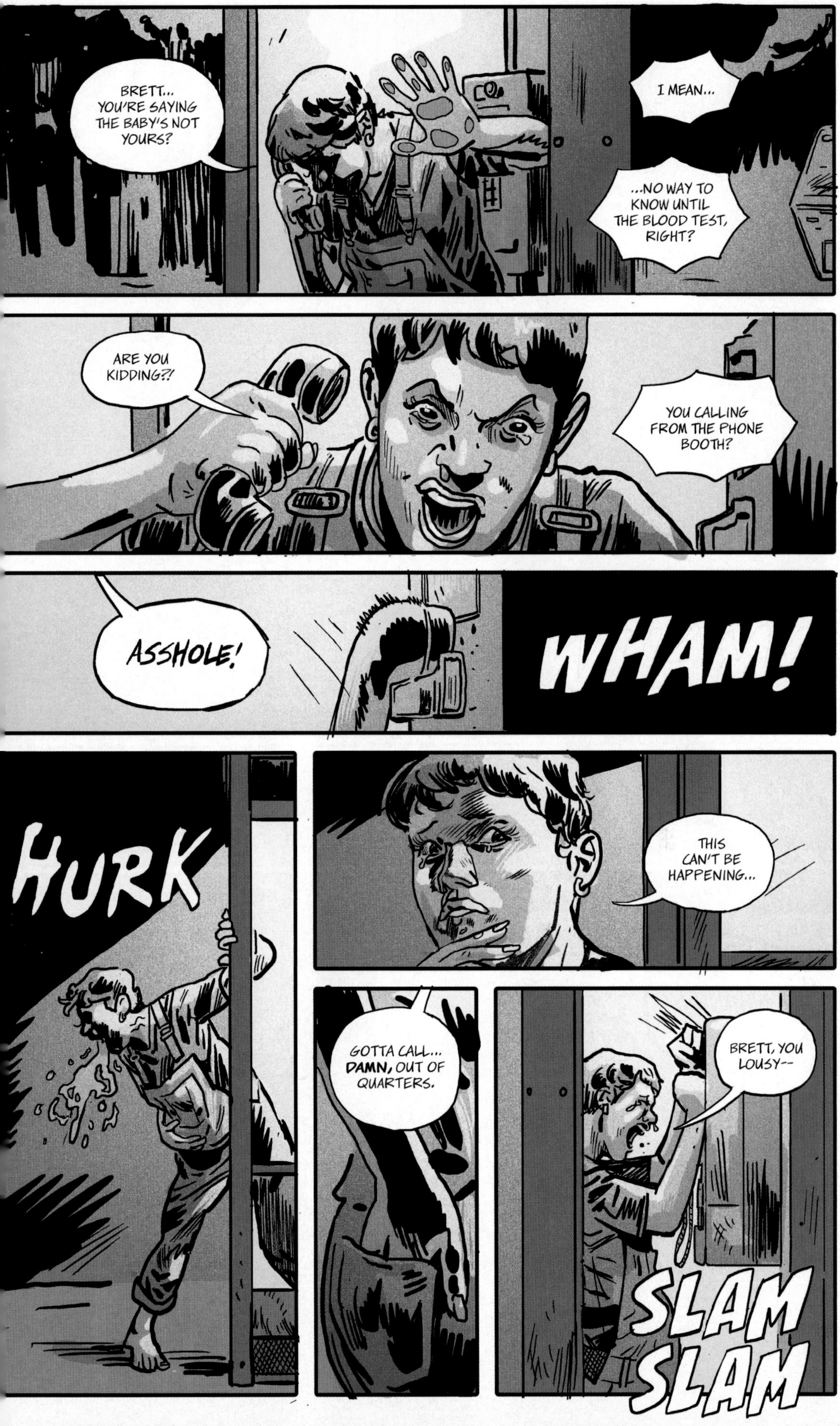
BRETT... YOU'RE SAYING THE BABY'S NOT YOURS?
I MEAN...
...NO WAY TO KNOW UNTIL THE BLOOD TEST, RIGHT?
ARE YOU KIDDING?!
YOU CALLING FROM THE PHONE BOOTH?
ASSHOLE!
WHAM!
HURK
THIS CAN'T BE HAPPENING...
GOTTA CALL... DAMN, OUT OF QUARTERS.
BRETT, YOU LOUSY--
SLAM
SLAM

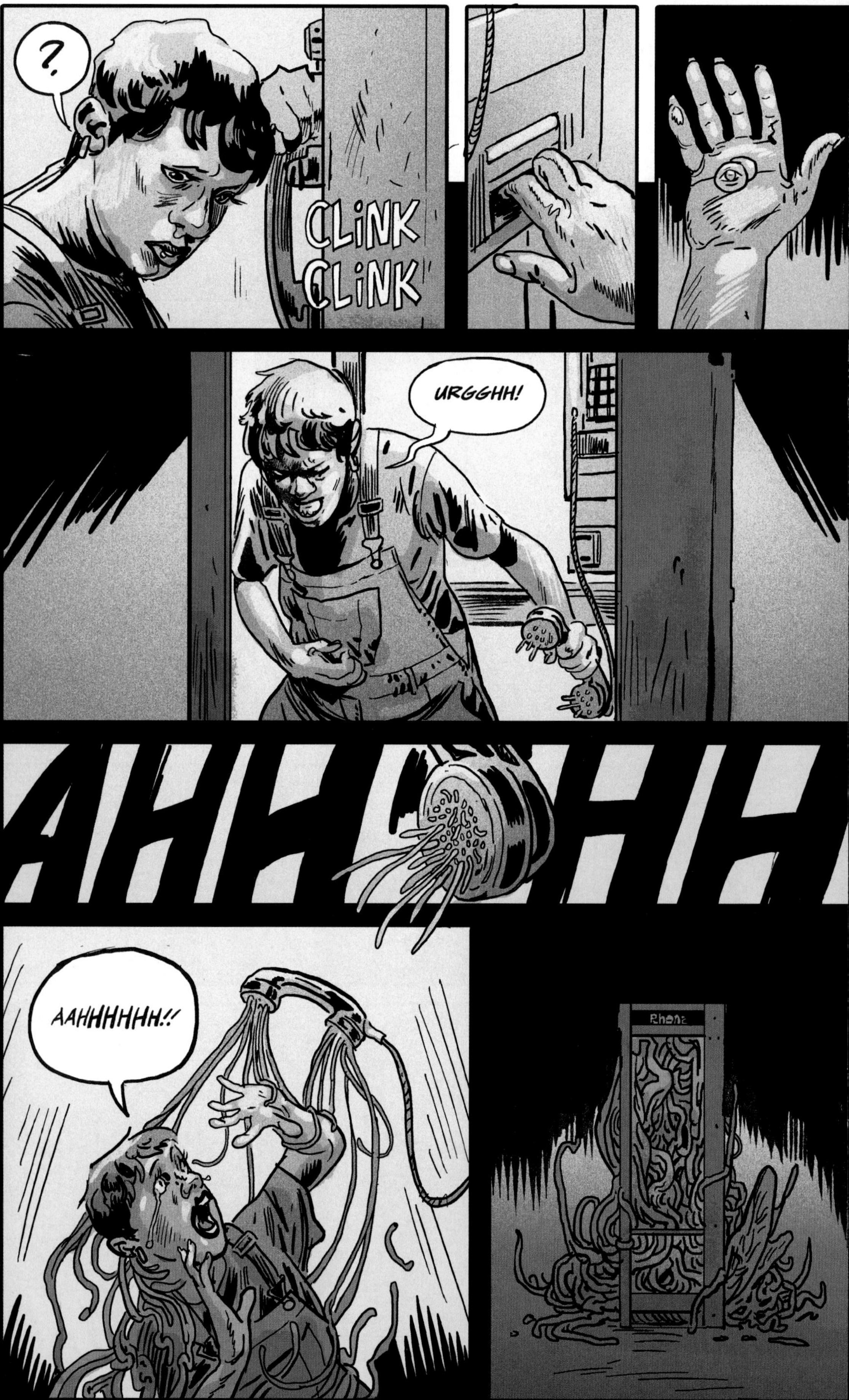
?
CLINK
CLINK
URGGHH!
AAHHHHHH!!

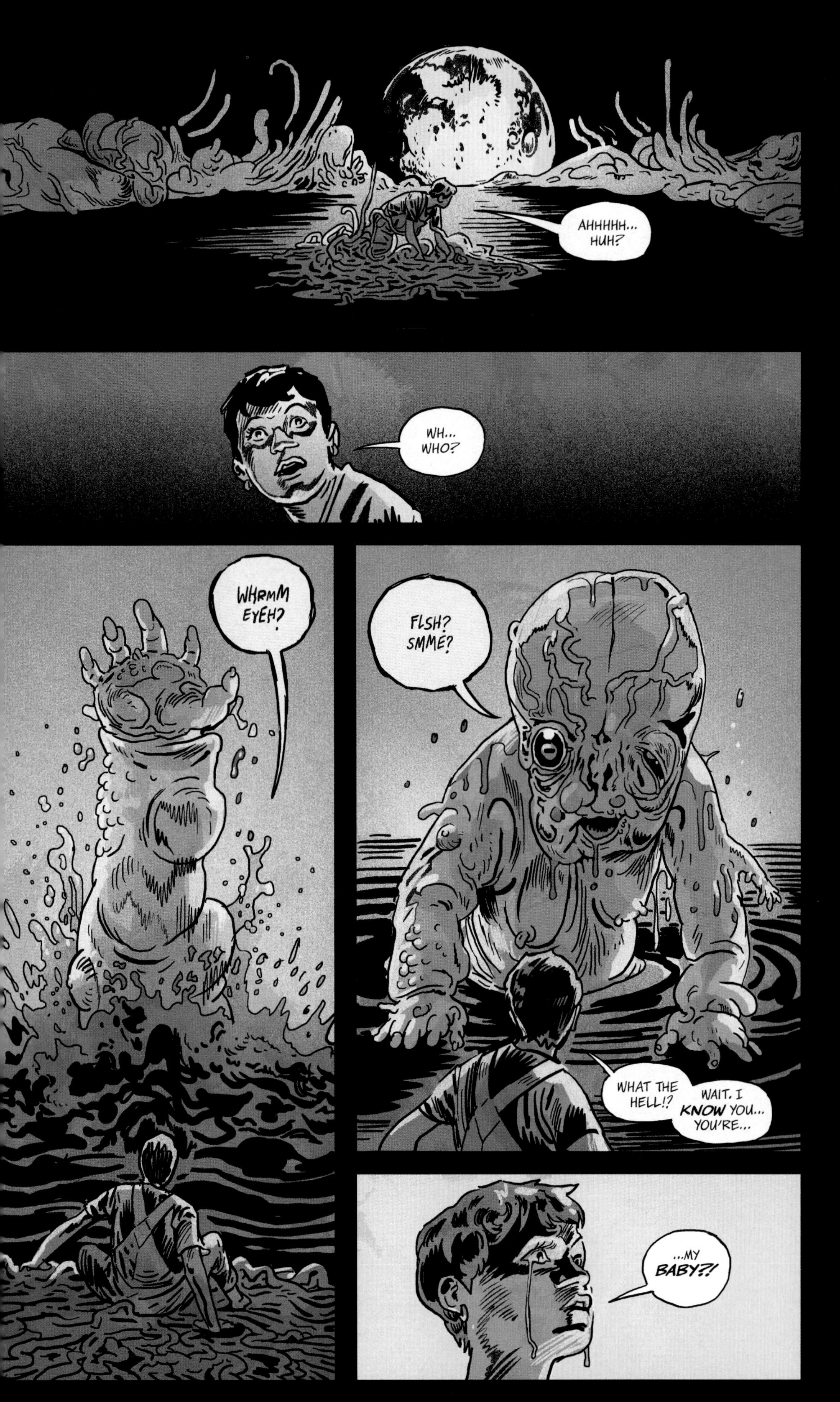
AHHHHH... HUH?
WH... WHO?
WHRMM EYEH?
FLSH? SMME?
WHAT THE HELL!?
WAIT. I **KNOW** YOU... YOU'RE...
...MY **BABY?!**

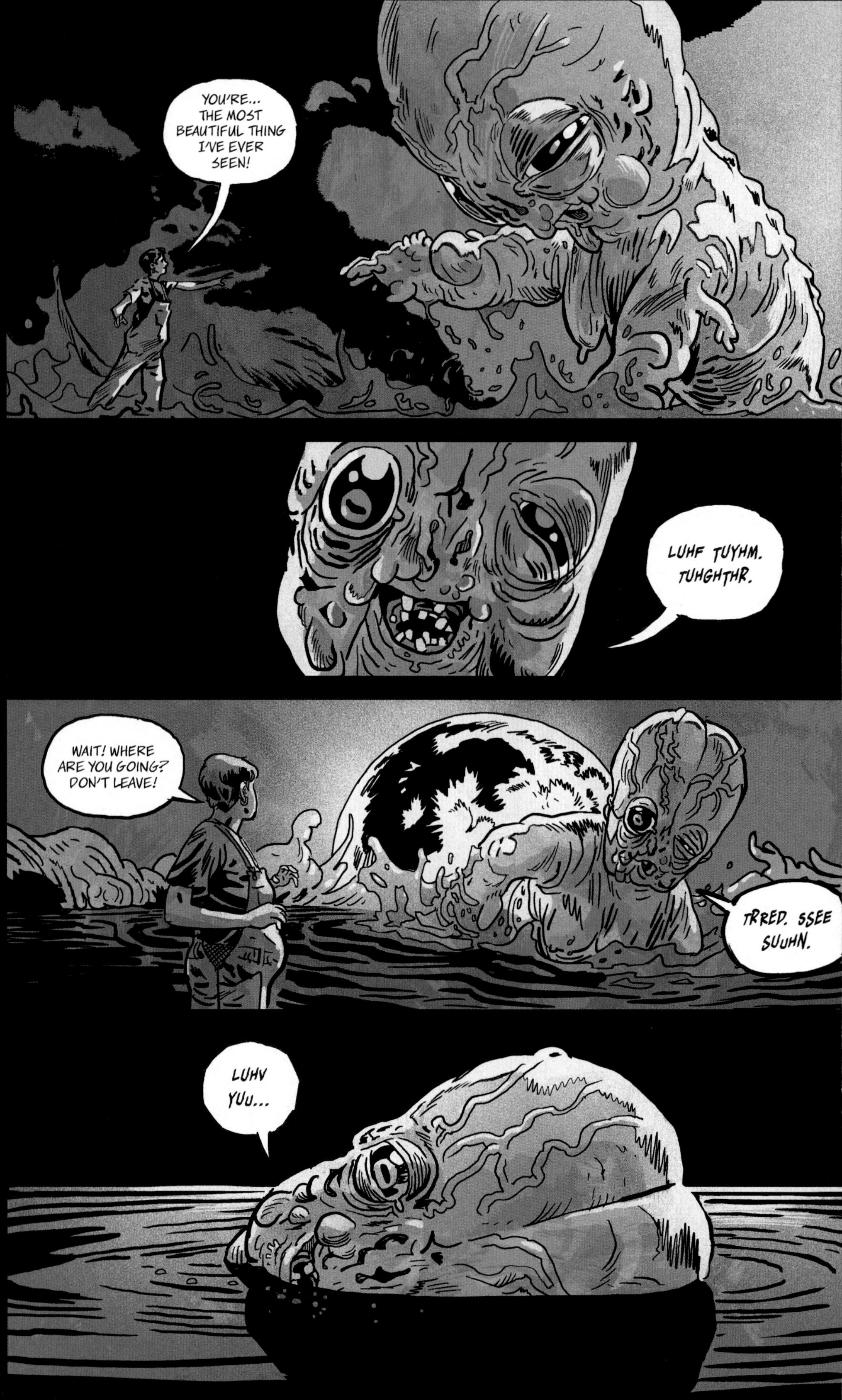
YOU'RE... THE MOST BEAUTIFUL THING I'VE EVER SEEN!
LUHF TUYHM. TUHGHTHR.
WAIT! WHERE ARE YOU GOING? DON'T LEAVE!
TRRED. SSEE SUUHN.
LUHV YUU...

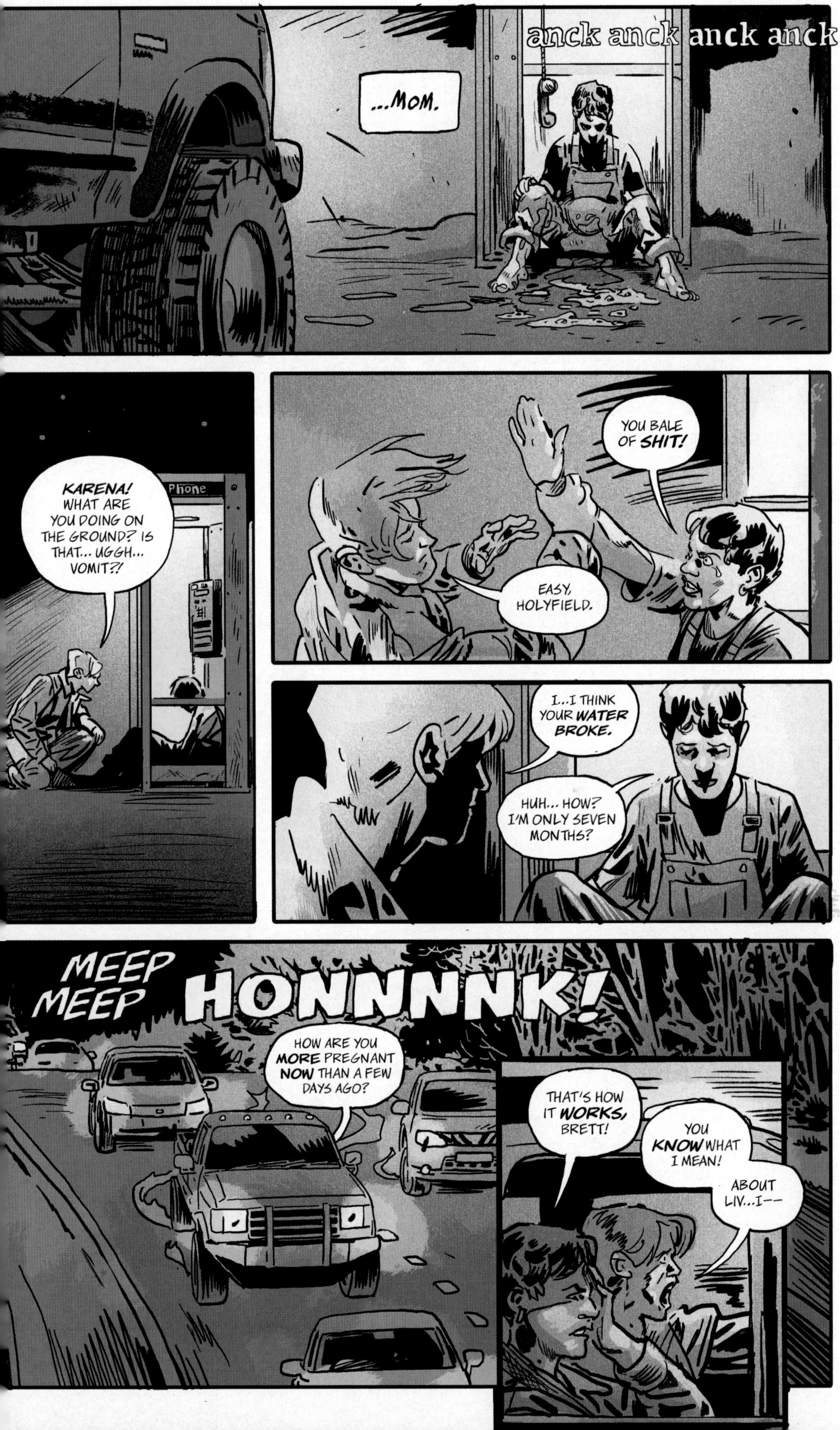

anck anck anck anck...
...MOM.
KARENA! WHAT ARE YOU DOING ON THE GROUND? IS THAT... UGGH... VOMIT?!
Phone
YOU BALE OF SHIT!
EASY, HOLYFIELD.
I...I THINK YOUR WATER BROKE.
HUH... HOW? I'M ONLY SEVEN MONTHS?
MEEP MEEP
HONNNNK!
HOW ARE YOU MORE PREGNANT NOW THAN A FEW DAYS AGO?
THAT'S HOW IT WORKS, BRETT!
YOU KNOW WHAT I MEAN!
ABOUT LIV...I--

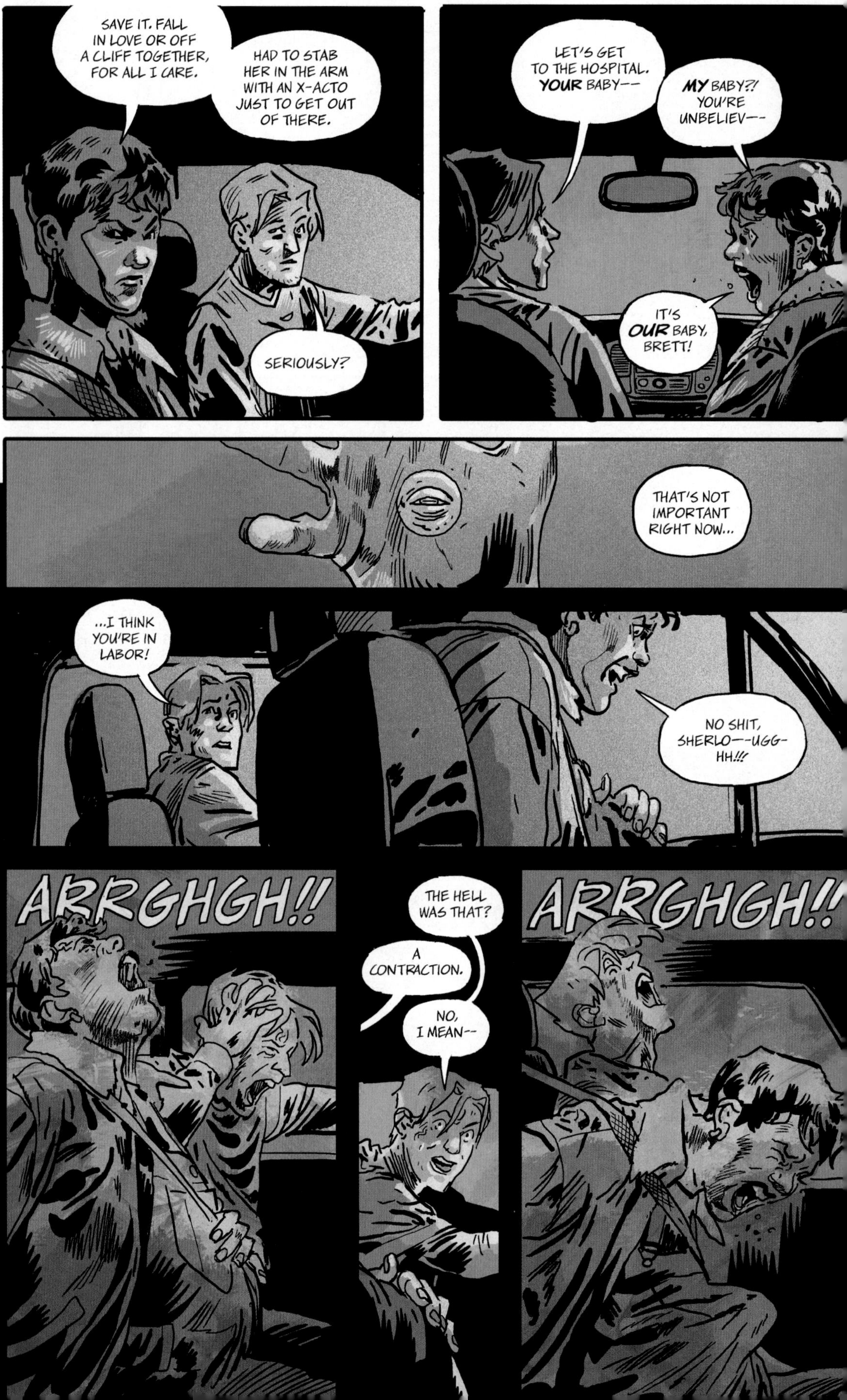
SAVE IT. FALL IN LOVE OR OFF A CLIFF TOGETHER, FOR ALL I CARE.
HAD TO STAB HER IN THE ARM WITH AN X-ACTO JUST TO GET OUT OF THERE.
SERIOUSLY?
LET'S GET TO THE HOSPITAL. YOUR BABY--
MY BABY?! YOU'RE UNBELIEV--
IT'S OUR BABY, BRETT!
THAT'S NOT IMPORTANT RIGHT NOW...
...I THINK YOU'RE IN LABOR!
NO SHIT, SHERLO--UGG-HH!!!
ARRGHGH!!
THE HELL WAS THAT?
A CONTRACTION.
NO, I MEAN--
ARRGHGH!!

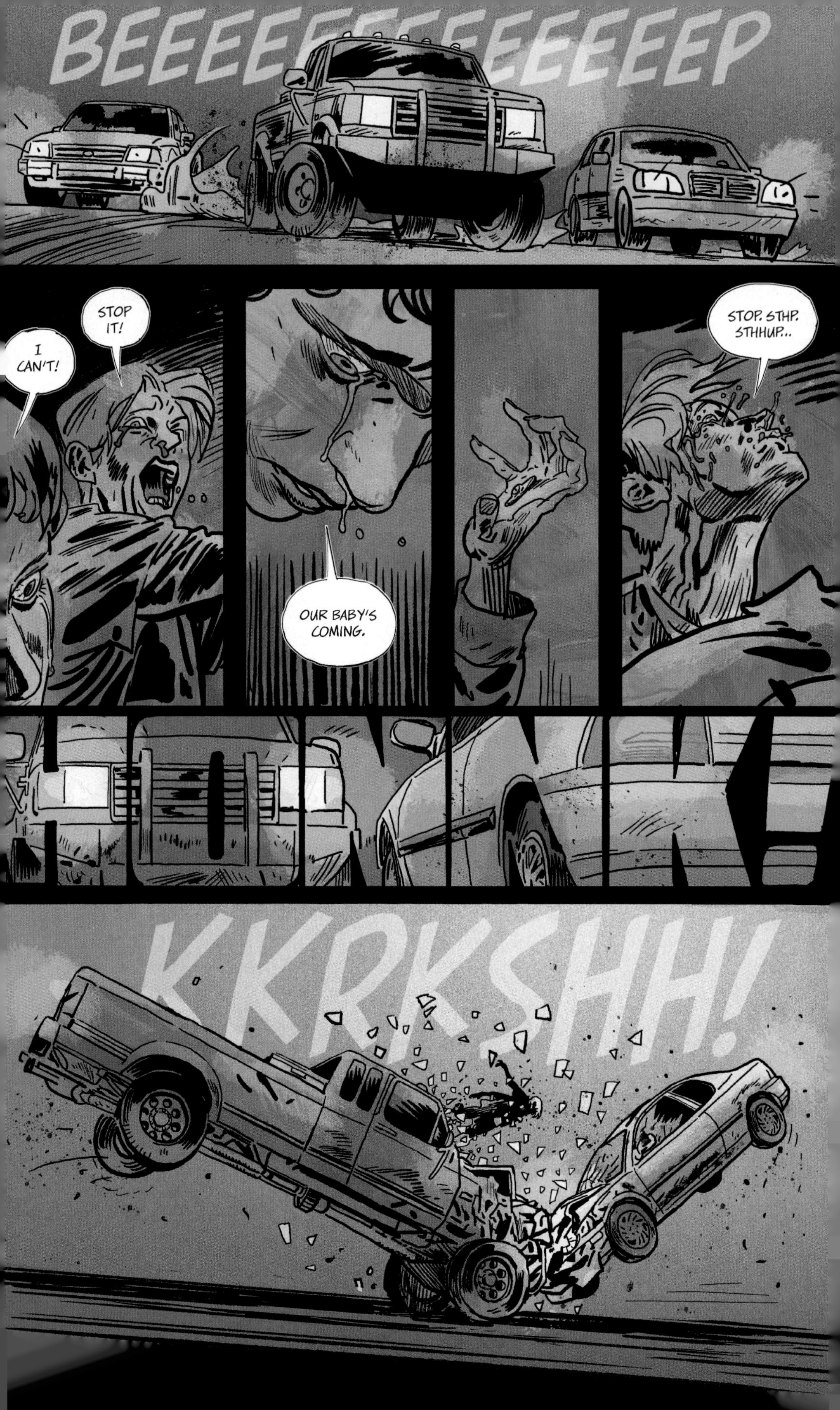
BEEEEEEEEEEEEEEEP
I CAN'T!
STOP IT!
OUR BABY'S COMING.
STOP. STHP. STHHUP...
HONK!
KKRKSHH!

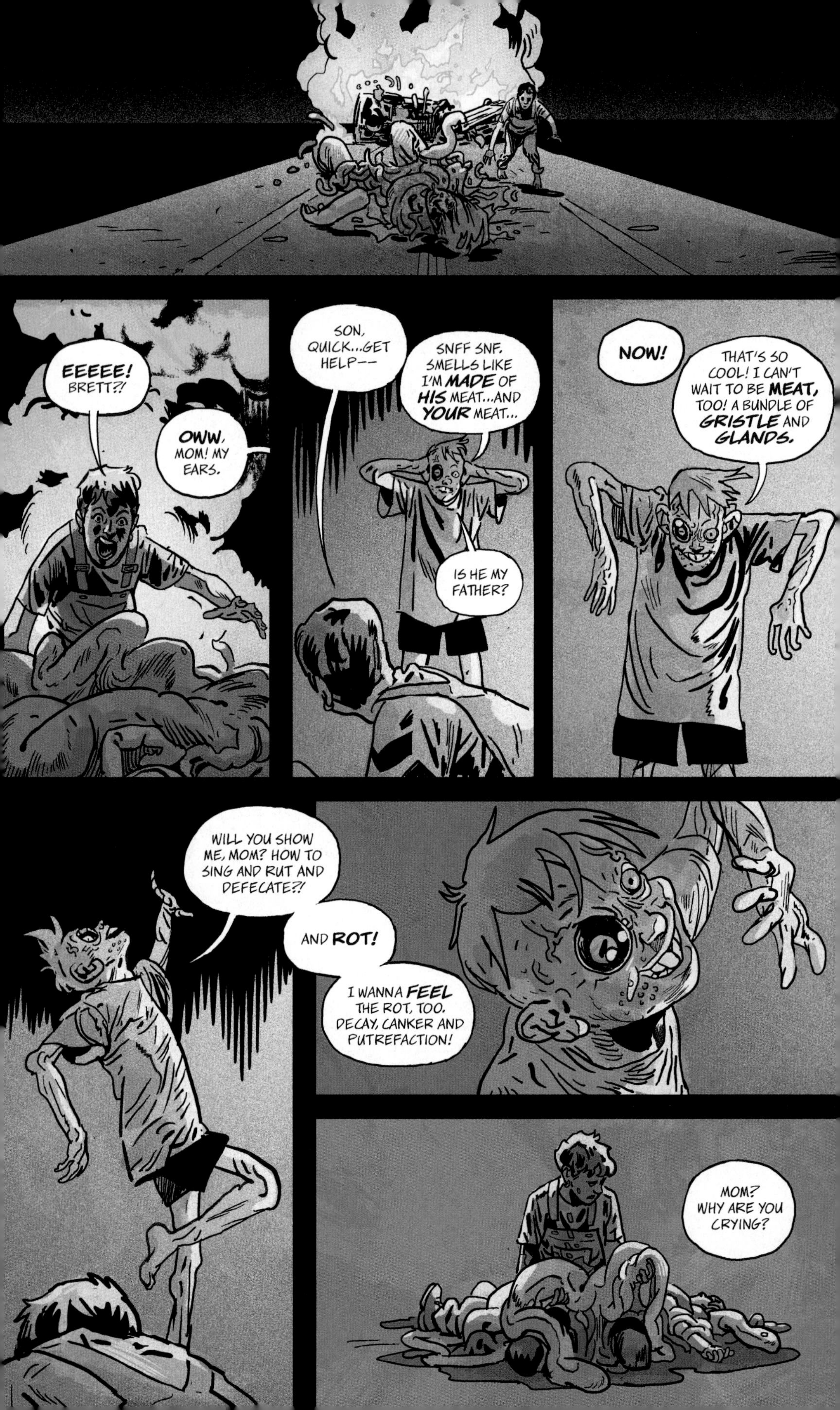
EEEEE! BRETT?!
OWW, MOM! MY EARS.
SON, QUICK...GET HELP--
SNFF SNF. SMELLS LIKE I'M MADE OF HIS MEAT...AND YOUR MEAT...
IS HE MY FATHER?
NOW!
THAT'S SO COOL! I CAN'T WAIT TO BE MEAT, TOO! A BUNDLE OF GRISTLE AND GLANDS.
WILL YOU SHOW ME, MOM? HOW TO SING AND RUT AND DEFECATE?!
AND ROT!
I WANNA FEEL THE ROT, TOO. DECAY, CANKER AND PUTREFACTION!
MOM? WHY ARE YOU CRYING?

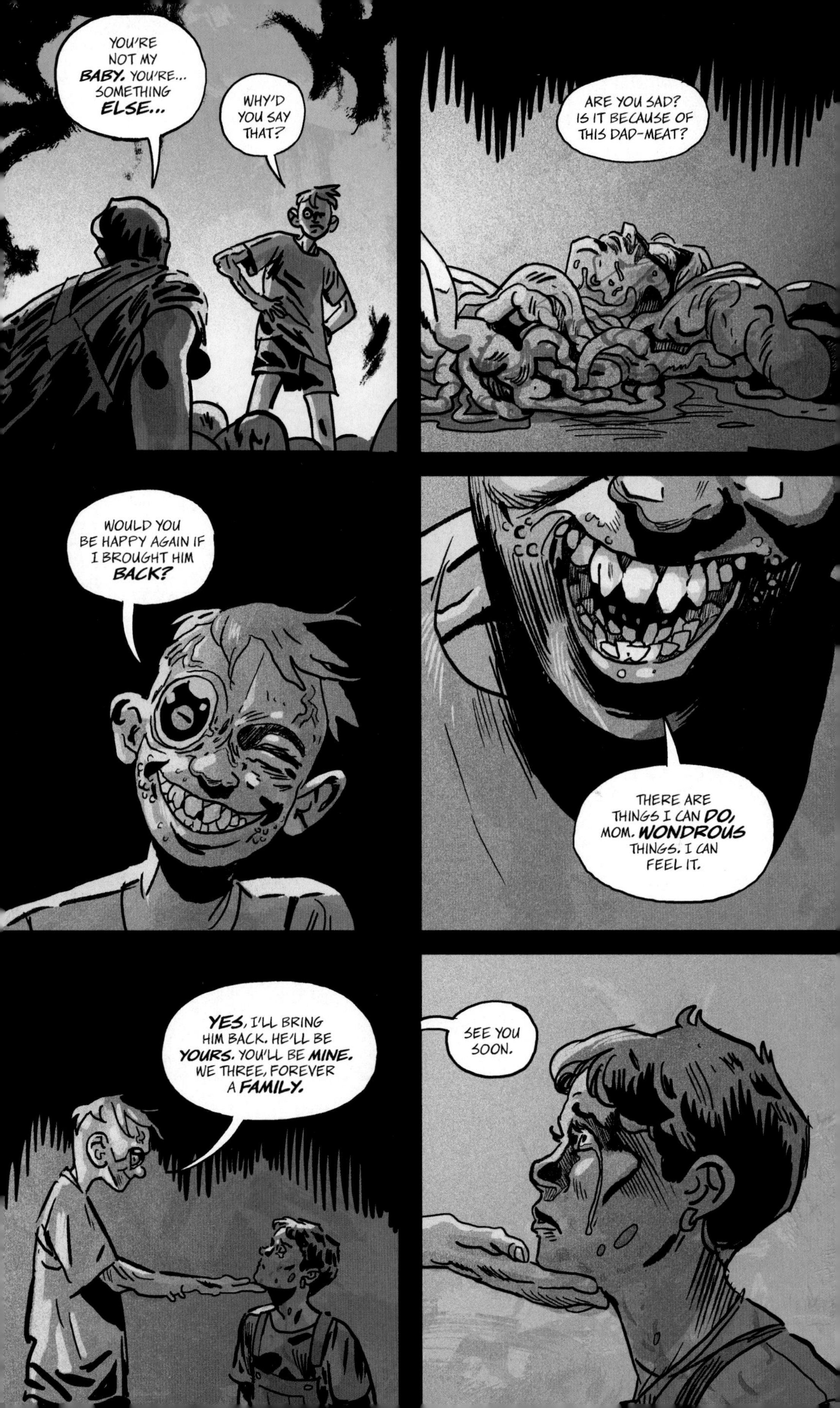
YOU'RE NOT MY BABY. YOU'RE... SOMETHING ELSE...
WHY'D YOU SAY THAT?
ARE YOU SAD? IS IT BECAUSE OF THIS DAD-MEAT?
WOULD YOU BE HAPPY AGAIN IF I BROUGHT HIM BACK?
THERE ARE THINGS I CAN DO, MOM. WONDROUS THINGS. I CAN FEEL IT.
YES, I'LL BRING HIM BACK. HE'LL BE YOURS. YOU'LL BE MINE. WE THREE, FOREVER A FAMILY.
SEE YOU SOON.

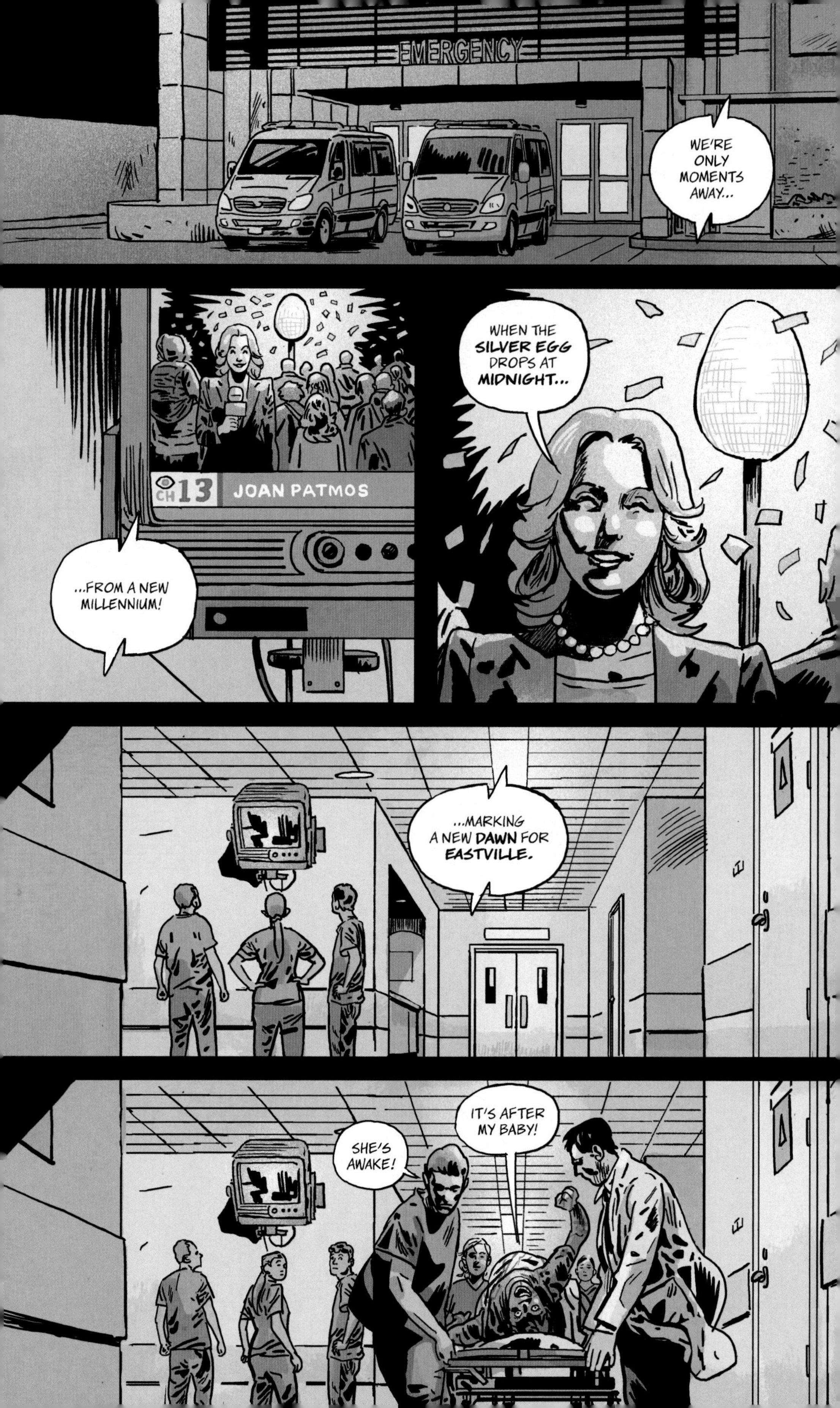
EMERGENCY
WE'RE ONLY MOMENTS AWAY...
CH 13 JOAN PATMOS
WHEN THE SILVER EGG DROPS AT MIDNIGHT...
...FROM A NEW MILLENNIUM!
...MARKING A NEW DAWN FOR EASTVILLE.
SHE'S AWAKE!
IT'S AFTER MY BABY!

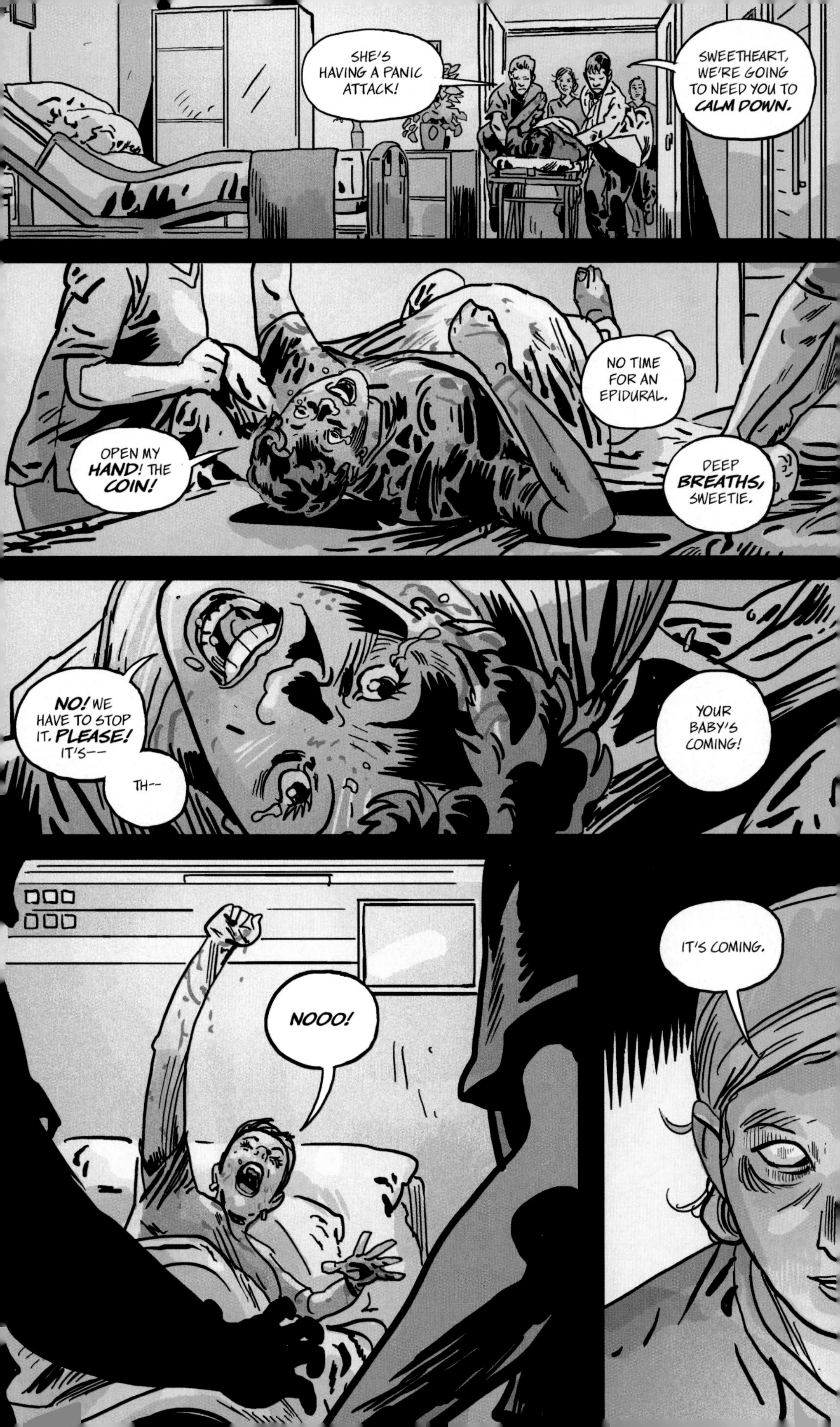
SHE'S HAVING A PANIC ATTACK!
SWEETHEART, WE'RE GOING TO NEED YOU TO CALM DOWN.
OPEN MY HAND! THE COIN!
NO TIME FOR AN EPIDURAL.
DEEP BREATHS, SWEETIE.
NO! WE HAVE TO STOP IT. PLEASE! IT'S--
TH--
YOUR BABY'S COMING!
NOOO!
IT'S COMING.

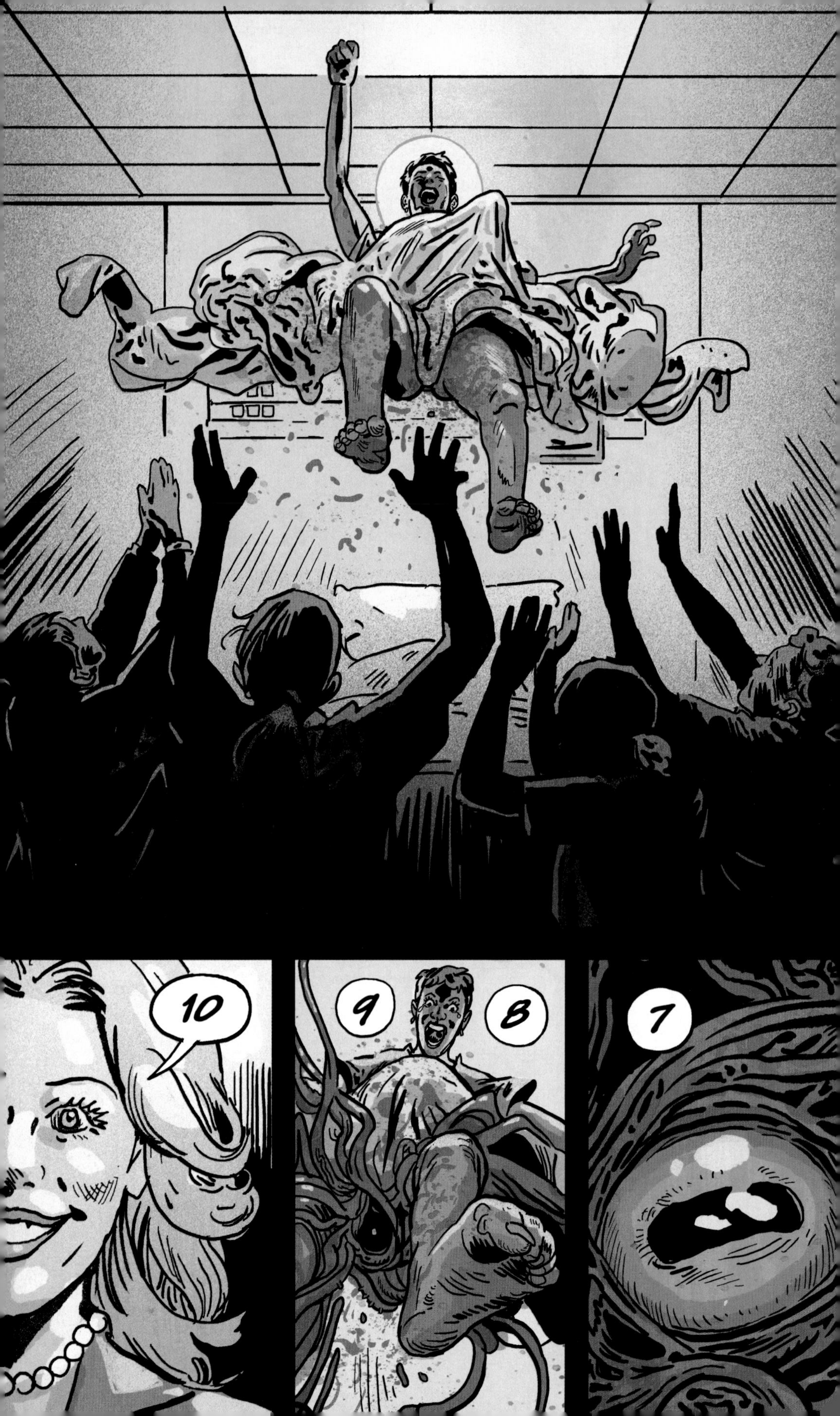
10
9
8
7

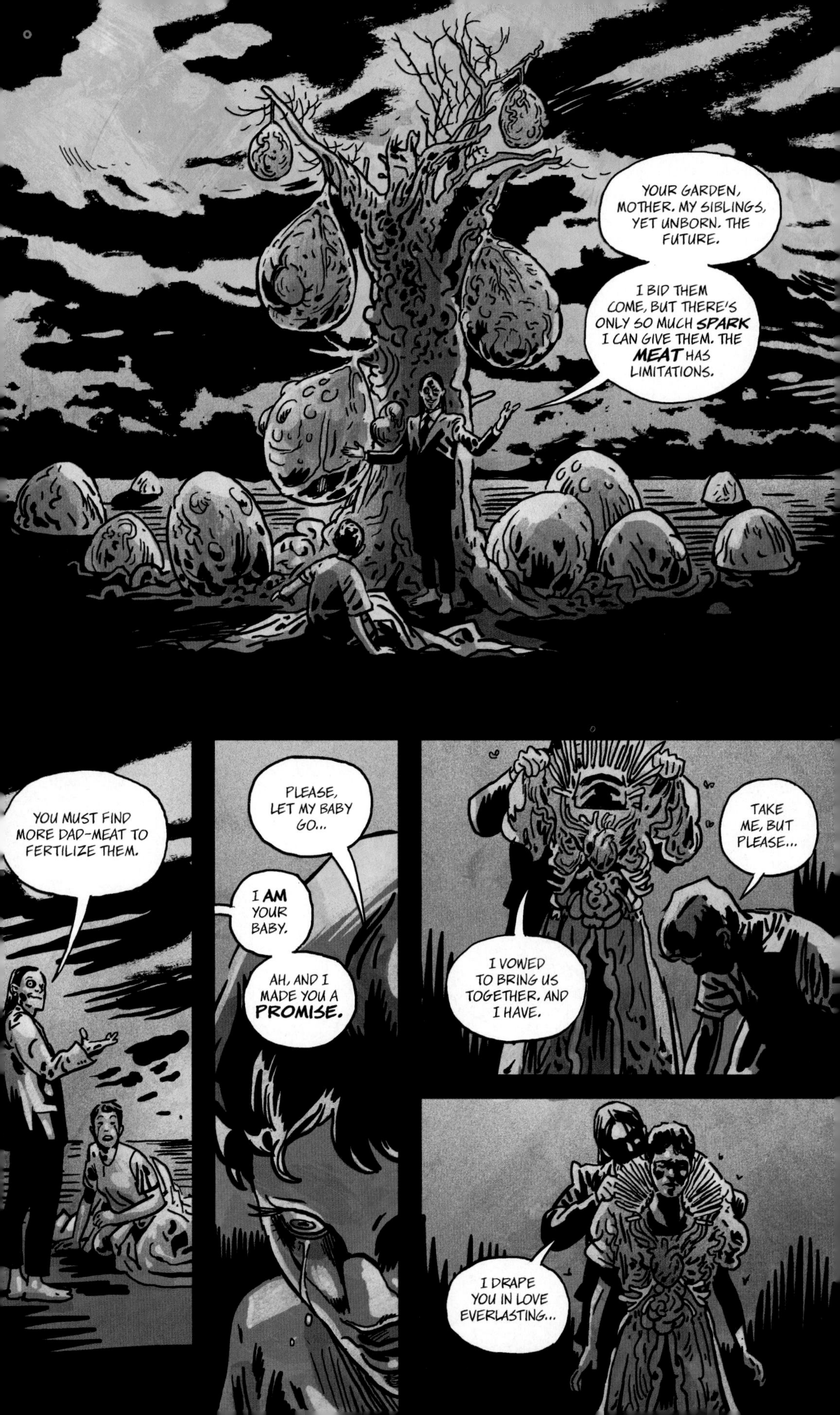
YOUR GARDEN, MOTHER. MY SIBLINGS, YET UNBORN. THE FUTURE.
I BID THEM COME, BUT THERE'S ONLY SO MUCH **SPARK** I CAN GIVE THEM. THE **MEAT** HAS LIMITATIONS.
YOU MUST FIND MORE DAD-MEAT TO FERTILIZE THEM.
PLEASE, LET MY BABY GO...
I **AM** YOUR BABY.
AH, AND I MADE YOU A **PROMISE.**
TAKE ME, BUT PLEASE...
I VOWED TO BRING US TOGETHER. AND I HAVE.
I DRAPE YOU IN LOVE EVERLASTING...

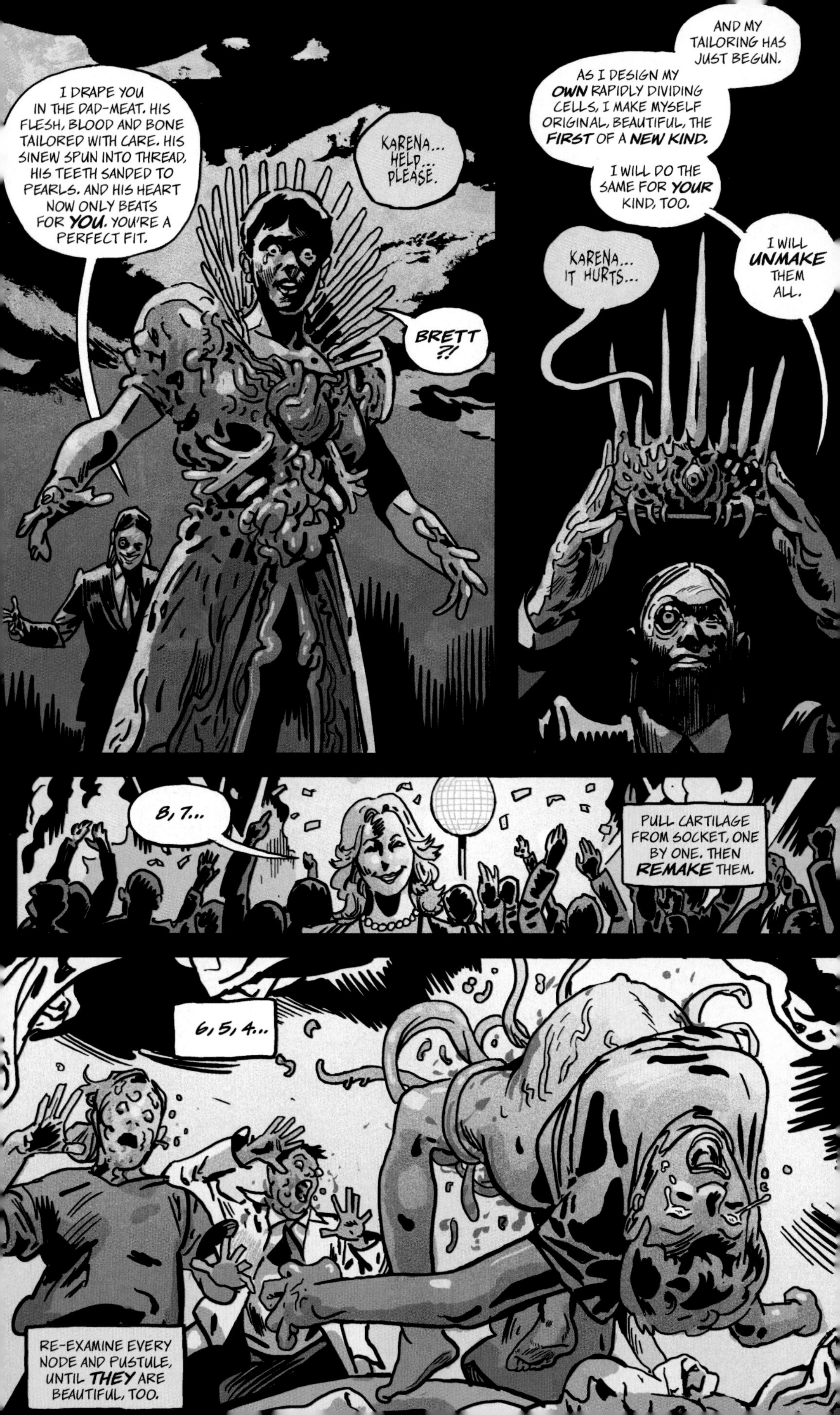

I DRAPE YOU IN THE DAD-MEAT. HIS FLESH, BLOOD AND BONE TAILORED WITH CARE. HIS SINEW SPUN INTO THREAD, HIS TEETH SANDED TO PEARLS. AND HIS HEART NOW ONLY BEATS FOR **YOU**. YOU'RE A PERFECT FIT.
KARENA... HELP... PLEASE.
BRETT ?!
AND MY TAILORING HAS JUST BEGUN.
AS I DESIGN MY **OWN** RAPIDLY DIVIDING CELLS, I MAKE MYSELF ORIGINAL, BEAUTIFUL, THE **FIRST** OF A **NEW KIND.**
I WILL DO THE SAME FOR **YOUR** KIND, TOO.
KARENA... IT HURTS...
I WILL **UNMAKE** THEM ALL.
8, 7...
PULL CARTILAGE FROM SOCKET, ONE BY ONE. THEN **REMAKE** THEM.
6, 5, 4...
RE-EXAMINE EVERY NODE AND PUSTULE, UNTIL **THEY** ARE BEAUTIFUL, TOO.

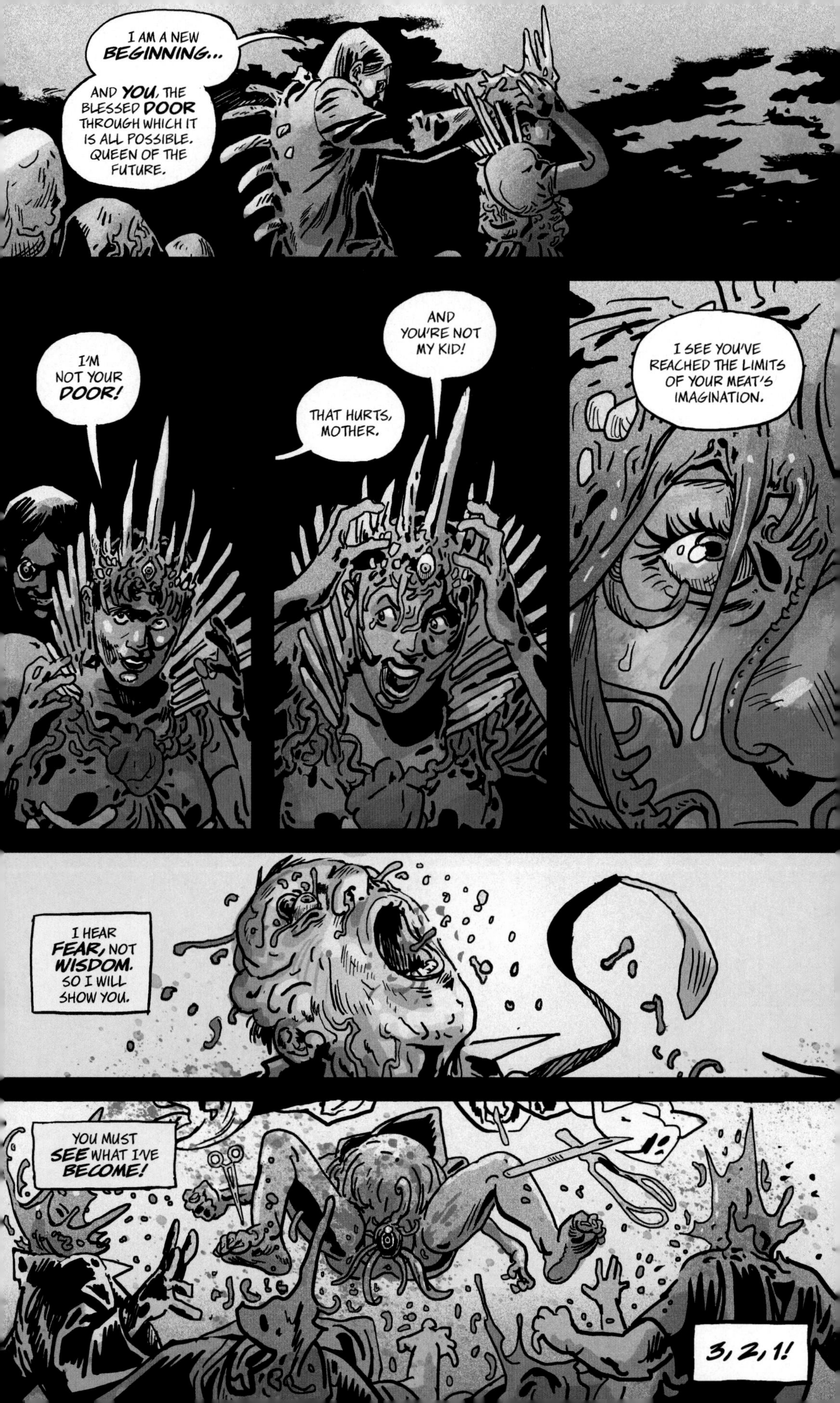
I AM A NEW BEGINNING...
AND YOU, THE BLESSED DOOR THROUGH WHICH IT IS ALL POSSIBLE. QUEEN OF THE FUTURE.
I'M NOT YOUR DOOR!
AND YOU'RE NOT MY KID!
THAT HURTS, MOTHER.
I SEE YOU'VE REACHED THE LIMITS OF YOUR MEAT'S IMAGINATION.
I HEAR FEAR, NOT WISDOM. SO I WILL SHOW YOU.
YOU MUST SEE WHAT I'VE BECOME!
3, 2, 1!

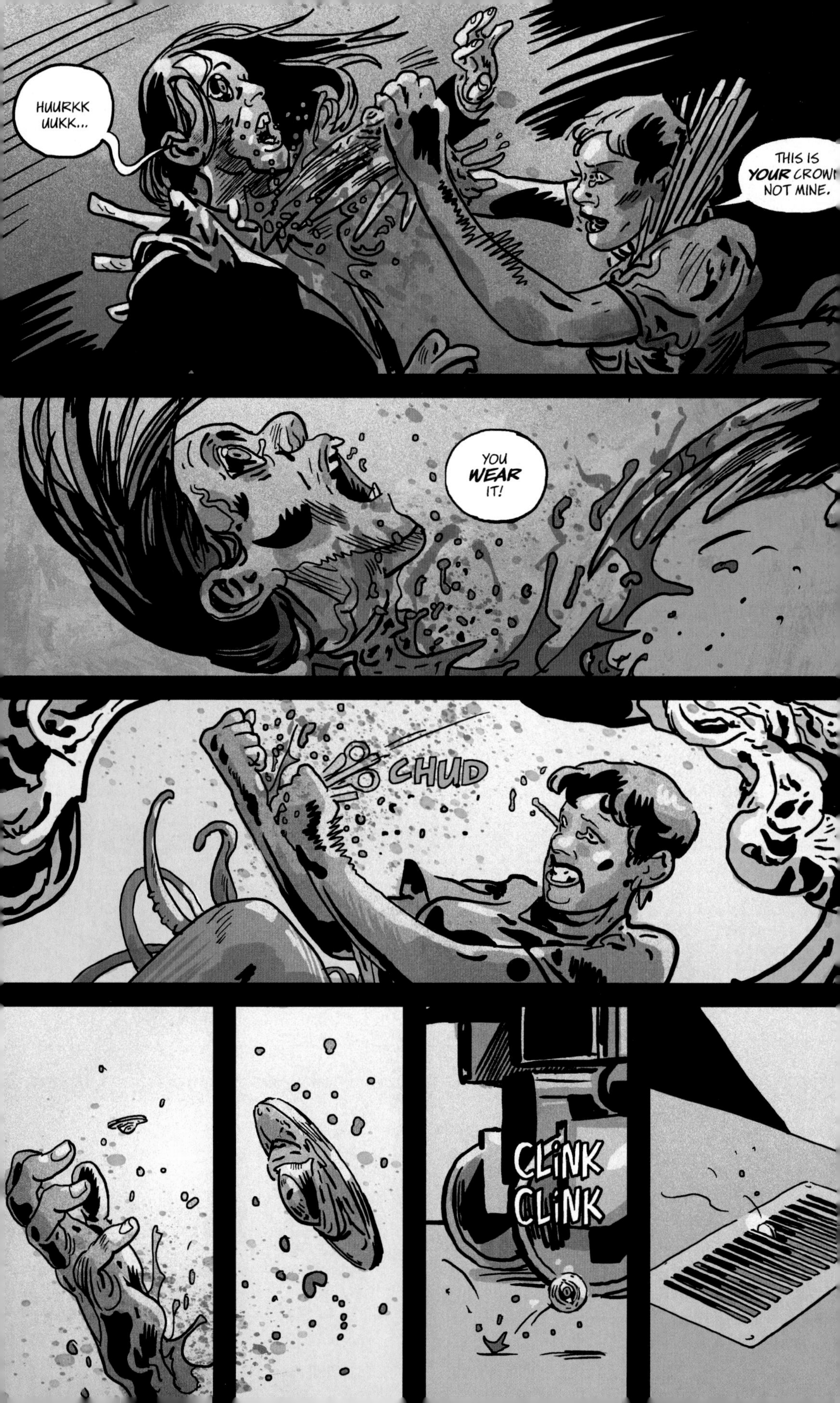
HUURKK UUKK...
THIS IS YOUR CROWN NOT MINE.
YOU WEAR IT!
CHUD
CLINK CLINK

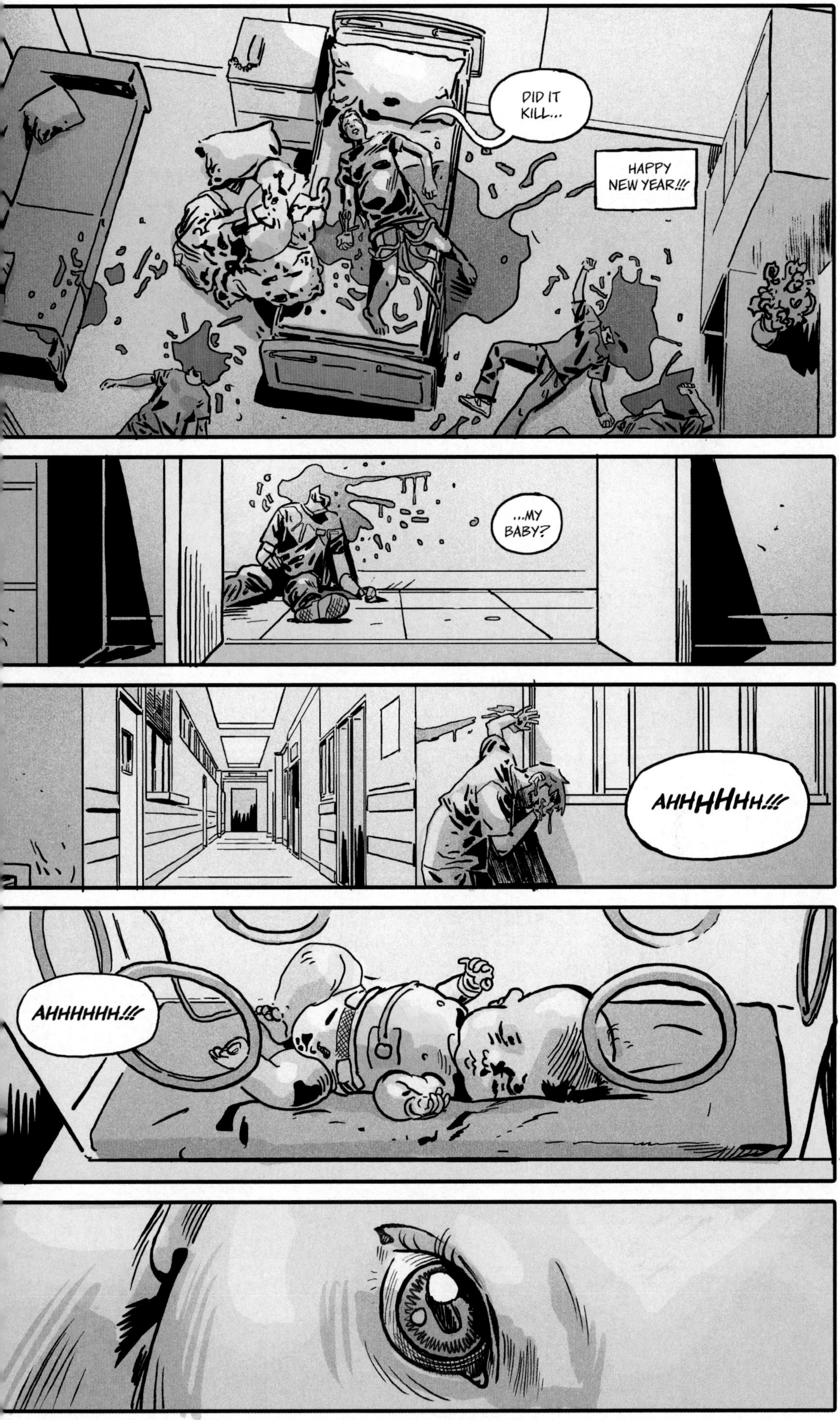
DID IT KILL...
HAPPY NEW YEAR!!!
...MY BABY?
AHHHHHH!!!
AHHHHHH!!!

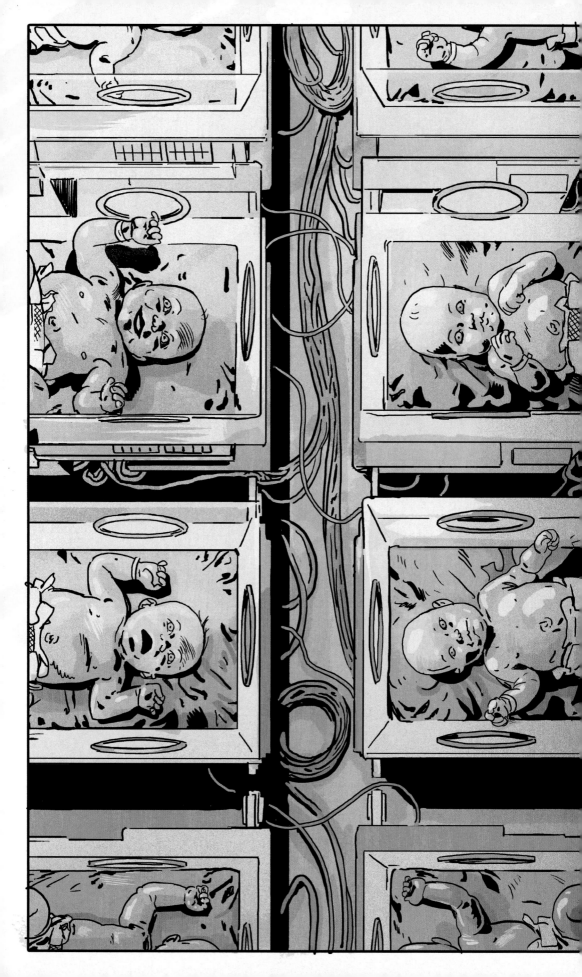

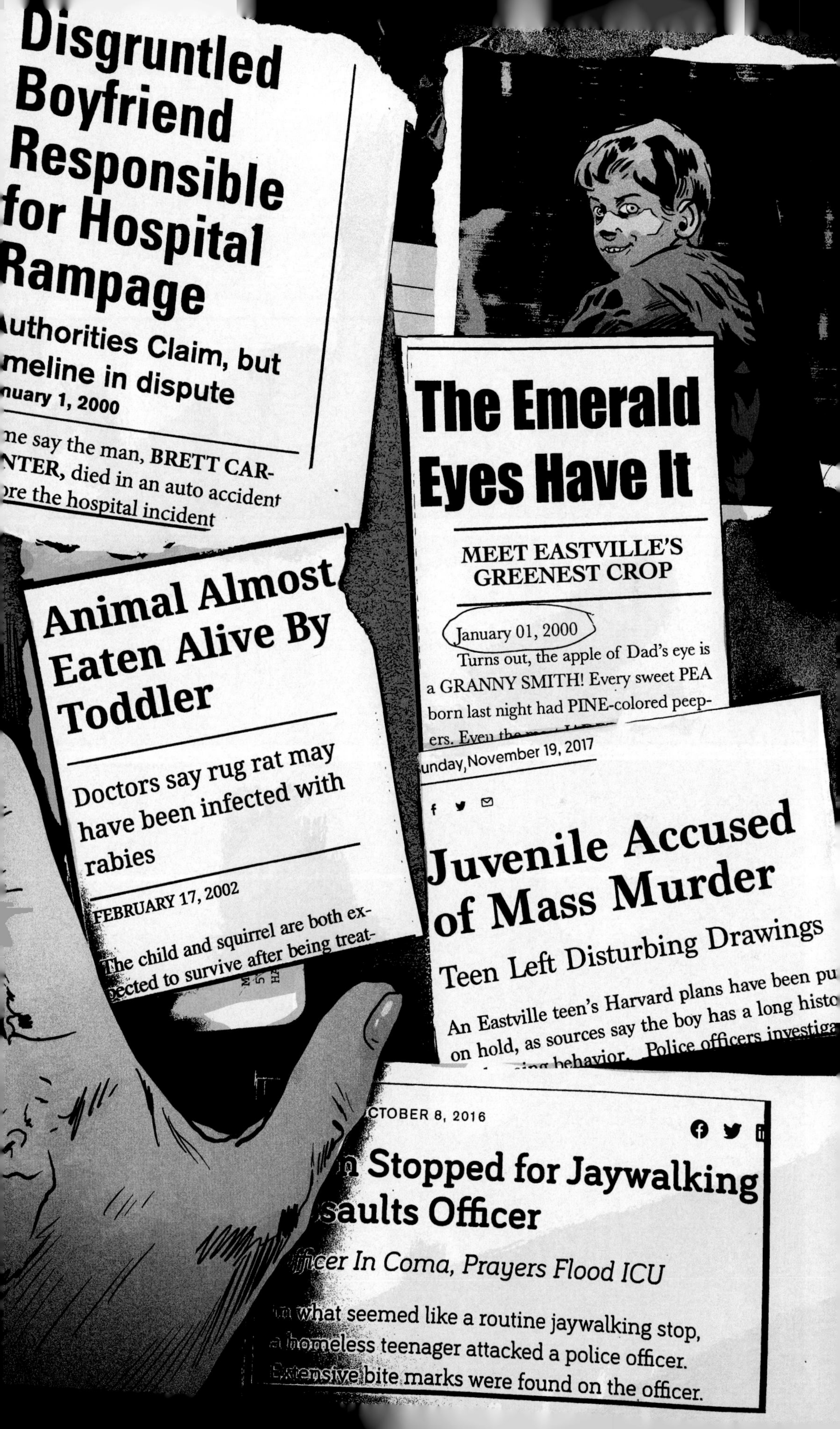
Disgruntled Boyfriend Responsible for Hospital Rampage
uthorities Claim, but
meline in dispute
nuary 1, 2000
ne say the man, BRETT CAR-
NTER, died in an auto accident
ore the hospital incident
The Emerald Eyes Have It
MEET EASTVILLE'S GREENEST CROP
January 01, 2000
Turns out, the apple of Dad's eye is a GRANNY SMITH! Every sweet PEA born last night had PINE-colored peepers.
Animal Almost Eaten Alive By Toddler
Doctors say rug rat may have been infected with rabies
FEBRUARY 17, 2002
The child and squirrel are both ex-
pected to survive after being treat-
unday, November 19, 2017
Juvenile Accused of Mass Murder
Teen Left Disturbing Drawings
An Eastville teen's Harvard plans have been pu
on hold, as sources say the boy has a long histo
CTOBER 8, 2016
n Stopped for Jaywalking
saults Officer
fficer In Coma, Prayers Flood ICU
what seemed like a routine jaywalking stop,
homeless teenager attacked a police officer.
Extensive bite marks were found on the officer.

December 31, 2019
New Year's Eve
COUNT WITH ME AS WE RING IN A NEW DECADE! IN 10, 9...
HAPPY BIRTHDAY, SAM.
7, 6, 5...
HAPPY NEW YEAR!
MOMMY LOVES YOU.
END.

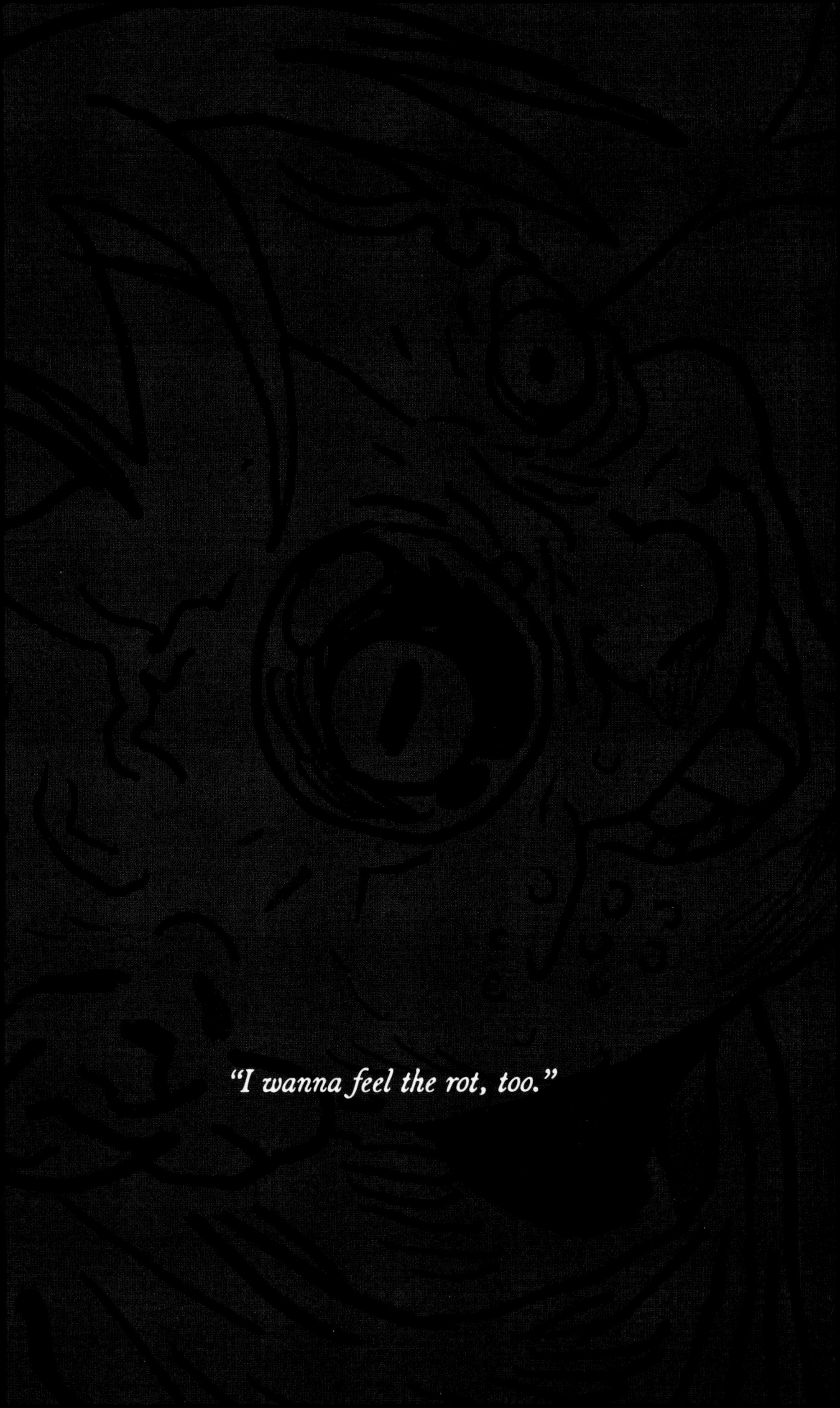
"I wanna feel the rot, too."

The Bad Year

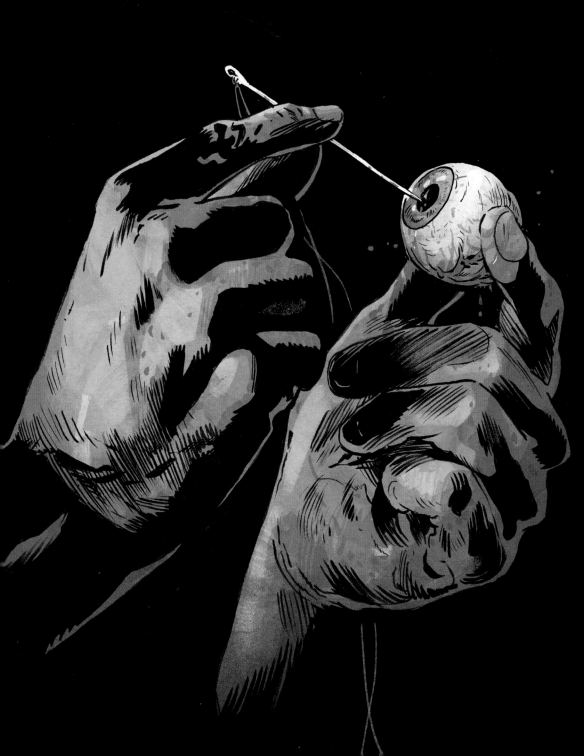

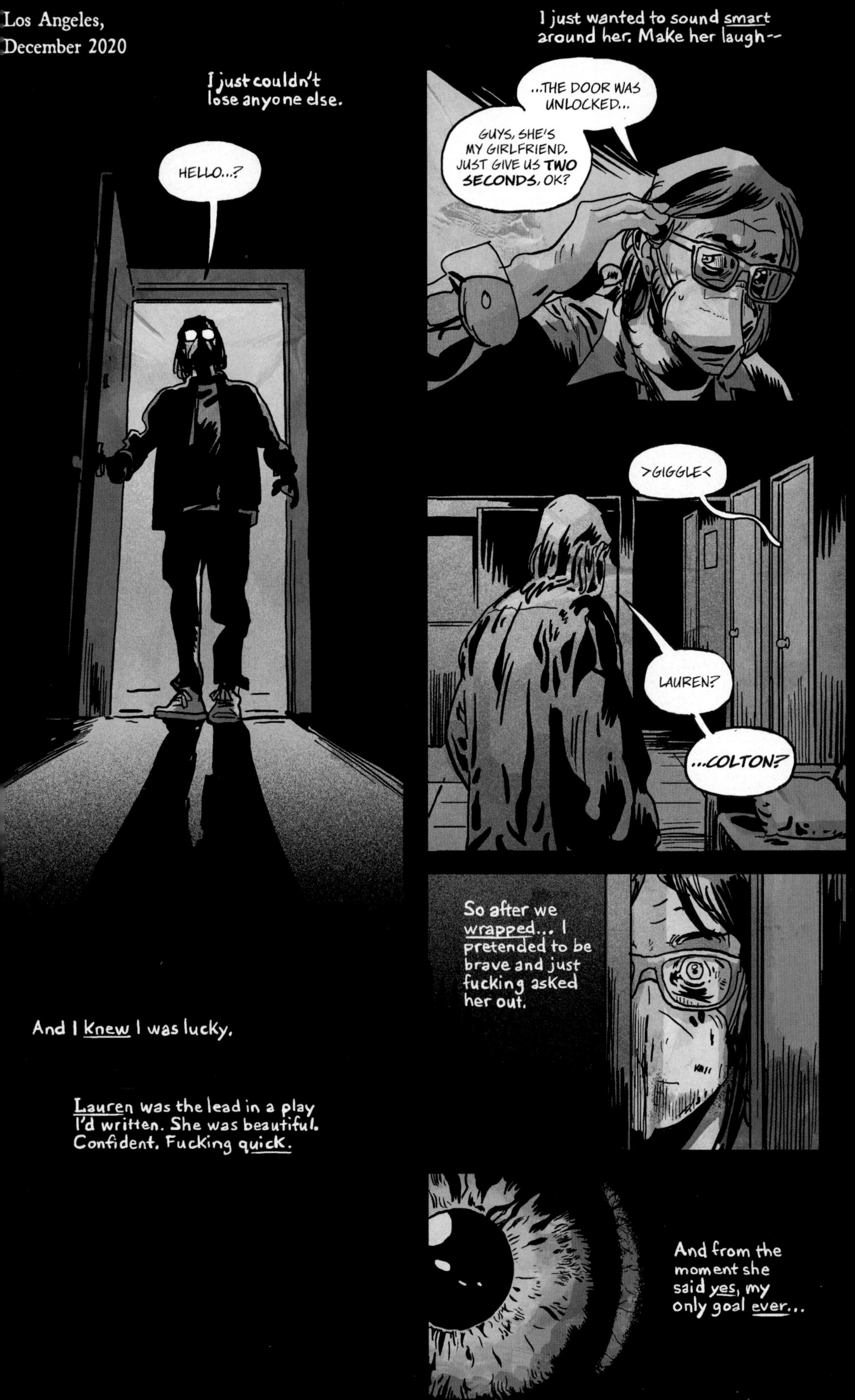

Los Angeles,
December 2020
I just couldn't lose anyone else.
HELLO...?
And I knew I was lucky.
Lauren was the lead in a play I'd written. She was beautiful. Confident. Fucking quick.
I just wanted to sound smart around her. Make her laugh--
...THE DOOR WAS UNLOCKED...
GUYS, SHE'S MY GIRLFRIEND. JUST GIVE US TWO SECONDS, OK?
>GIGGLE<
LAUREN?
...COLTON?
So after we wrapped... I pretended to be brave and just fucking asked her out.
And from the moment she said yes, my only goal ever...

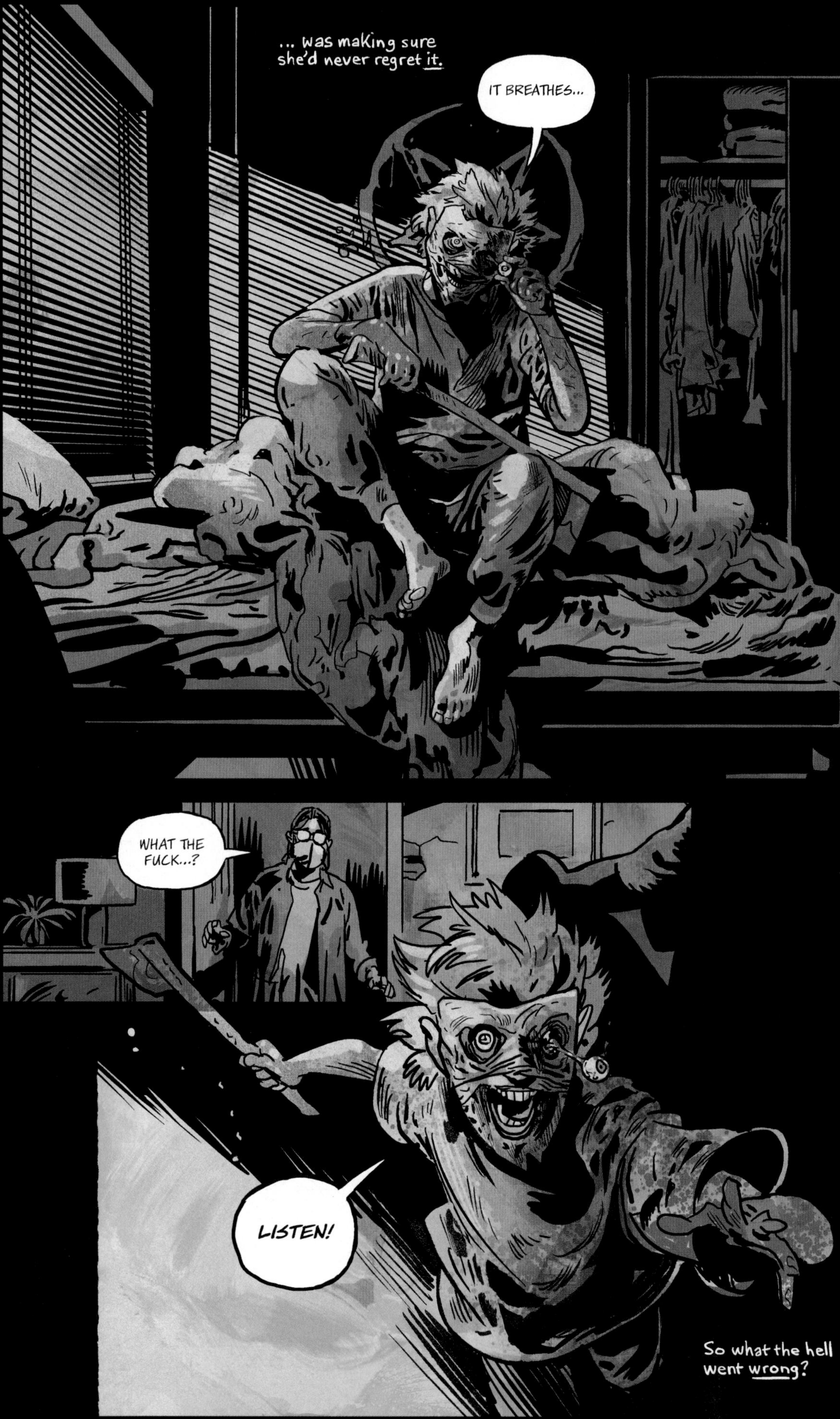
... was making sure she'd never regret it.
IT BREATHES...
WHAT THE FUCK...?
LISTEN!
So what the hell went wrong?

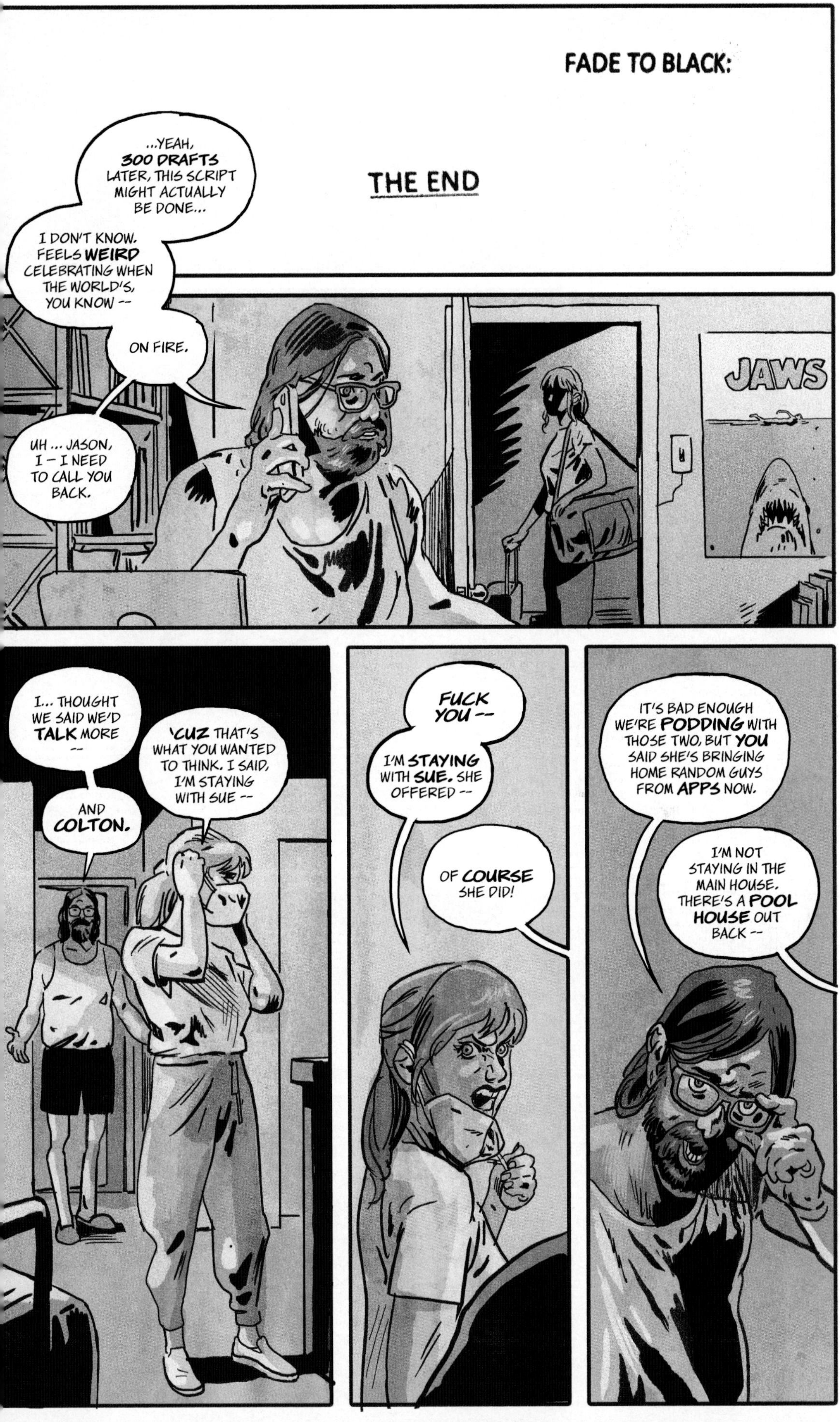
FADE TO BLACK:
THE END
...YEAH, 300 DRAFTS LATER, THIS SCRIPT MIGHT ACTUALLY BE DONE...
I DON'T KNOW. FEELS WEIRD CELEBRATING WHEN THE WORLD'S, YOU KNOW --
ON FIRE.
UH ... JASON, I -- I NEED TO CALL YOU BACK.
JAWS
I... THOUGHT WE SAID WE'D TALK MORE --
AND COLTON.
'CUZ THAT'S WHAT YOU WANTED TO THINK. I SAID, I'M STAYING WITH SUE --
FUCK YOU --
I'M STAYING WITH SUE. SHE OFFERED --
OF COURSE SHE DID!
IT'S BAD ENOUGH WE'RE PODDING WITH THOSE TWO, BUT YOU SAID SHE'S BRINGING HOME RANDOM GUYS FROM APPS NOW.
I'M NOT STAYING IN THE MAIN HOUSE. THERE'S A POOL HOUSE OUT BACK --

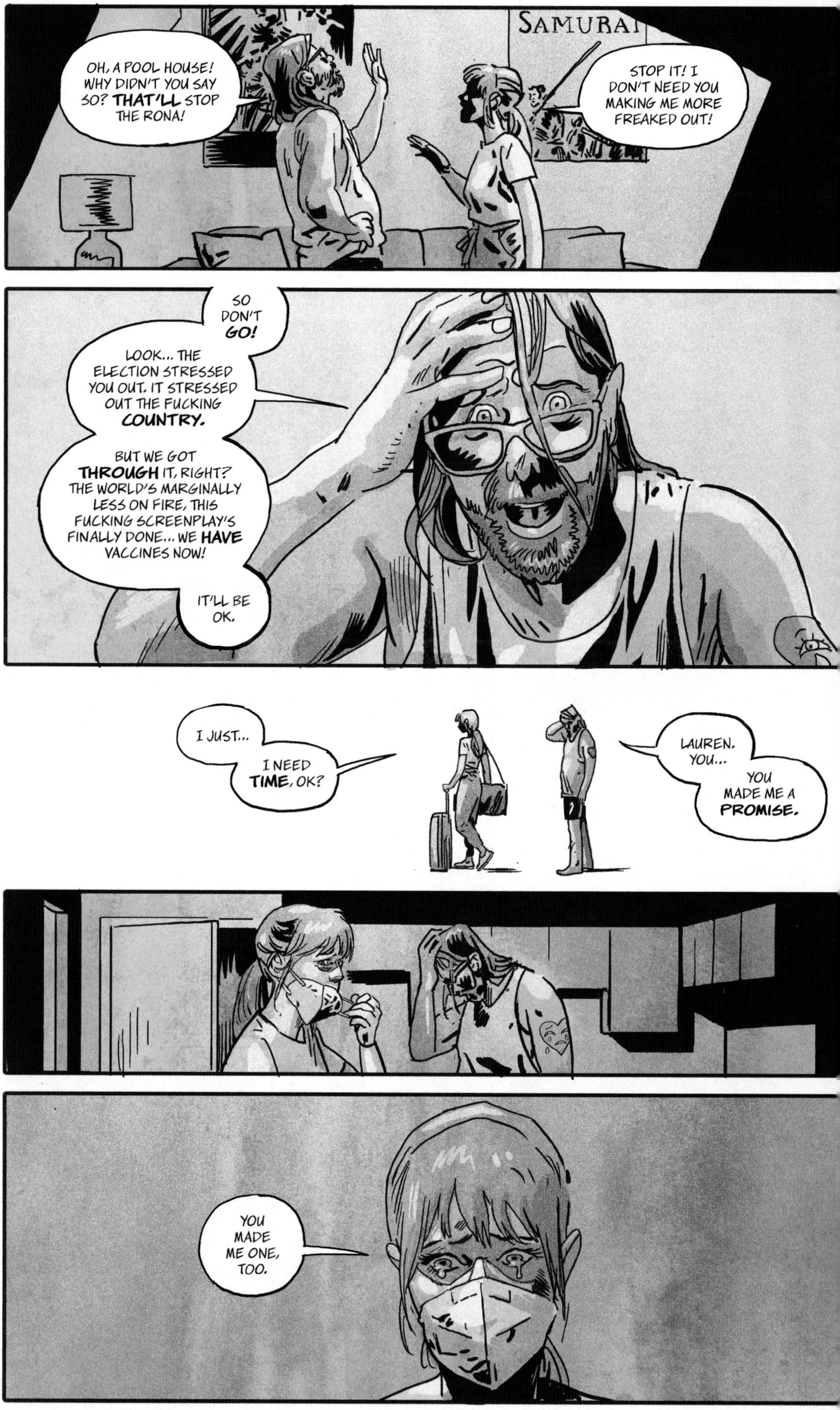
OH, A POOL HOUSE! WHY DIDN'T YOU SAY SO? THAT'LL STOP THE RONA!
STOP IT! I DON'T NEED YOU MAKING ME MORE FREAKED OUT!
SAMURAI
SO DON'T GO!
LOOK... THE ELECTION STRESSED YOU OUT. IT STRESSED OUT THE FUCKING COUNTRY.
BUT WE GOT THROUGH IT, RIGHT? THE WORLD'S MARGINALLY LESS ON FIRE, THIS FUCKING SCREENPLAY'S FINALLY DONE... WE HAVE VACCINES NOW!
IT'LL BE OK.
I JUST...
I NEED TIME, OK?
LAUREN. YOU...
YOU MADE ME A PROMISE.
YOU MADE ME ONE, TOO.

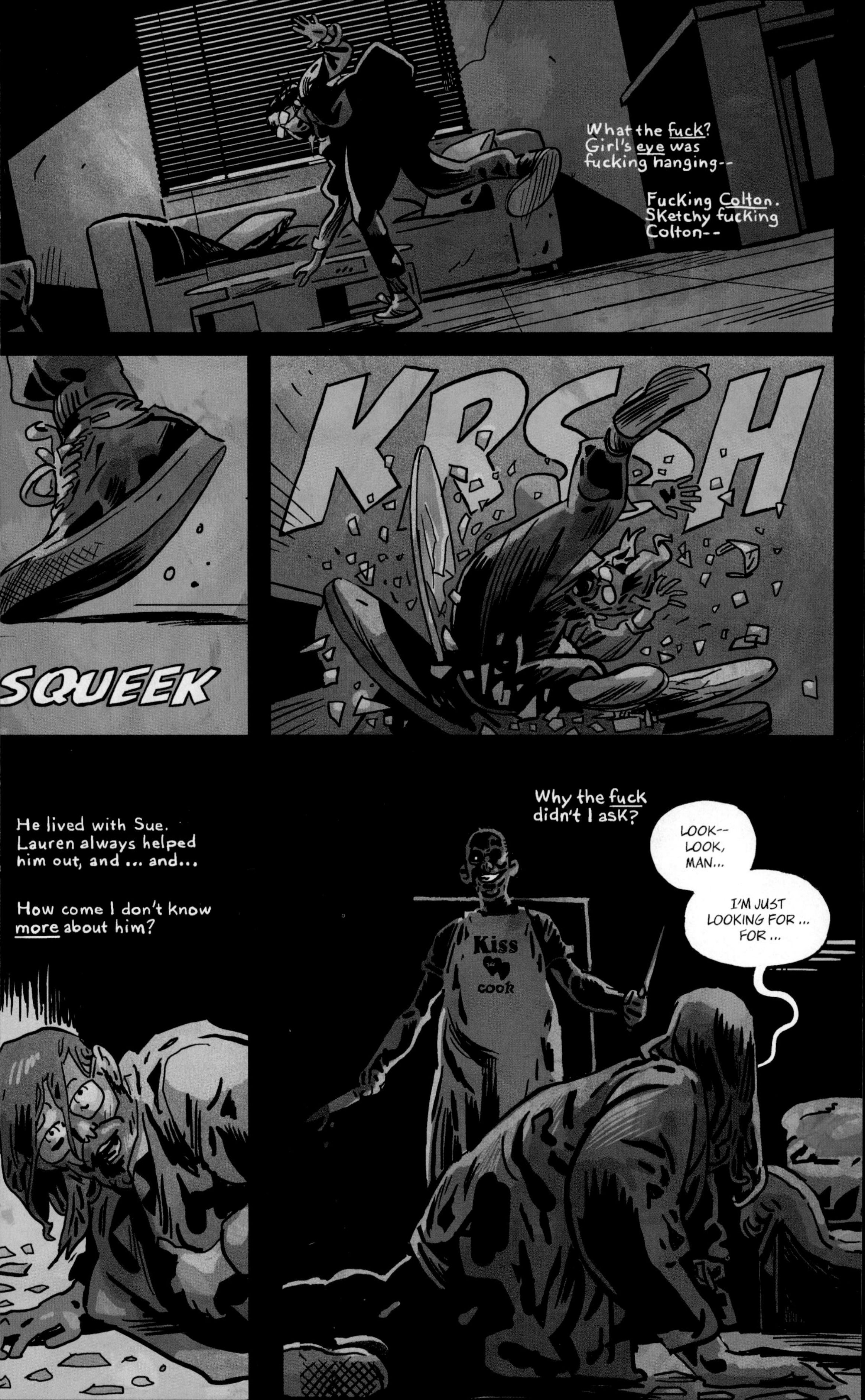
What the fuck? Girl's eye was fucking hanging--
Fucking Colton. Sketchy fucking Colton--
SQUEEK
KRSSH
He lived with Sue. Lauren always helped him out, and ... and...
How come I don't know more about him?
Why the fuck didn't I ask?
LOOK-- LOOK, MAN...
I'M JUST LOOKING FOR ... FOR ...
Kiss cook

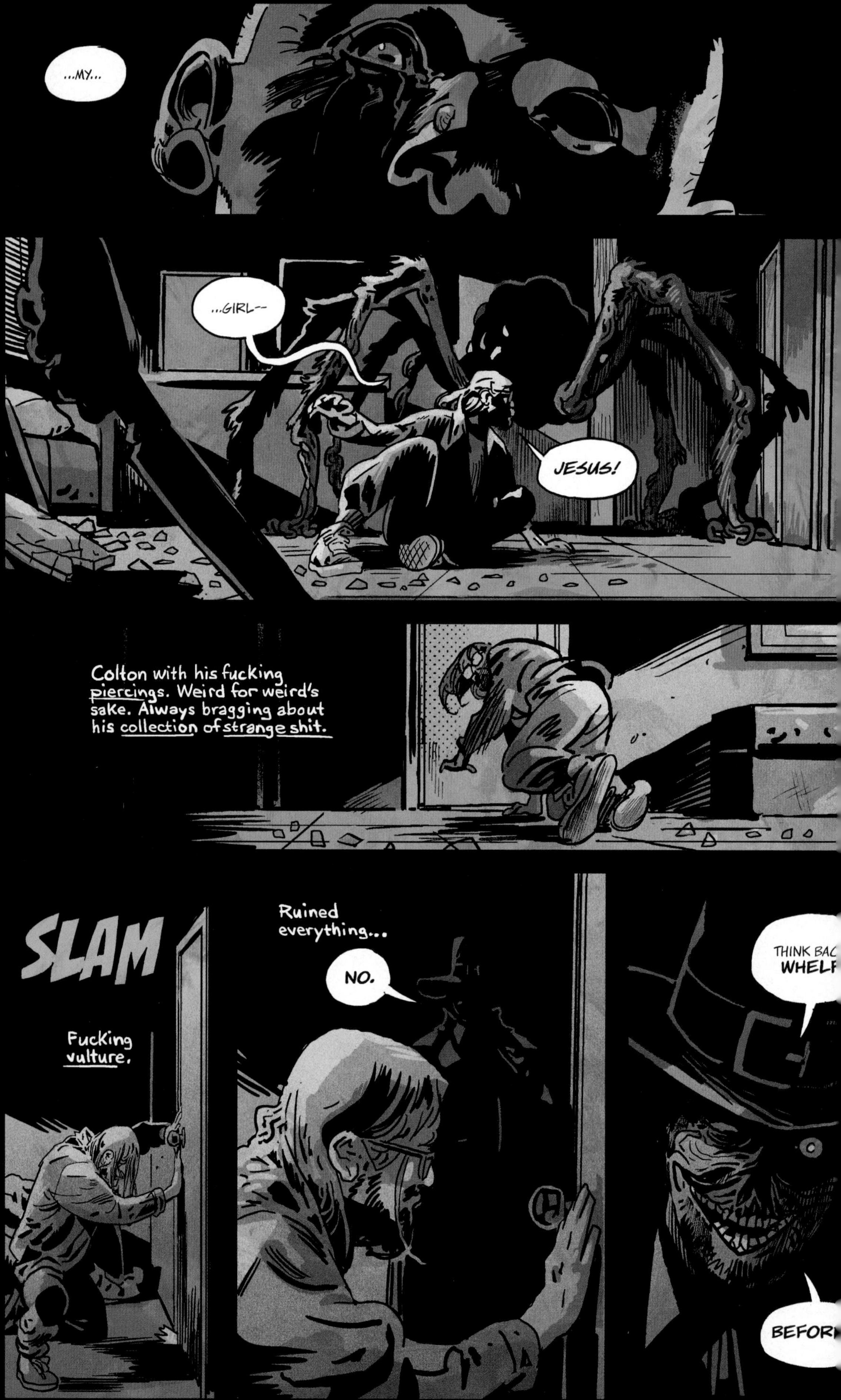
...MY...
...GIRL--
JESUS!
Colton with his fucking piercings. Weird for weird's sake. Always bragging about his collection of strange shit.
SLAM
Fucking vulture.
Ruined everything...
NO.

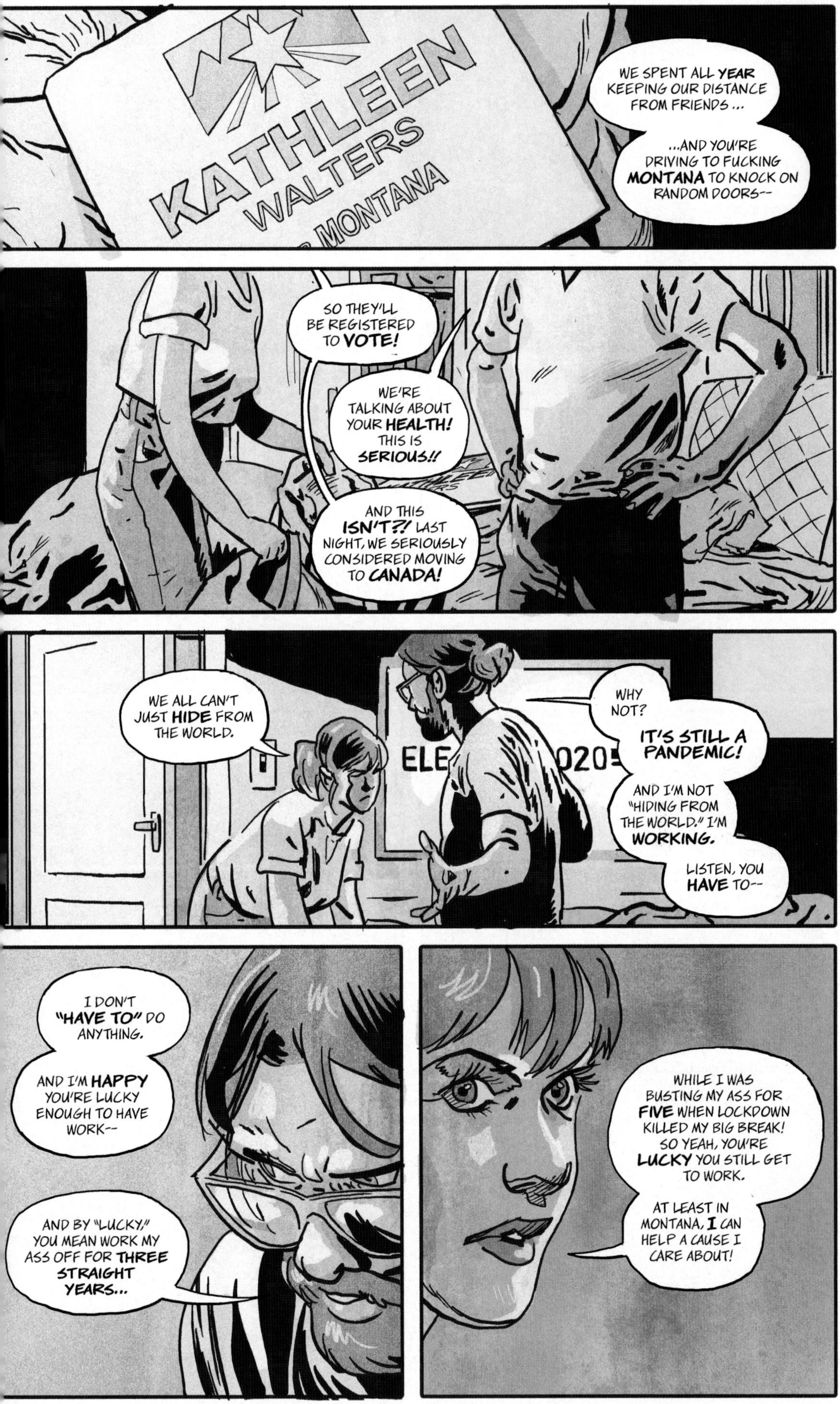
KATHLEEN
WALTERS
MONTANA
WE SPENT ALL YEAR KEEPING OUR DISTANCE FROM FRIENDS ...
...AND YOU'RE DRIVING TO FUCKING MONTANA TO KNOCK ON RANDOM DOORS--
SO THEY'LL BE REGISTERED TO VOTE!
WE'RE TALKING ABOUT YOUR HEALTH! THIS IS SERIOUS!!
AND THIS ISN'T?! LAST NIGHT, WE SERIOUSLY CONSIDERED MOVING TO CANADA!
WE ALL CAN'T JUST HIDE FROM THE WORLD.
WHY NOT?
IT'S STILL A PANDEMIC!
AND I'M NOT "HIDING FROM THE WORLD." I'M WORKING.
LISTEN, YOU HAVE TO--
I DON'T "HAVE TO" DO ANYTHING.
AND I'M HAPPY YOU'RE LUCKY ENOUGH TO HAVE WORK--
AND BY "LUCKY," YOU MEAN WORK MY ASS OFF FOR THREE STRAIGHT YEARS...
WHILE I WAS BUSTING MY ASS FOR FIVE WHEN LOCKDOWN KILLED MY BIG BREAK! SO YEAH, YOU'RE LUCKY YOU STILL GET TO WORK.
AT LEAST IN MONTANA, I CAN HELP A CAUSE I CARE ABOUT!

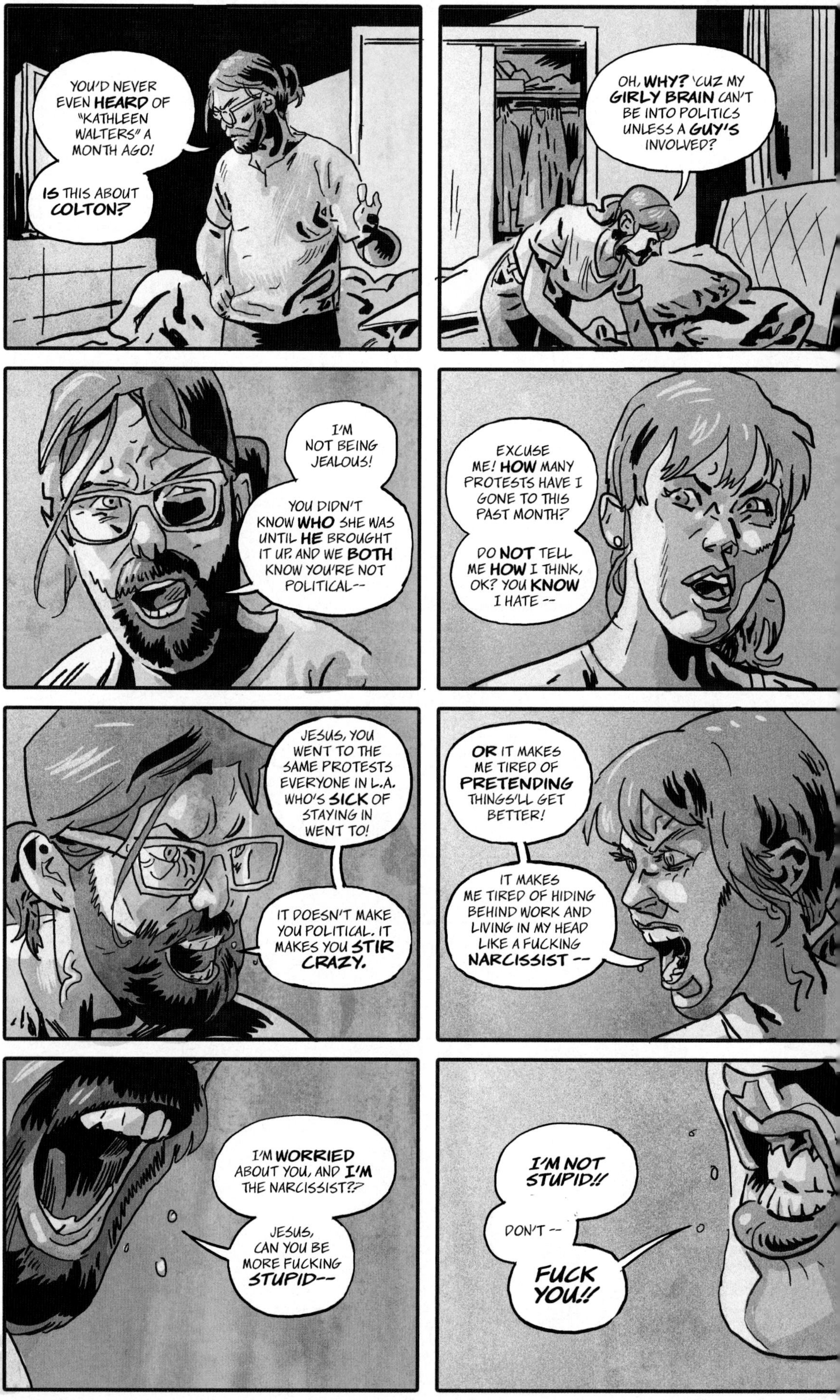
YOU'D NEVER EVEN HEARD OF "KATHLEEN WALTERS" A MONTH AGO!
IS THIS ABOUT COLTON?
OH, WHY? 'CUZ MY GIRLY BRAIN CAN'T BE INTO POLITICS UNLESS A GUY'S INVOLVED?
I'M NOT BEING JEALOUS!
YOU DIDN'T KNOW WHO SHE WAS UNTIL HE BROUGHT IT UP. AND WE BOTH KNOW YOU'RE NOT POLITICAL--
EXCUSE ME! HOW MANY PROTESTS HAVE I GONE TO THIS PAST MONTH?
DO NOT TELL ME HOW I THINK, OK? YOU KNOW I HATE --
JESUS, YOU WENT TO THE SAME PROTESTS EVERYONE IN L.A. WHO'S SICK OF STAYING IN WENT TO!
IT DOESN'T MAKE YOU POLITICAL. IT MAKES YOU STIR CRAZY.
OR IT MAKES ME TIRED OF PRETENDING THINGS'LL GET BETTER!
IT MAKES ME TIRED OF HIDING BEHIND WORK AND LIVING IN MY HEAD LIKE A FUCKING NARCISSIST --
I'M WORRIED ABOUT YOU, AND I'M THE NARCISSIST?!?
JESUS, CAN YOU BE MORE FUCKING STUPID--
I'M NOT STUPID!!
DON'T --
FUCK YOU!!

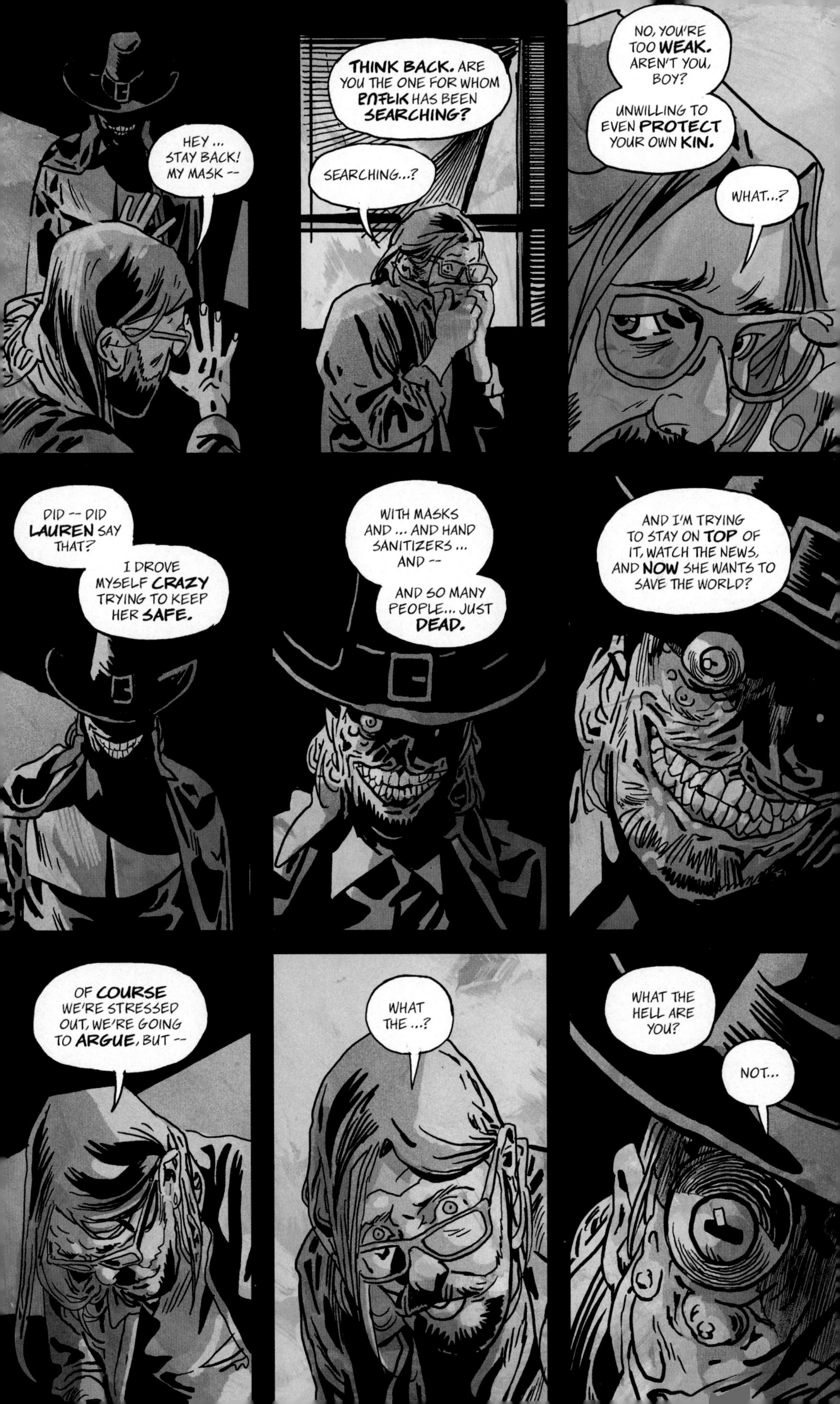
HEY ... STAY BACK! MY MASK --
THINK BACK. ARE YOU THE ONE FOR WHOM ƐՈŦŁIK HAS BEEN SEARCHING?
SEARCHING...?
NO, YOU'RE TOO WEAK. AREN'T YOU, BOY?
UNWILLING TO EVEN PROTECT YOUR OWN KIN.
WHAT...?
DID -- DID LAUREN SAY THAT?
I DROVE MYSELF CRAZY TRYING TO KEEP HER SAFE.
WITH MASKS AND ... AND HAND SANITIZERS ... AND --
AND SO MANY PEOPLE... JUST DEAD.
AND I'M TRYING TO STAY ON TOP OF IT, WATCH THE NEWS, AND NOW SHE WANTS TO SAVE THE WORLD?
OF COURSE WE'RE STRESSED OUT, WE'RE GOING TO ARGUE, BUT --
WHAT THE ...?
WHAT THE HELL ARE YOU?
NOT...

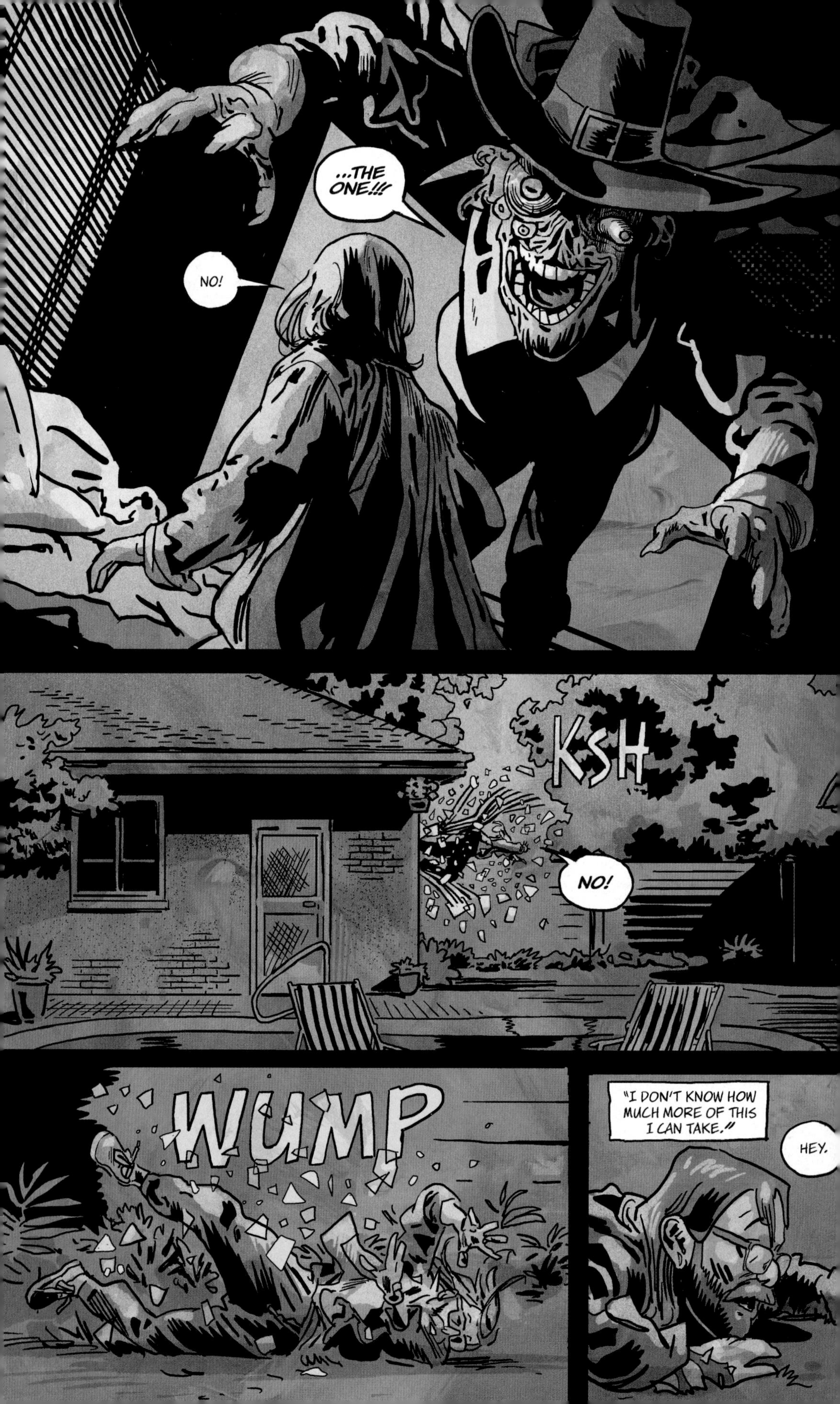
...THE ONE!!!
NO!
KSH
NO!
WUMP
"I DON'T KNOW HOW MUCH MORE OF THIS I CAN TAKE."
HEY.

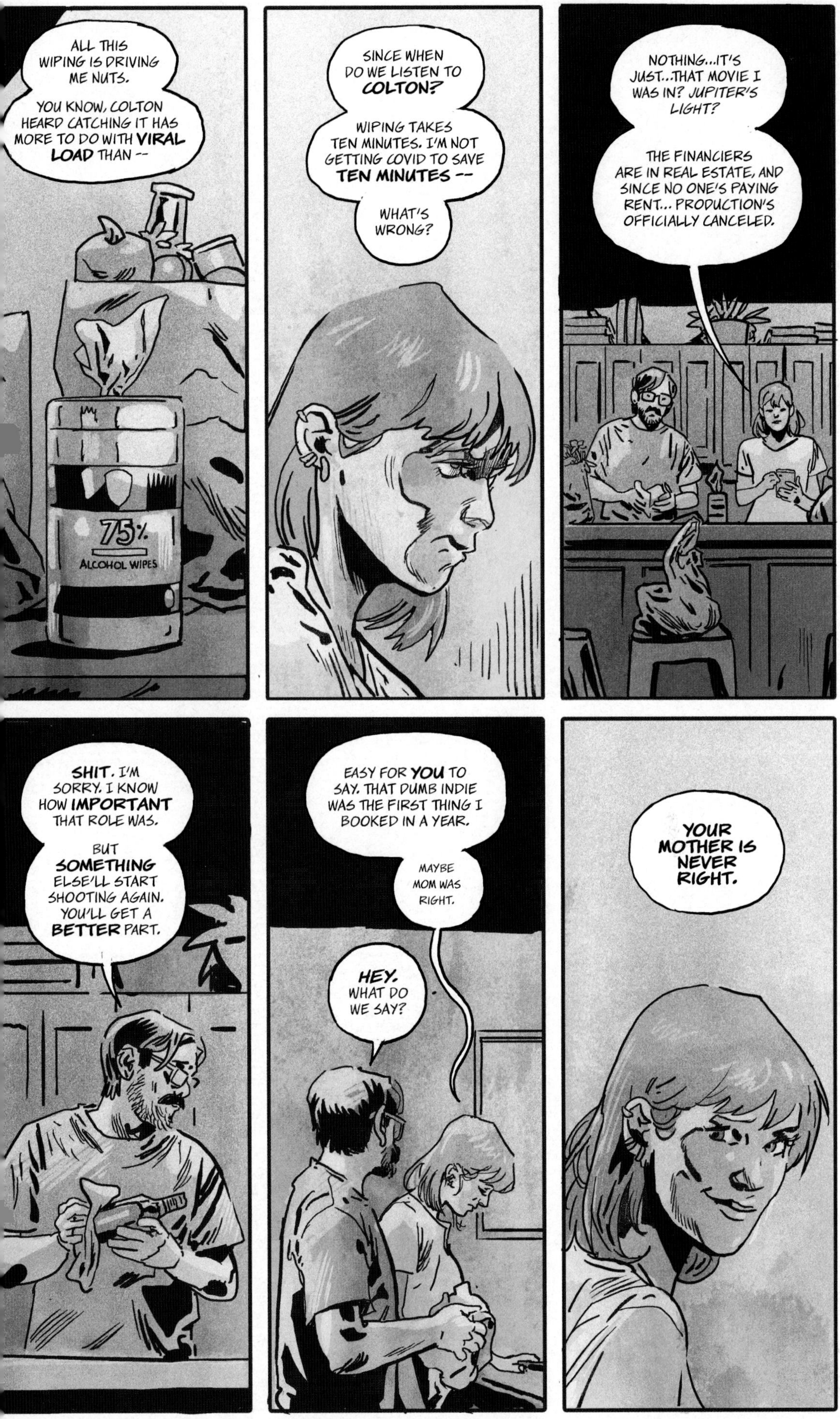
ALL THIS WIPING IS DRIVING ME NUTS.
YOU KNOW, COLTON HEARD CATCHING IT HAS MORE TO DO WITH VIRAL LOAD THAN --
SINCE WHEN DO WE LISTEN TO COLTON?
WIPING TAKES TEN MINUTES. I'M NOT GETTING COVID TO SAVE TEN MINUTES --
WHAT'S WRONG?
NOTHING...IT'S JUST...THAT MOVIE I WAS IN? JUPITER'S LIGHT?
THE FINANCIERS ARE IN REAL ESTATE, AND SINCE NO ONE'S PAYING RENT... PRODUCTION'S OFFICIALLY CANCELED.
75% ALCOHOL WIPES
SHIT. I'M SORRY. I KNOW HOW IMPORTANT THAT ROLE WAS.
BUT SOMETHING ELSE'LL START SHOOTING AGAIN. YOU'LL GET A BETTER PART.
EASY FOR YOU TO SAY. THAT DUMB INDIE WAS THE FIRST THING I BOOKED IN A YEAR.
MAYBE MOM WAS RIGHT.
HEY. WHAT DO WE SAY?
YOUR MOTHER IS NEVER RIGHT.

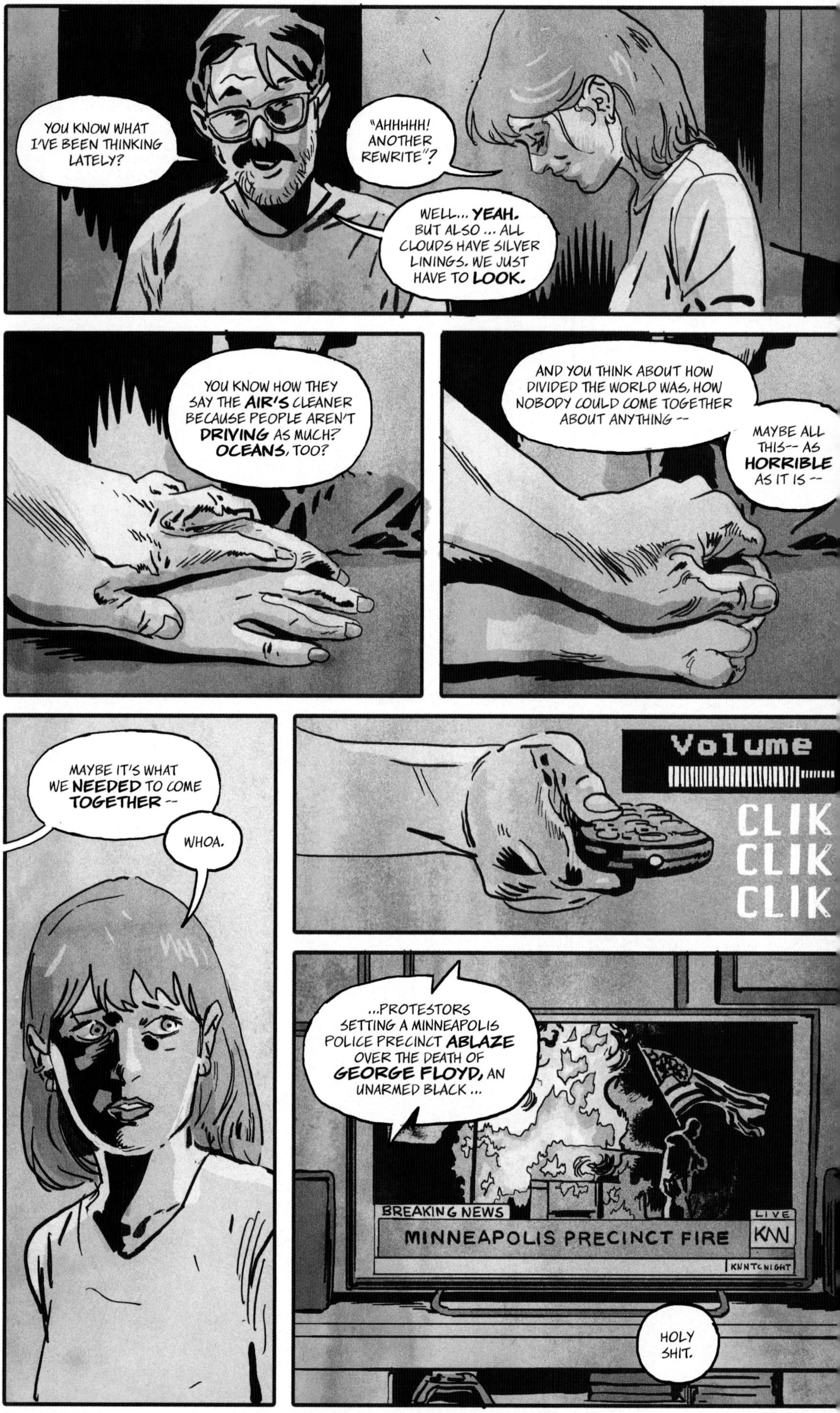
YOU KNOW WHAT I'VE BEEN THINKING LATELY?
"AHHHHH! ANOTHER REWRITE"?
WELL... YEAH. BUT ALSO ... ALL CLOUDS HAVE SILVER LININGS. WE JUST HAVE TO LOOK.
YOU KNOW HOW THEY SAY THE AIR'S CLEANER BECAUSE PEOPLE AREN'T DRIVING AS MUCH? OCEANS, TOO?
AND YOU THINK ABOUT HOW DIVIDED THE WORLD WAS, HOW NOBODY COULD COME TOGETHER ABOUT ANYTHING --
MAYBE ALL THIS-- AS HORRIBLE AS IT IS --
MAYBE IT'S WHAT WE NEEDED TO COME TOGETHER --
WHOA.
Volume
CLIK CLIK CLIK
...PROTESTORS SETTING A MINNEAPOLIS POLICE PRECINCT ABLAZE OVER THE DEATH OF GEORGE FLOYD, AN UNARMED BLACK ...
BREAKING NEWS
MINNEAPOLIS PRECINCT FIRE
LIVE
KNN
KNNTONIGHT
HOLY SHIT.

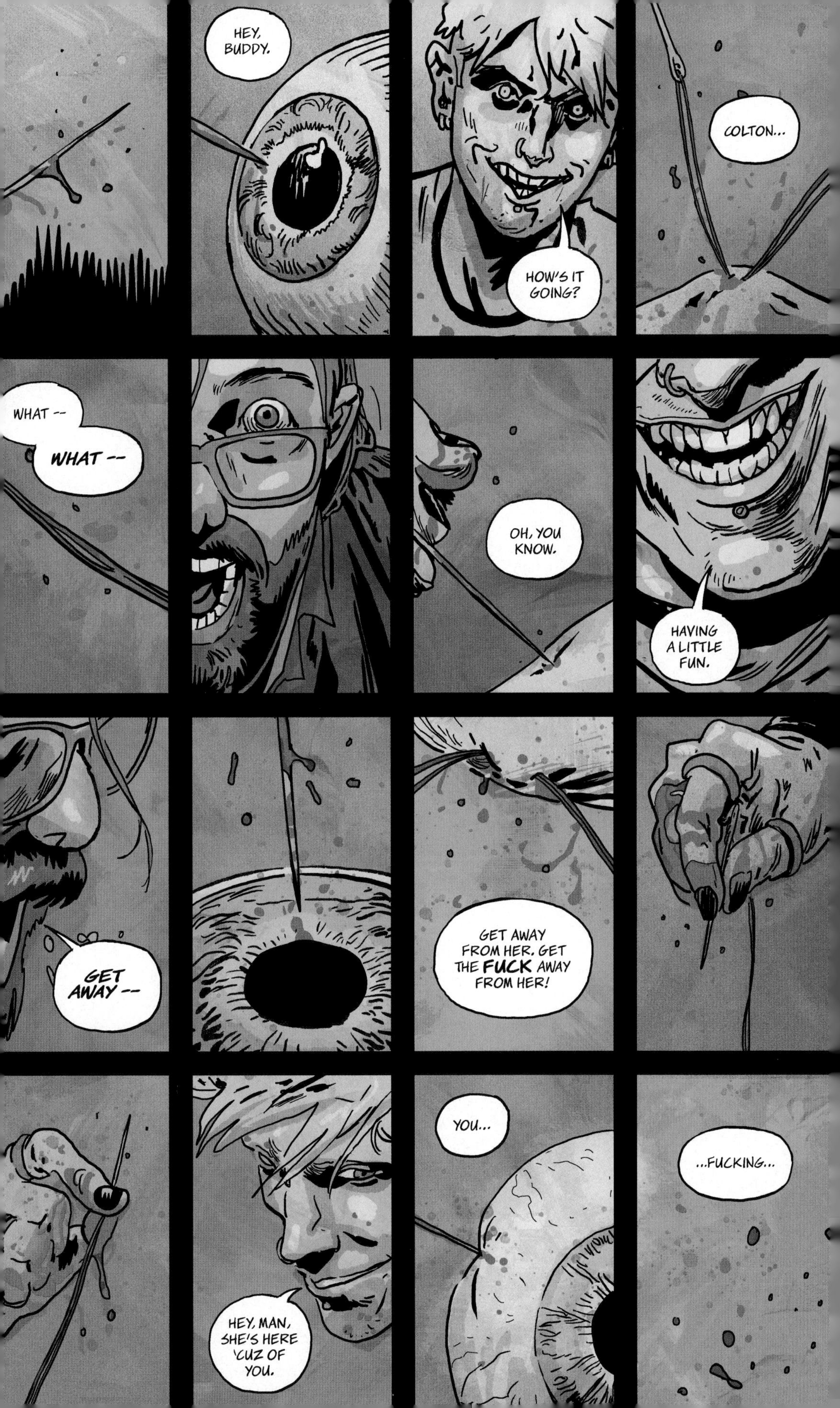
HEY, BUDDY.
HOW'S IT GOING?
COLTON...
WHAT --
WHAT --
OH, YOU KNOW.
HAVING A LITTLE FUN.
GET AWAY --
GET AWAY FROM HER. GET THE FUCK AWAY FROM HER!
HEY, MAN, SHE'S HERE 'CUZ OF YOU.
YOU...
...FUCKING...

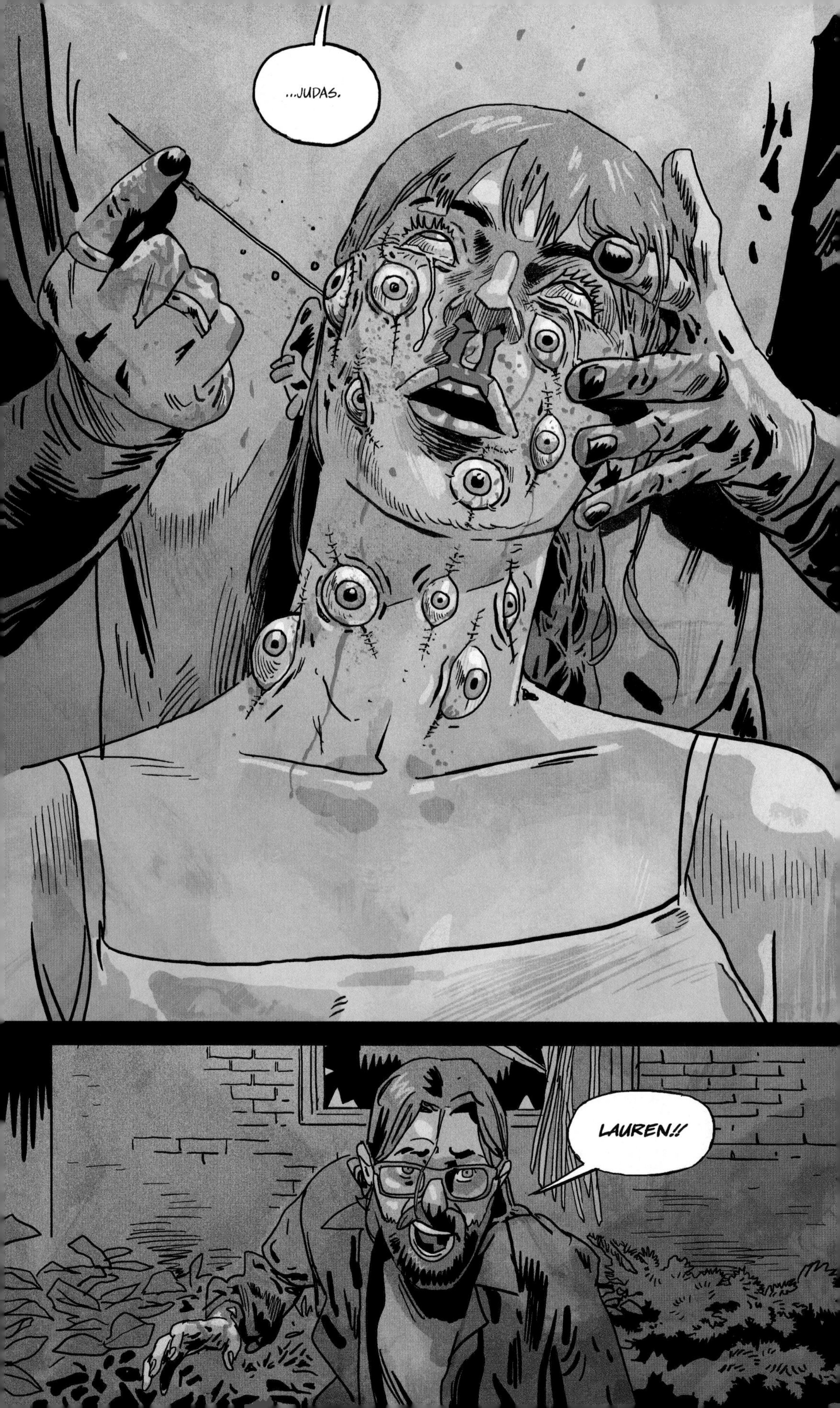
...JUDAS.
LAUREN!!

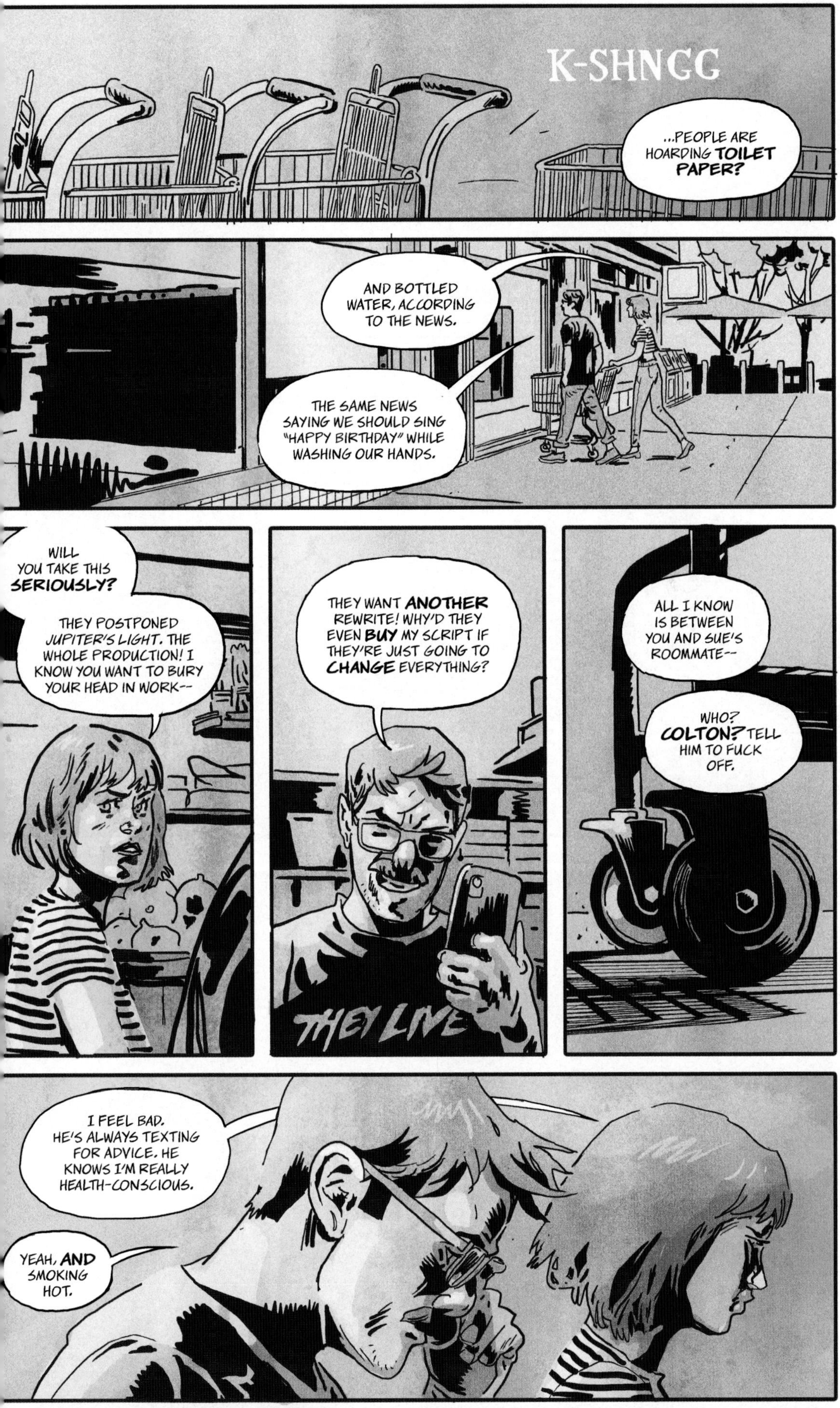
K-SHNGG
...PEOPLE ARE HOARDING TOILET PAPER?
AND BOTTLED WATER, ACCORDING TO THE NEWS.
THE SAME NEWS SAYING WE SHOULD SING "HAPPY BIRTHDAY" WHILE WASHING OUR HANDS.
WILL YOU TAKE THIS SERIOUSLY?
THEY POSTPONED JUPITER'S LIGHT. THE WHOLE PRODUCTION! I KNOW YOU WANT TO BURY YOUR HEAD IN WORK--
THEY WANT ANOTHER REWRITE! WHY'D THEY EVEN BUY MY SCRIPT IF THEY'RE JUST GOING TO CHANGE EVERYTHING?
THEY LIVE
ALL I KNOW IS BETWEEN YOU AND SUE'S ROOMMATE--
WHO? COLTON? TELL HIM TO FUCK OFF.
I FEEL BAD. HE'S ALWAYS TEXTING FOR ADVICE. HE KNOWS I'M REALLY HEALTH-CONSCIOUS.
YEAH, AND SMOKING HOT.

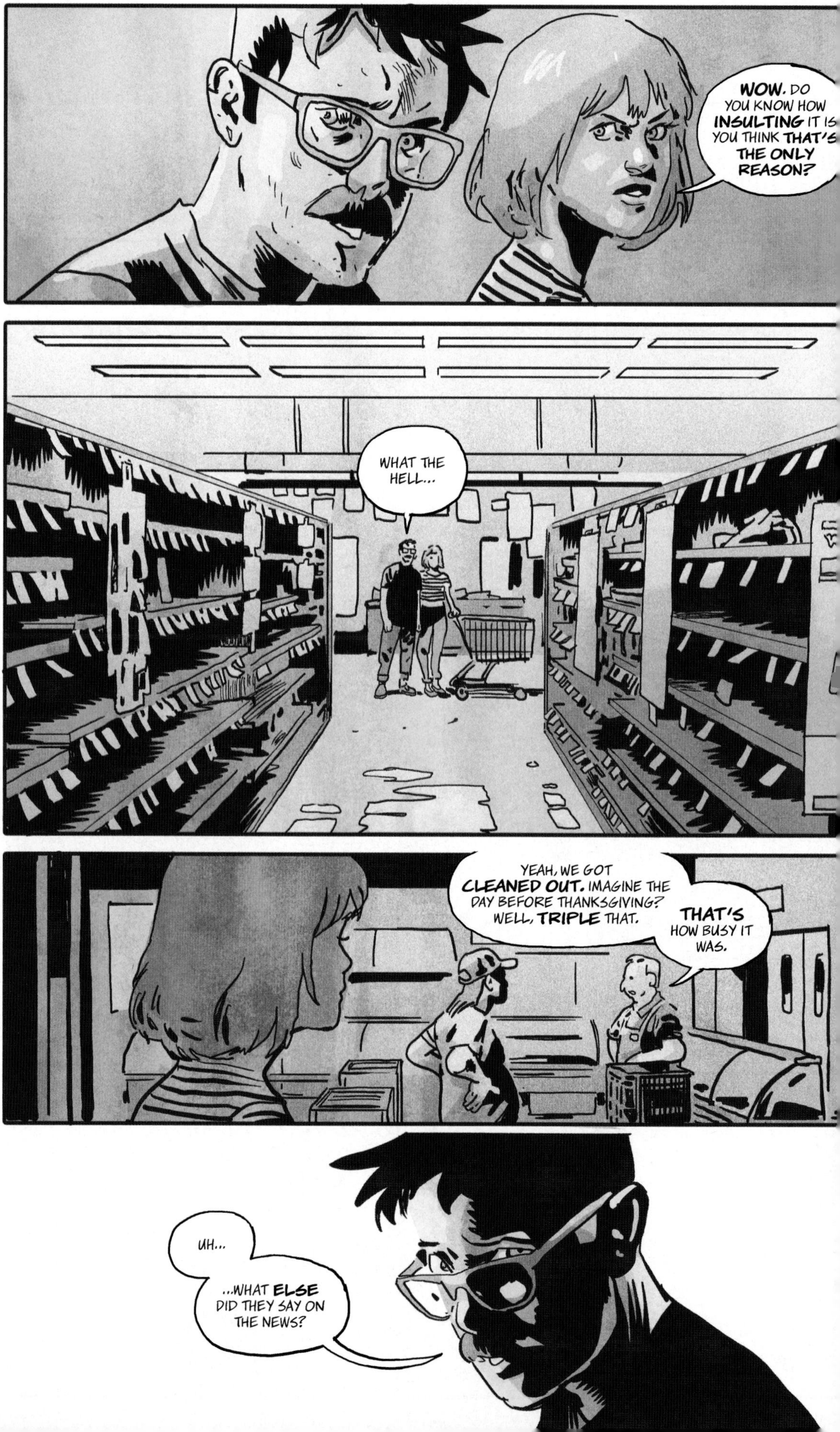
WOW. DO YOU KNOW HOW INSULTING IT IS YOU THINK THAT'S THE ONLY REASON?
WHAT THE HELL...
YEAH, WE GOT CLEANED OUT. IMAGINE THE DAY BEFORE THANKSGIVING? WELL, TRIPLE THAT.
THAT'S HOW BUSY IT WAS.
UH...
...WHAT ELSE DID THEY SAY ON THE NEWS?

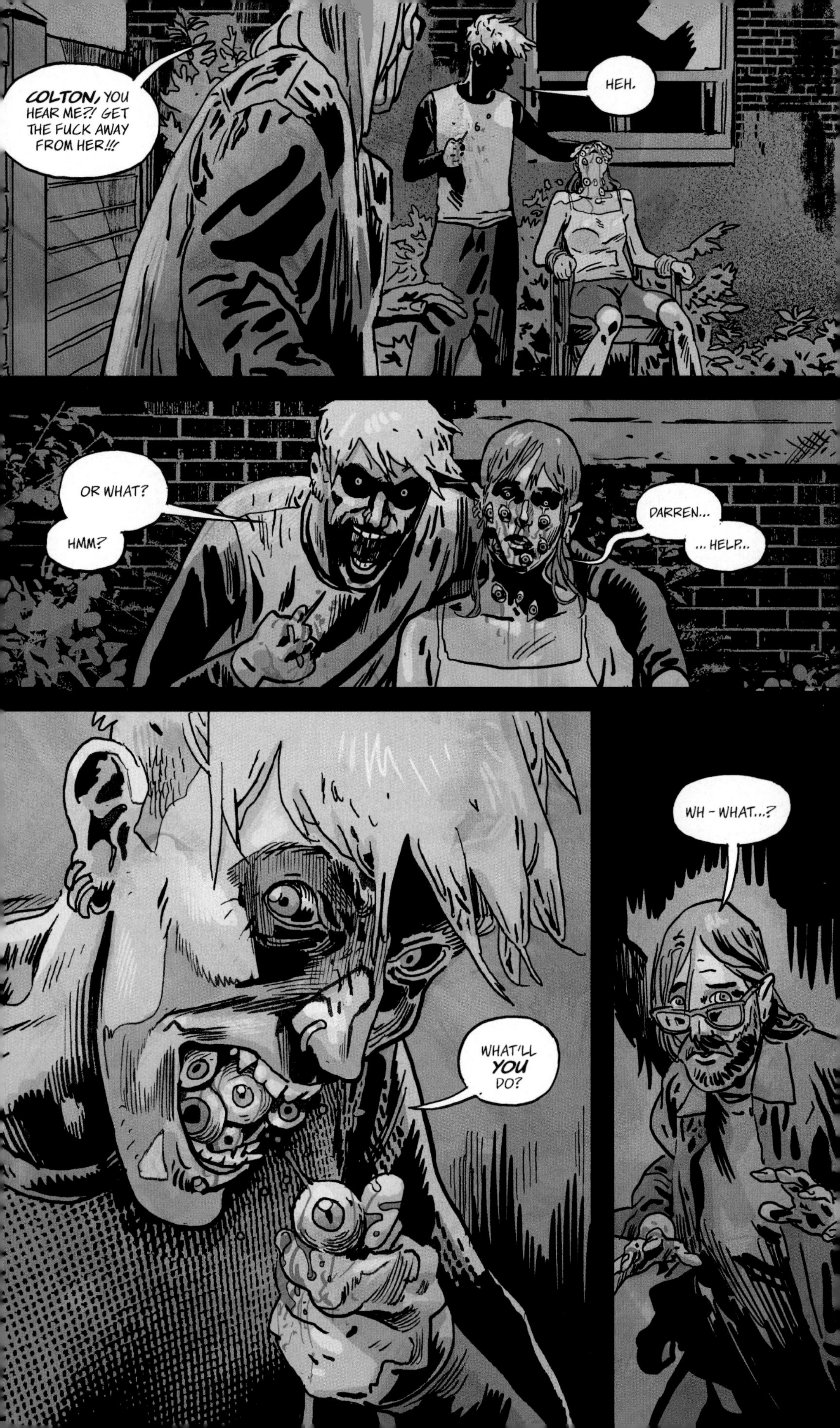
COLTON, YOU HEAR ME?! GET THE FUCK AWAY FROM HER!!!
HEH.
OR WHAT?
HMM?
DARREN...
...HELP...
WHAT'LL YOU DO?
WH - WHAT...?

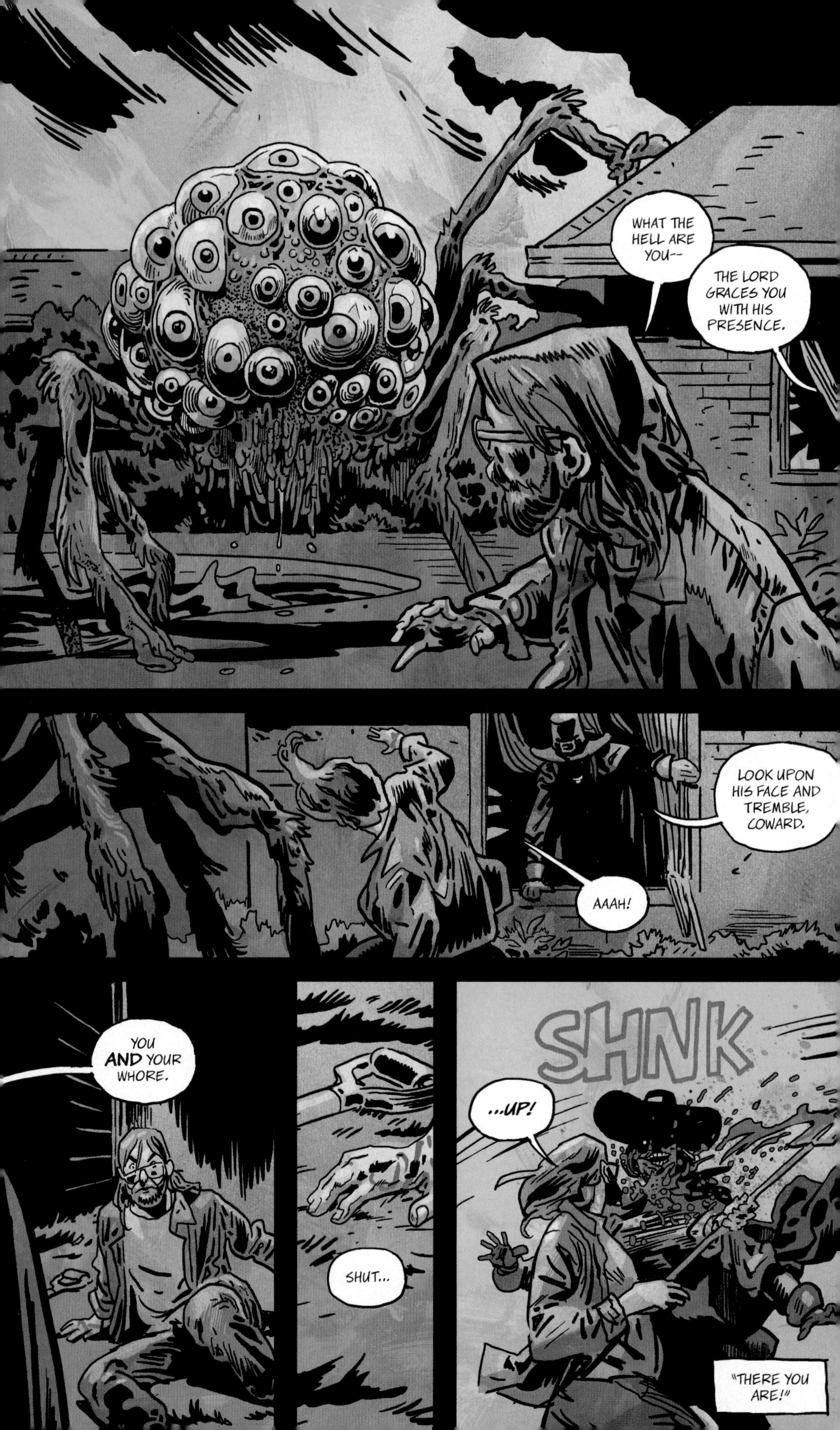
WHAT THE HELL ARE YOU--
THE LORD GRACES YOU WITH HIS PRESENCE.
LOOK UPON HIS FACE AND TREMBLE, COWARD.
AAAH!
YOU AND YOUR WHORE.
SHUT...
SHNK
...UP!
"THERE YOU ARE!"

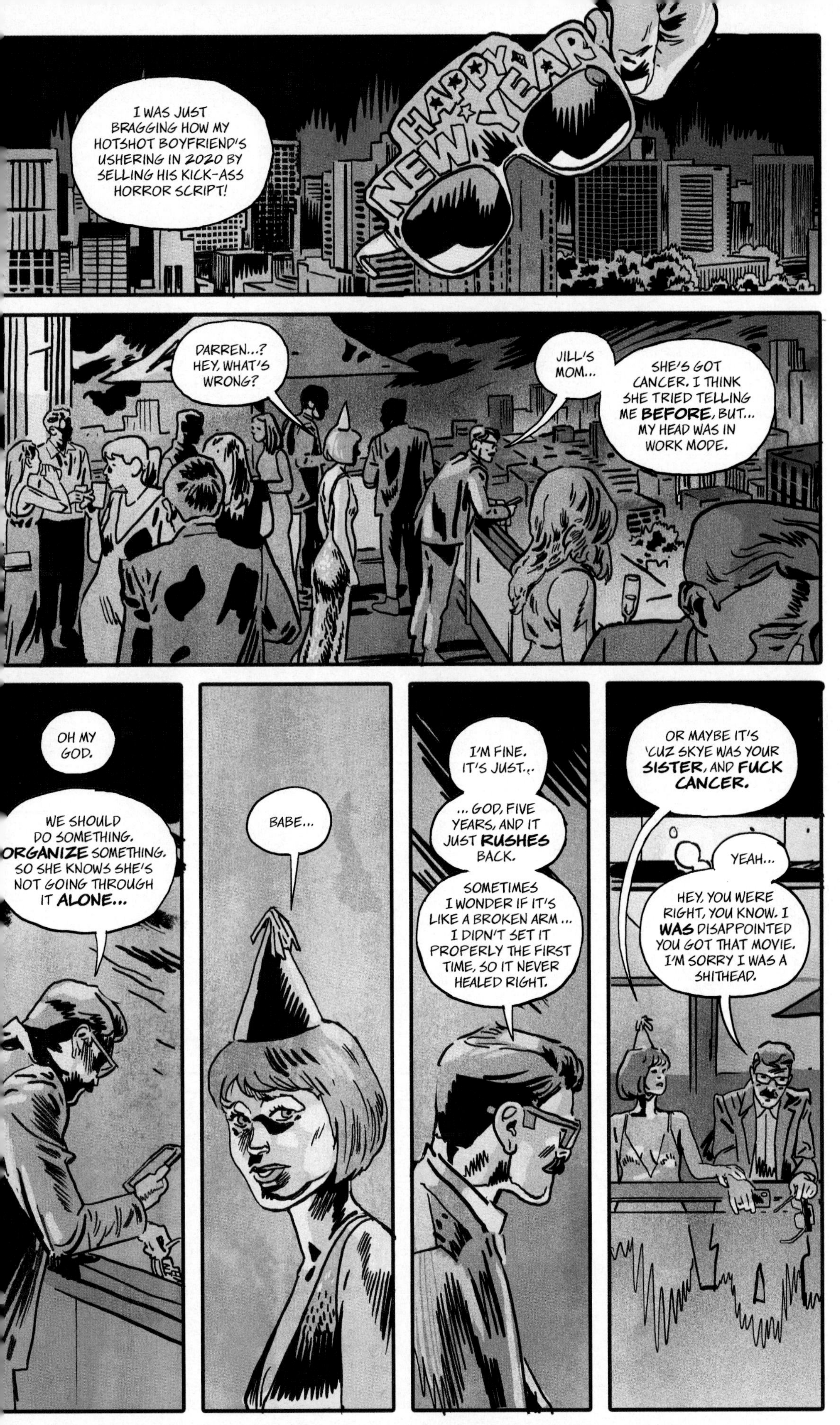
I WAS JUST BRAGGING HOW MY HOTSHOT BOYFRIEND'S USHERING IN 2020 BY SELLING HIS KICK-ASS HORROR SCRIPT!
HAPPY NEW YEAR!
DARREN...? HEY, WHAT'S WRONG?
JILL'S MOM...
SHE'S GOT CANCER. I THINK SHE TRIED TELLING ME **BEFORE**, BUT... MY HEAD WAS IN WORK MODE.
OH MY GOD.
WE SHOULD DO SOMETHING. **ORGANIZE** SOMETHING. SO SHE KNOWS SHE'S NOT GOING THROUGH IT **ALONE...**
BABE...
I'M FINE. IT'S JUST...
... GOD, FIVE YEARS, AND IT JUST **RUSHES** BACK.
SOMETIMES I WONDER IF IT'S LIKE A BROKEN ARM ... I DIDN'T SET IT PROPERLY THE FIRST TIME, SO IT NEVER HEALED RIGHT.
OR MAYBE IT'S 'CUZ SKYE WAS YOUR **SISTER**, AND **FUCK CANCER.**
YEAH...
HEY, YOU WERE RIGHT, YOU KNOW. I **WAS** DISAPPOINTED YOU GOT THAT MOVIE. I'M SORRY I WAS A SHITHEAD.

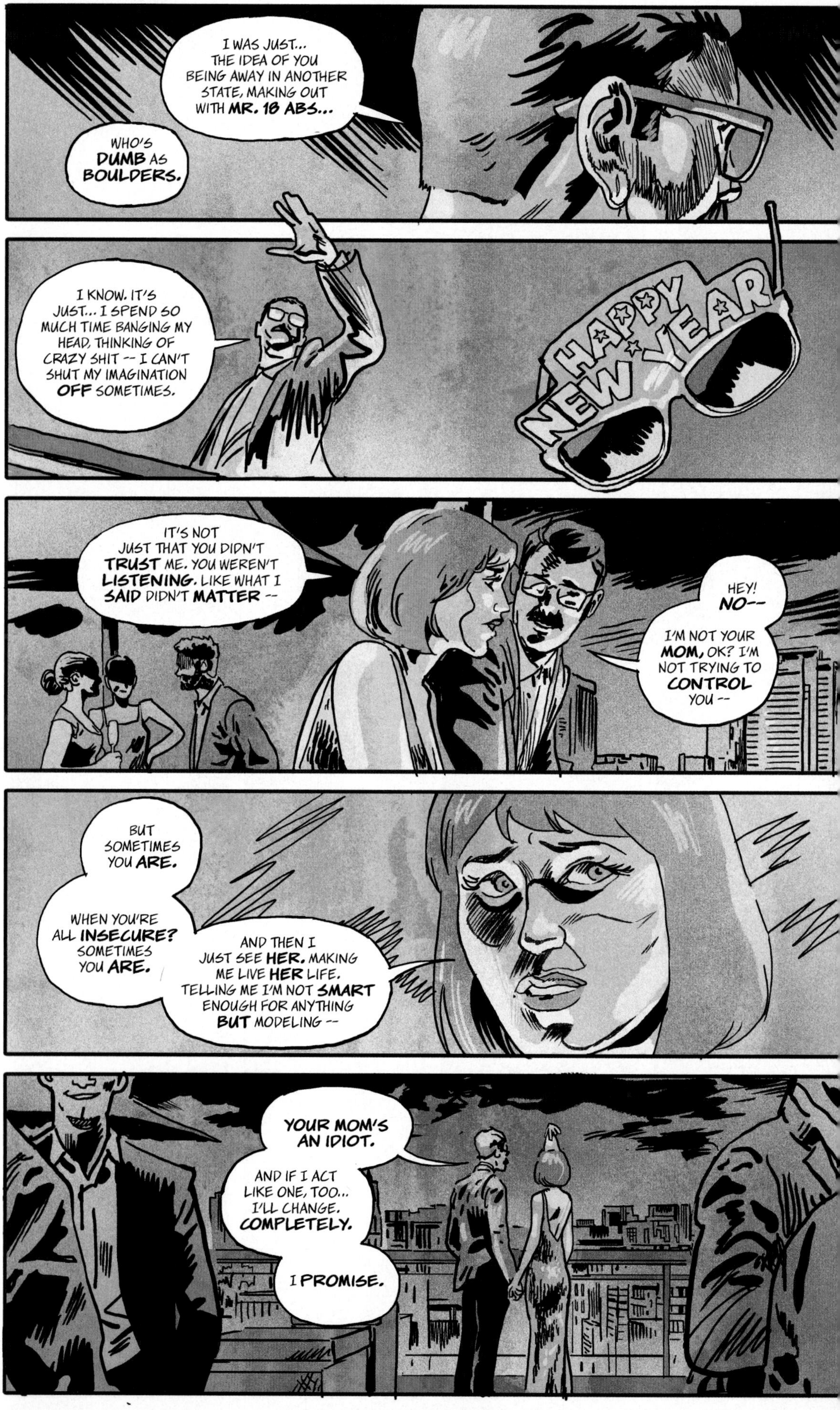

I WAS JUST... THE IDEA OF YOU BEING AWAY IN ANOTHER STATE, MAKING OUT WITH MR. 18 ABS...
WHO'S DUMB AS BOULDERS.
I KNOW. IT'S JUST... I SPEND SO MUCH TIME BANGING MY HEAD, THINKING OF CRAZY SHIT -- I CAN'T SHUT MY IMAGINATION OFF SOMETIMES.
HAPPY NEW YEAR
IT'S NOT JUST THAT YOU DIDN'T TRUST ME. YOU WEREN'T LISTENING. LIKE WHAT I SAID DIDN'T MATTER --
HEY! NO--
I'M NOT YOUR MOM, OK? I'M NOT TRYING TO CONTROL YOU --
BUT SOMETIMES YOU ARE.
WHEN YOU'RE ALL INSECURE? SOMETIMES YOU ARE.
AND THEN I JUST SEE HER. MAKING ME LIVE HER LIFE. TELLING ME I'M NOT SMART ENOUGH FOR ANYTHING BUT MODELING --
YOUR MOM'S AN IDIOT.
AND IF I ACT LIKE ONE, TOO... I'LL CHANGE. COMPLETELY.
I PROMISE.

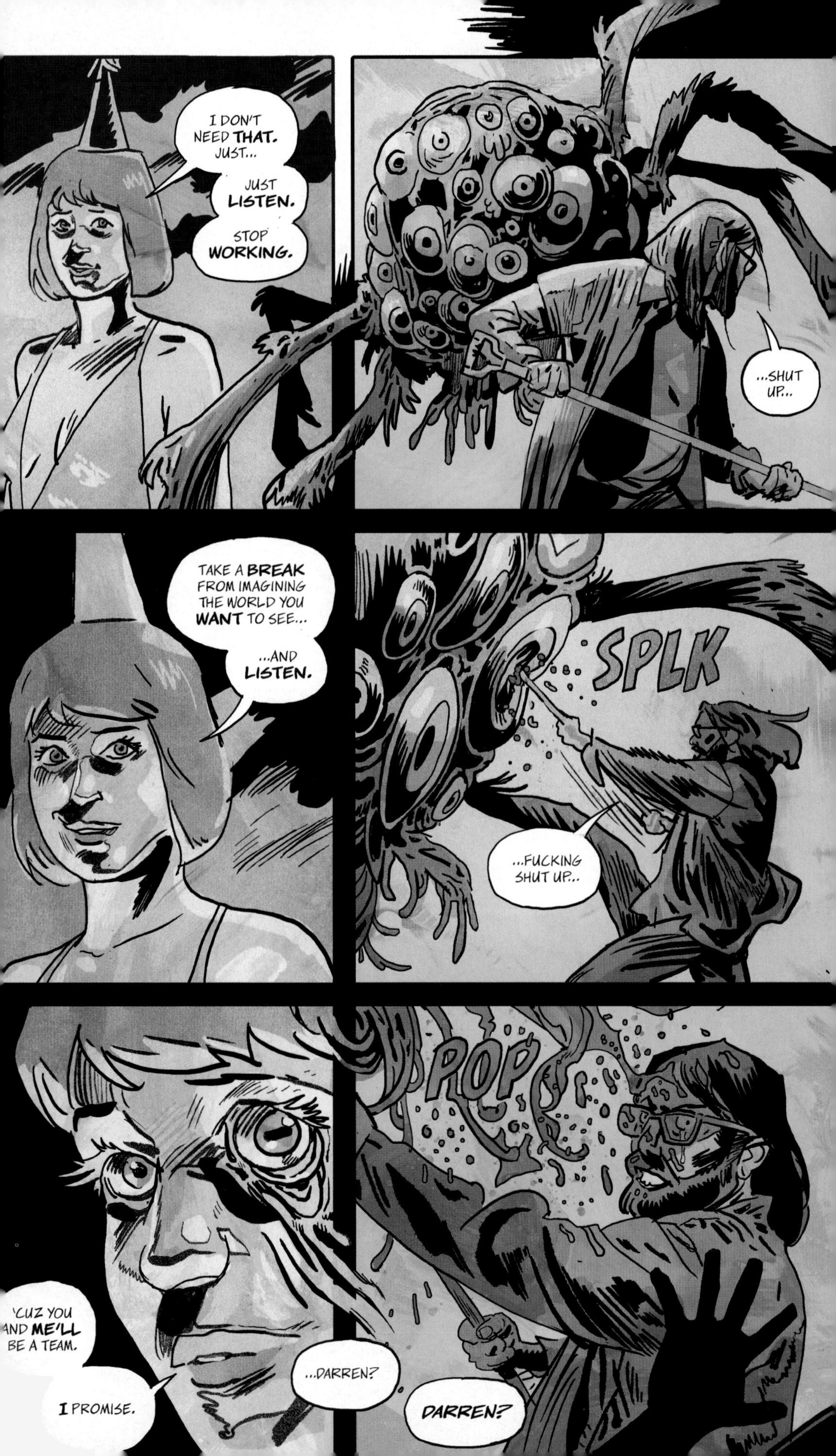
I DON'T NEED THAT. JUST...
JUST LISTEN.
STOP WORKING.
...SHUT UP...
TAKE A BREAK FROM IMAGINING THE WORLD YOU WANT TO SEE...
...AND LISTEN.
SPLK
...FUCKING SHUT UP...
'CUZ YOU AND ME'LL BE A TEAM.
I PROMISE.
POP
...DARREN?
DARREN?

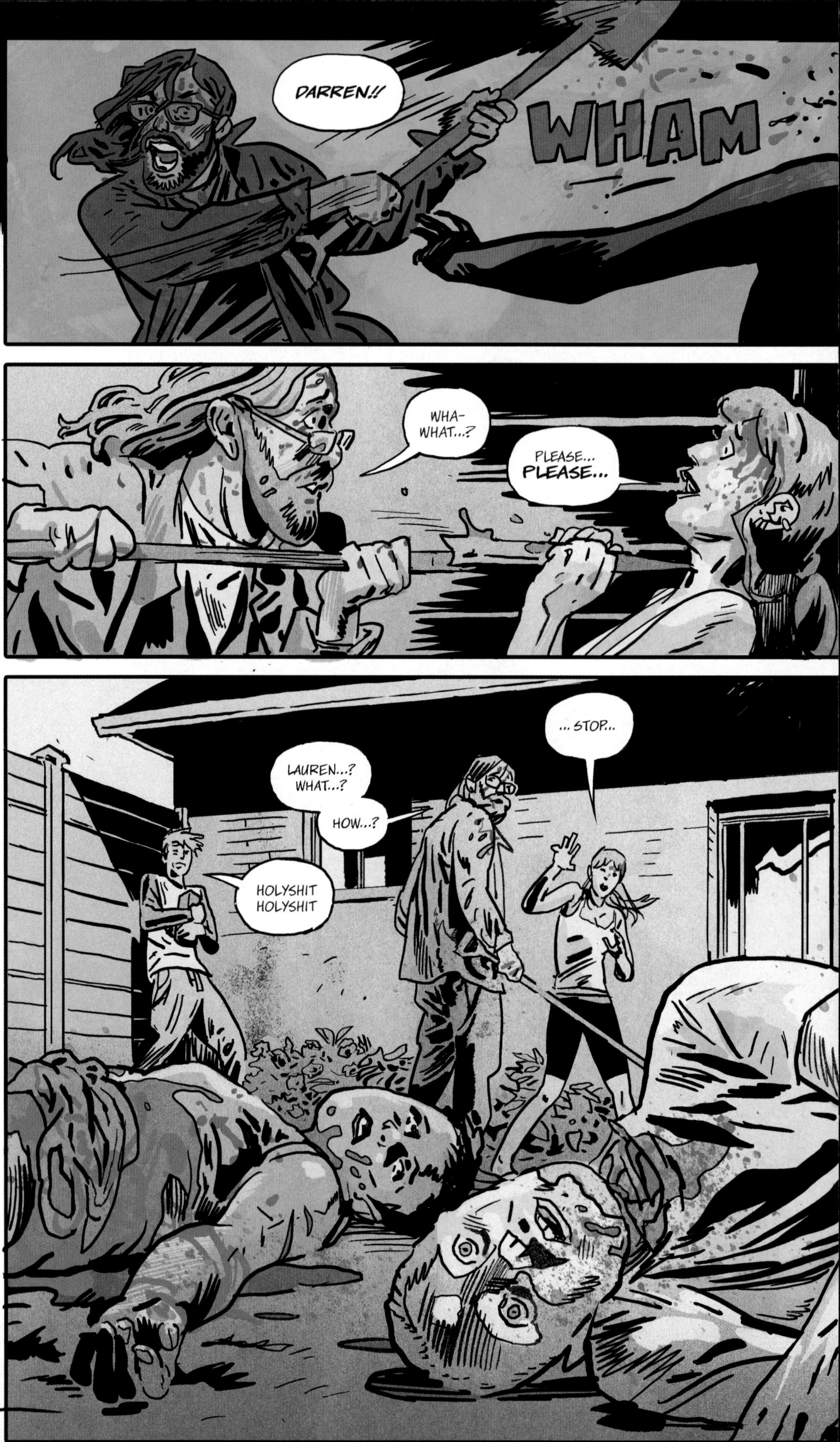
DARREN!!
WHAM
WHA-
WHAT...?
PLEASE...
PLEASE...
... STOP...
LAUREN...?
WHAT...?
HOW...?
HOLYSHIT
HOLYSHIT

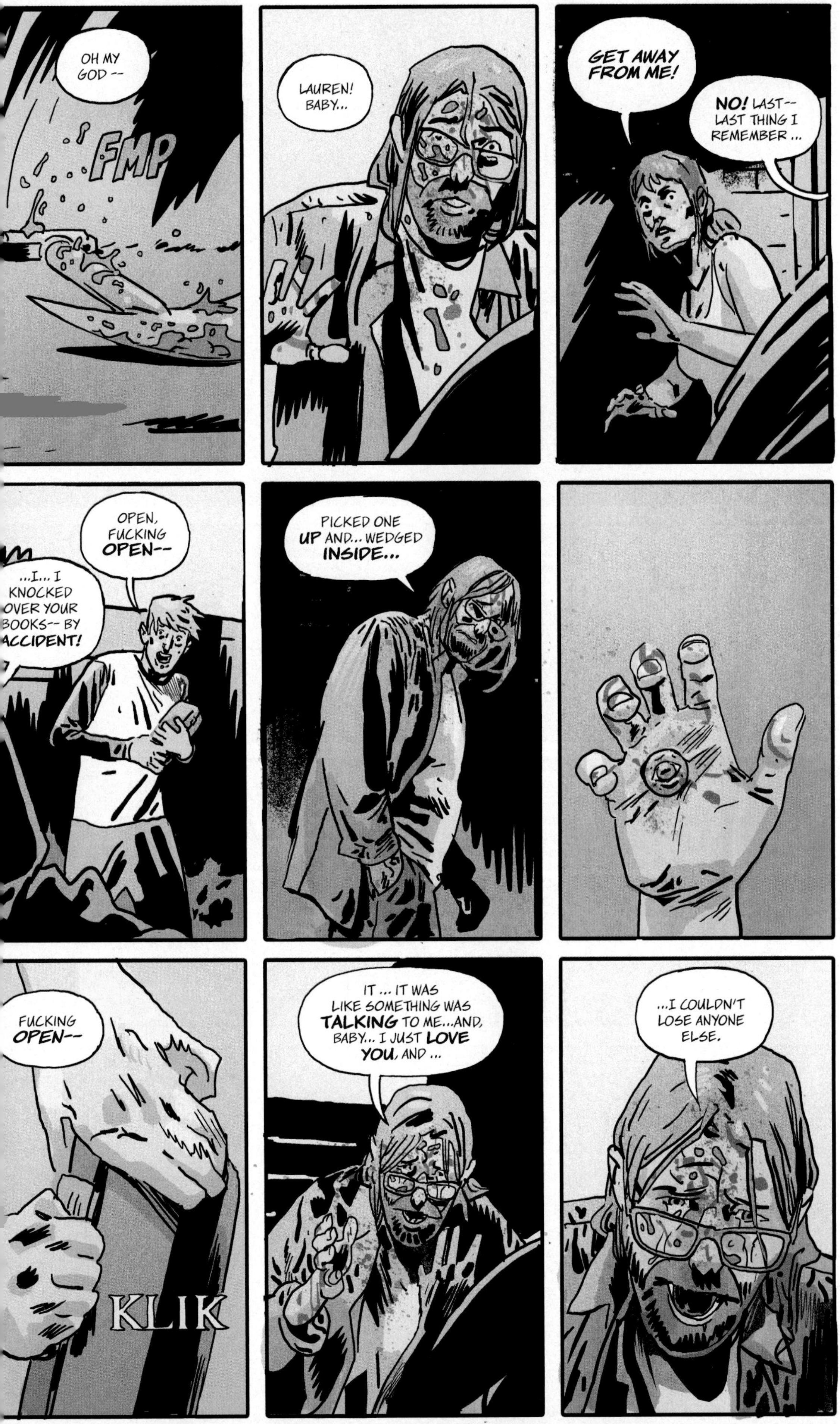
OH MY GOD --
FMP
LAUREN! BABY...
GET AWAY FROM ME!
NO! LAST-- LAST THING I REMEMBER ...
OPEN, FUCKING OPEN--
...I... I KNOCKED OVER YOUR BOOKS-- BY ACCIDENT!
PICKED ONE UP AND... WEDGED INSIDE...
FUCKING OPEN--
KLIK
IT ... IT WAS LIKE SOMETHING WAS TALKING TO ME...AND, BABY... I JUST LOVE YOU, AND ...
...I COULDN'T LOSE ANYONE ELSE.

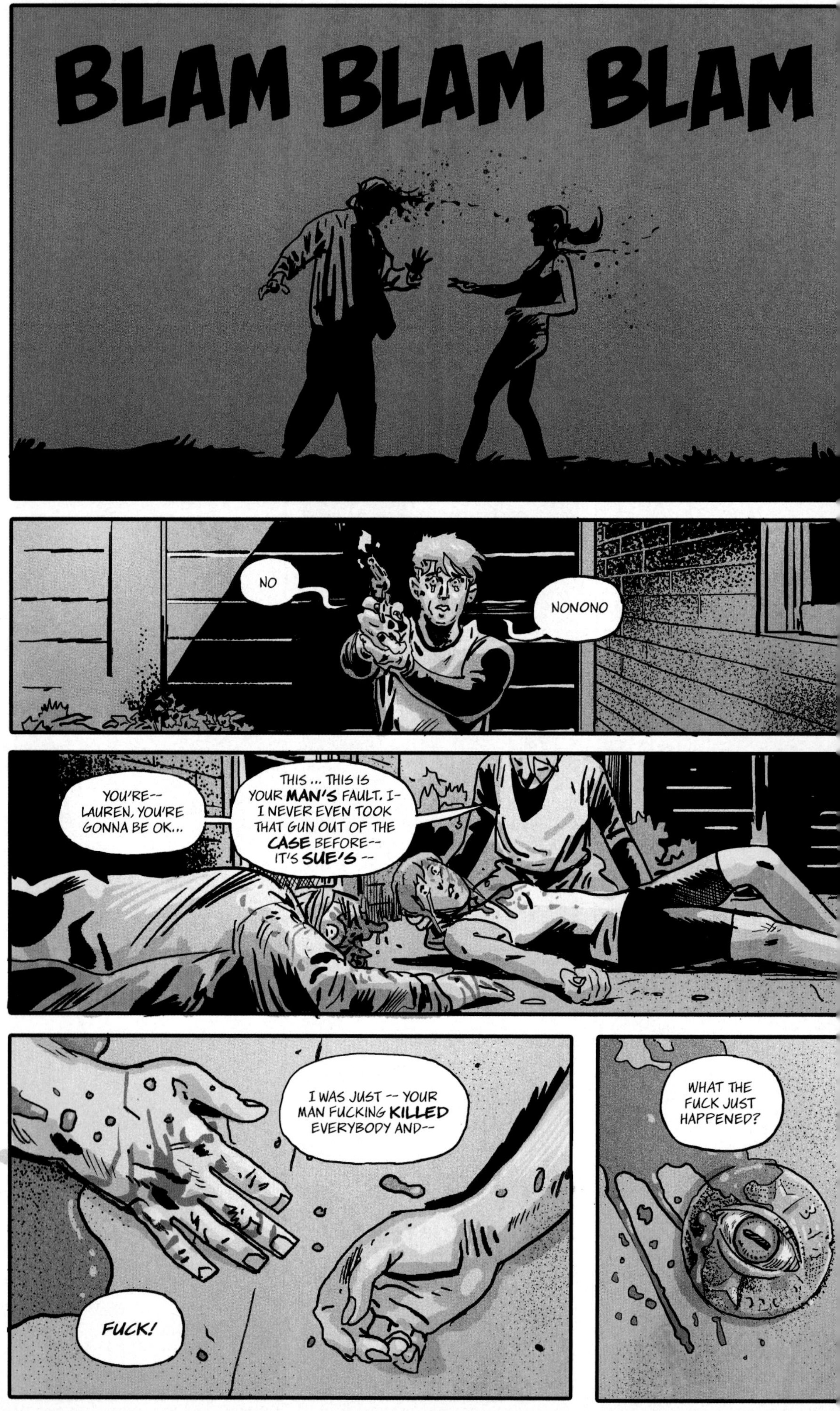
BLAM BLAM BLAM
NO
NONONO
YOU'RE-- LAUREN, YOU'RE GONNA BE OK...
THIS ... THIS IS YOUR MAN'S FAULT. I-I NEVER EVEN TOOK THAT GUN OUT OF THE CASE BEFORE-- IT'S SUE'S --
I WAS JUST -- YOUR MAN FUCKING KILLED EVERYBODY AND--
FUCK!
WHAT THE FUCK JUST HAPPENED?

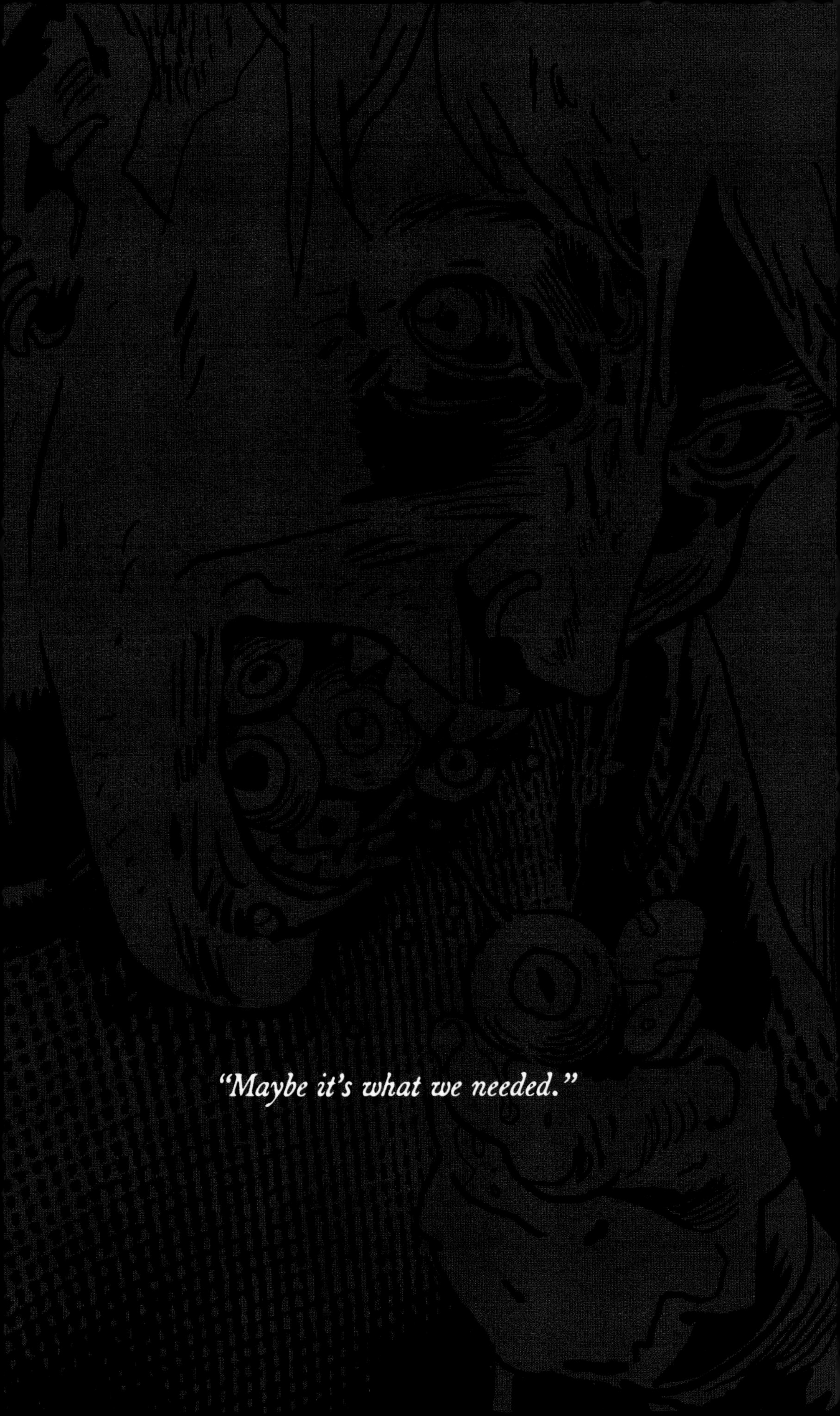
"Maybe it's what we needed."

Into the Fire

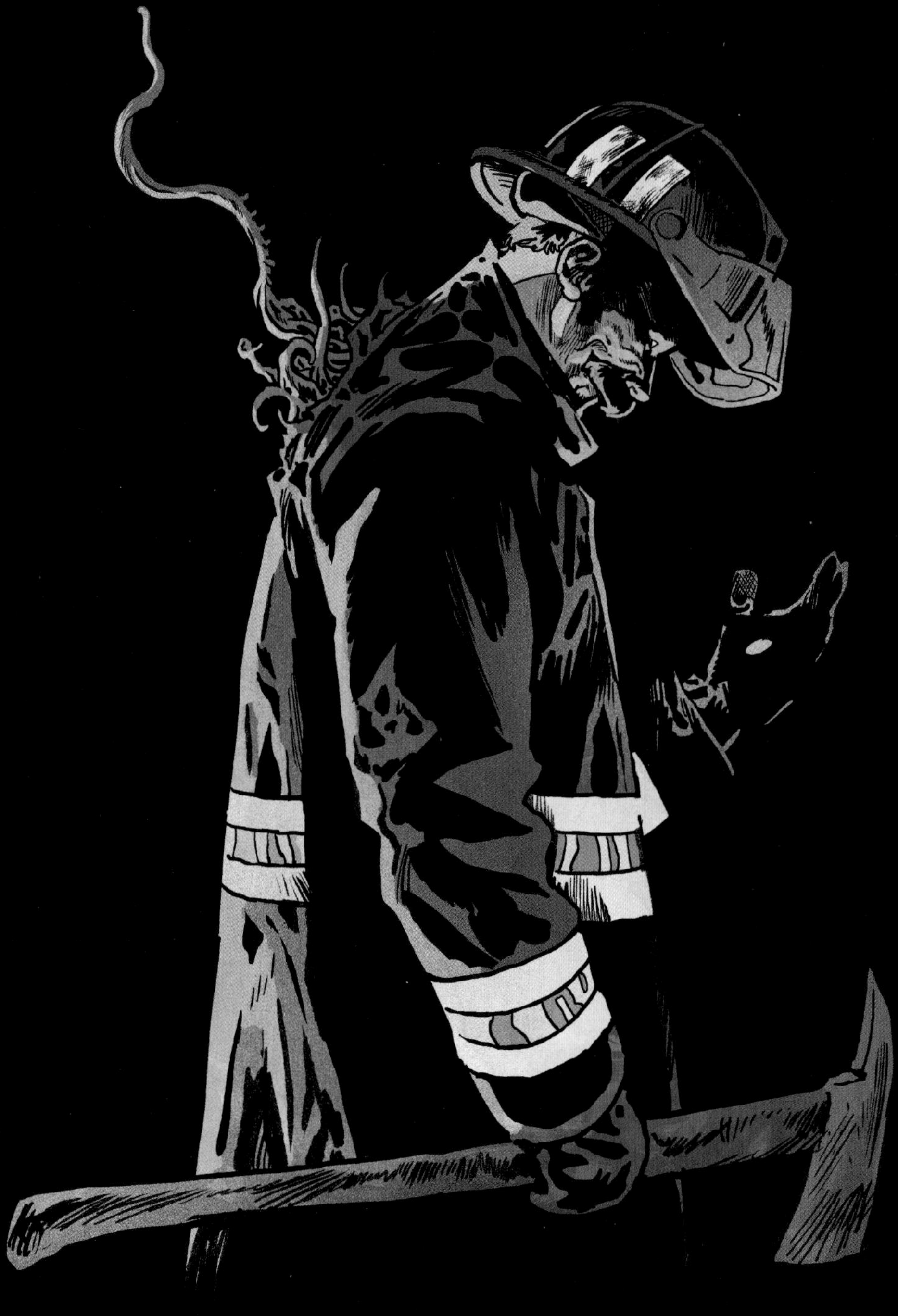

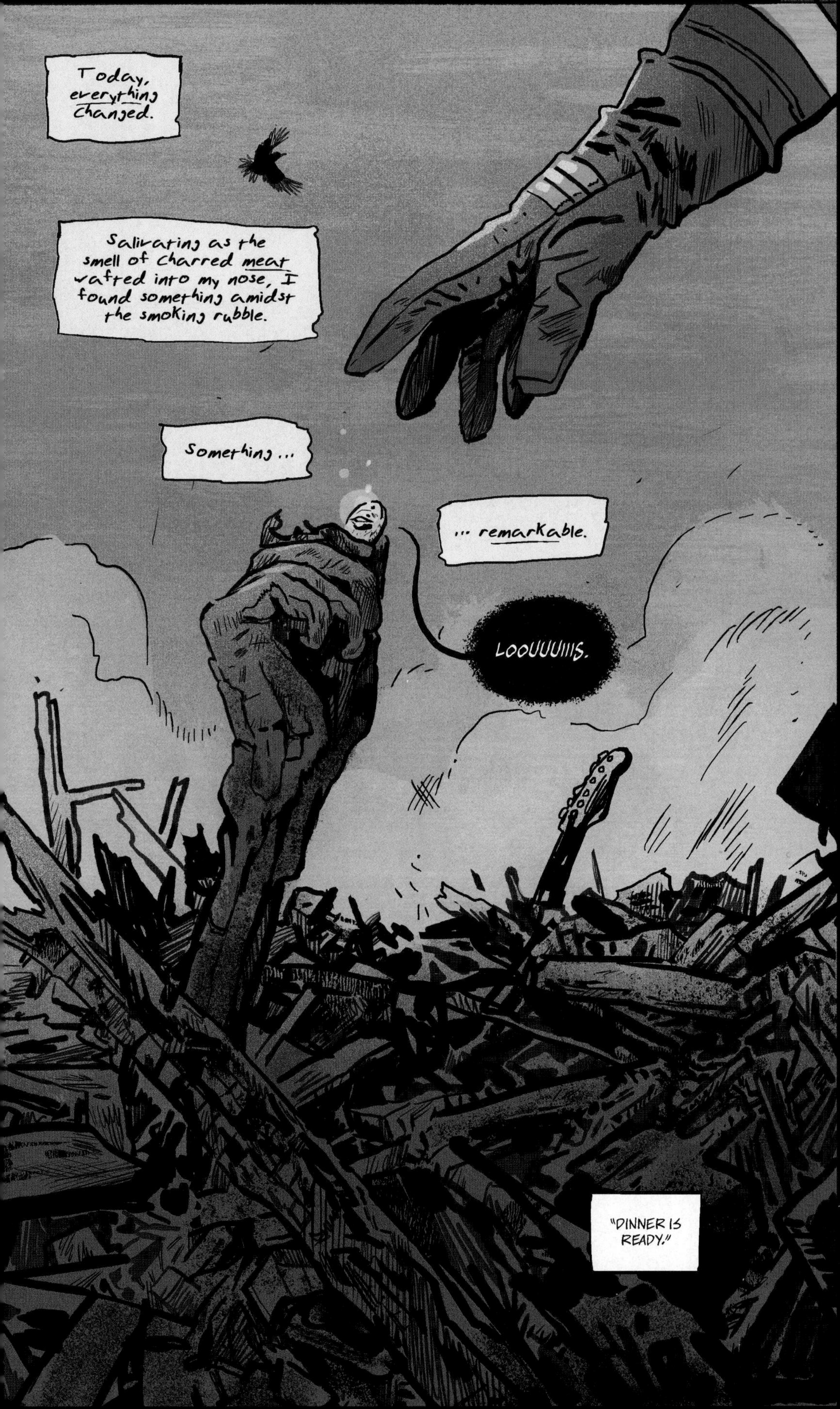
Today, everything changed.
Salivating as the smell of charred meat wafted into my nose, I found something amidst the smoking rubble.
Something...
...remarkable.
LOOUUUIIIS.
"DINNER IS READY."

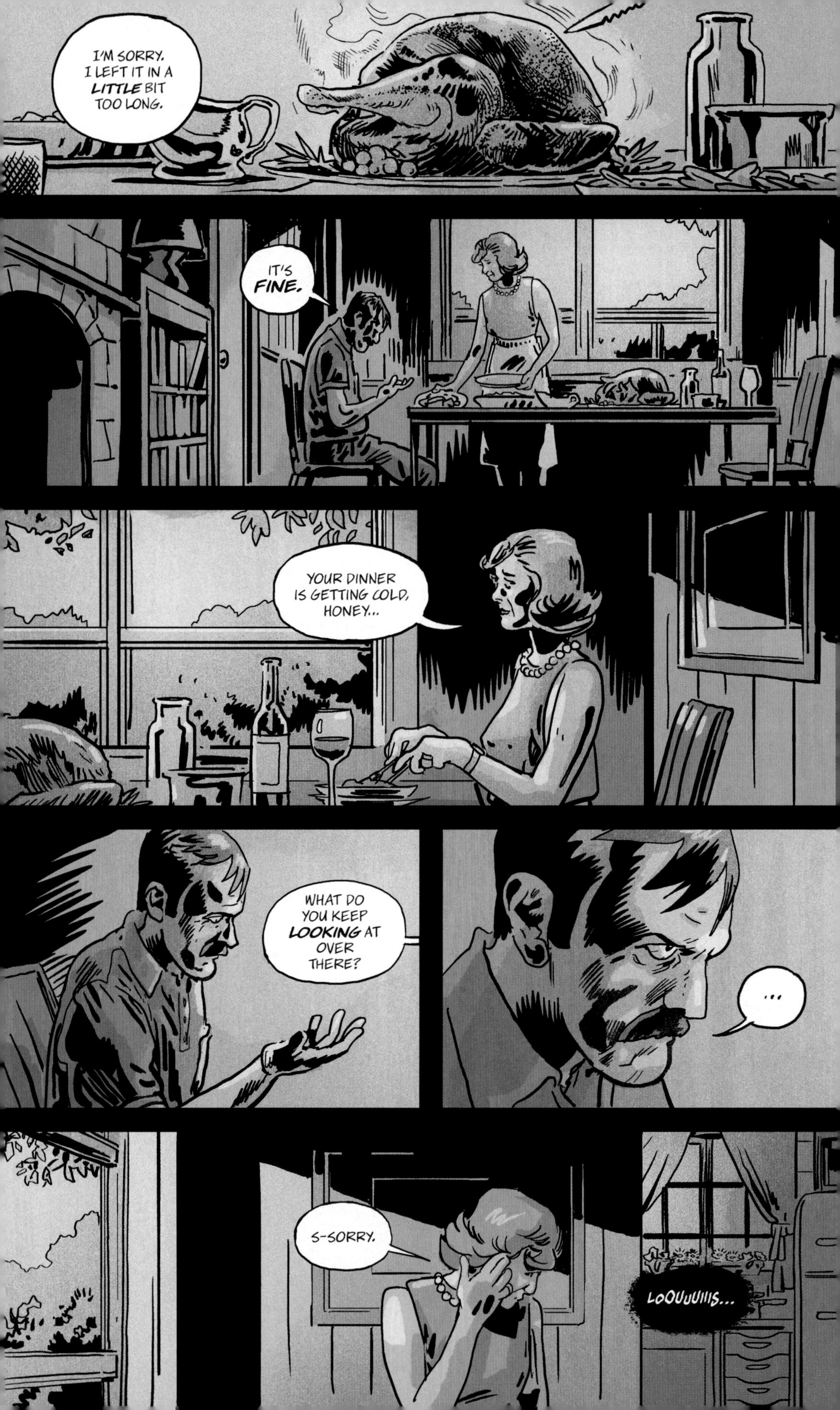
I'M SORRY. I LEFT IT IN A LITTLE BIT TOO LONG.
IT'S FINE.
YOUR DINNER IS GETTING COLD, HONEY...
WHAT DO YOU KEEP LOOKING AT OVER THERE?
...
S-SORRY.
LOOUUUIIIS...

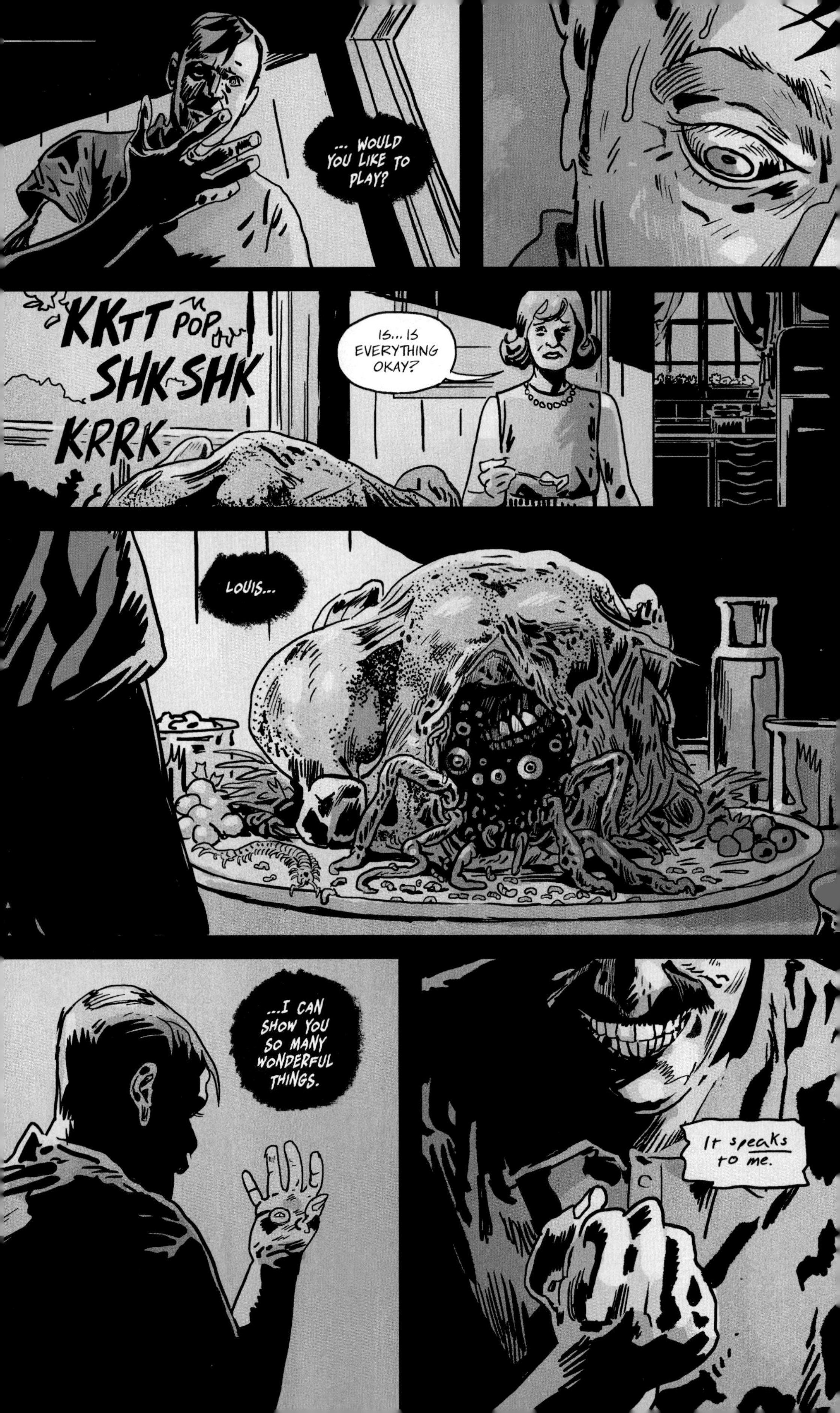
... WOULD YOU LIKE TO PLAY?
KKTT POP
SHK SHK
KRRK
IS... IS EVERYTHING OKAY?
LOUIS...
...I CAN SHOW YOU SO MANY WONDERFUL THINGS.
It speaks to me.

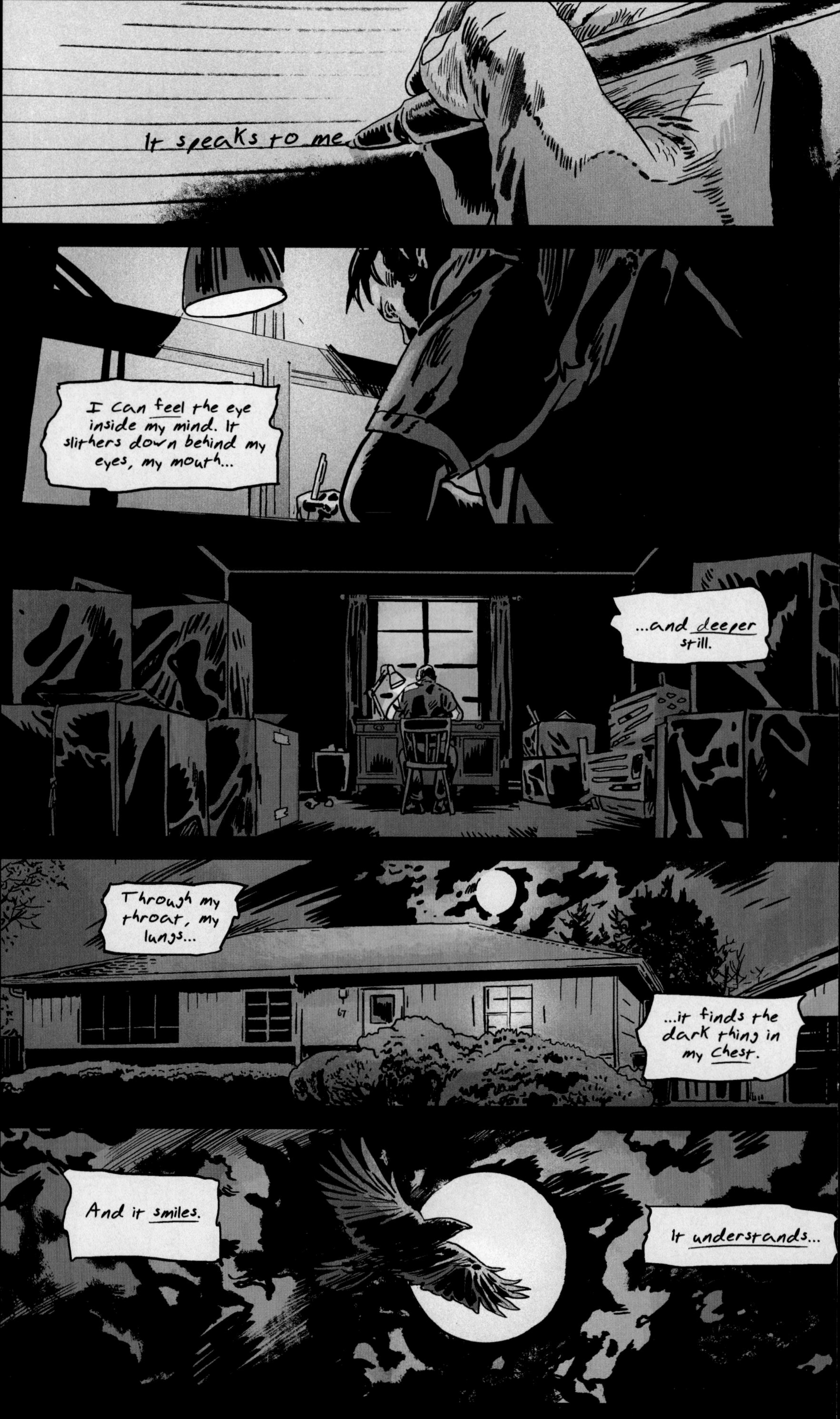
It speaks to me
I can feel the eye inside my mind. It slithers down behind my eyes, my mouth...
...and deeper still.
Through my throat, my lungs...
67
...it finds the dark thing in my chest.
And it smiles.
It understands...

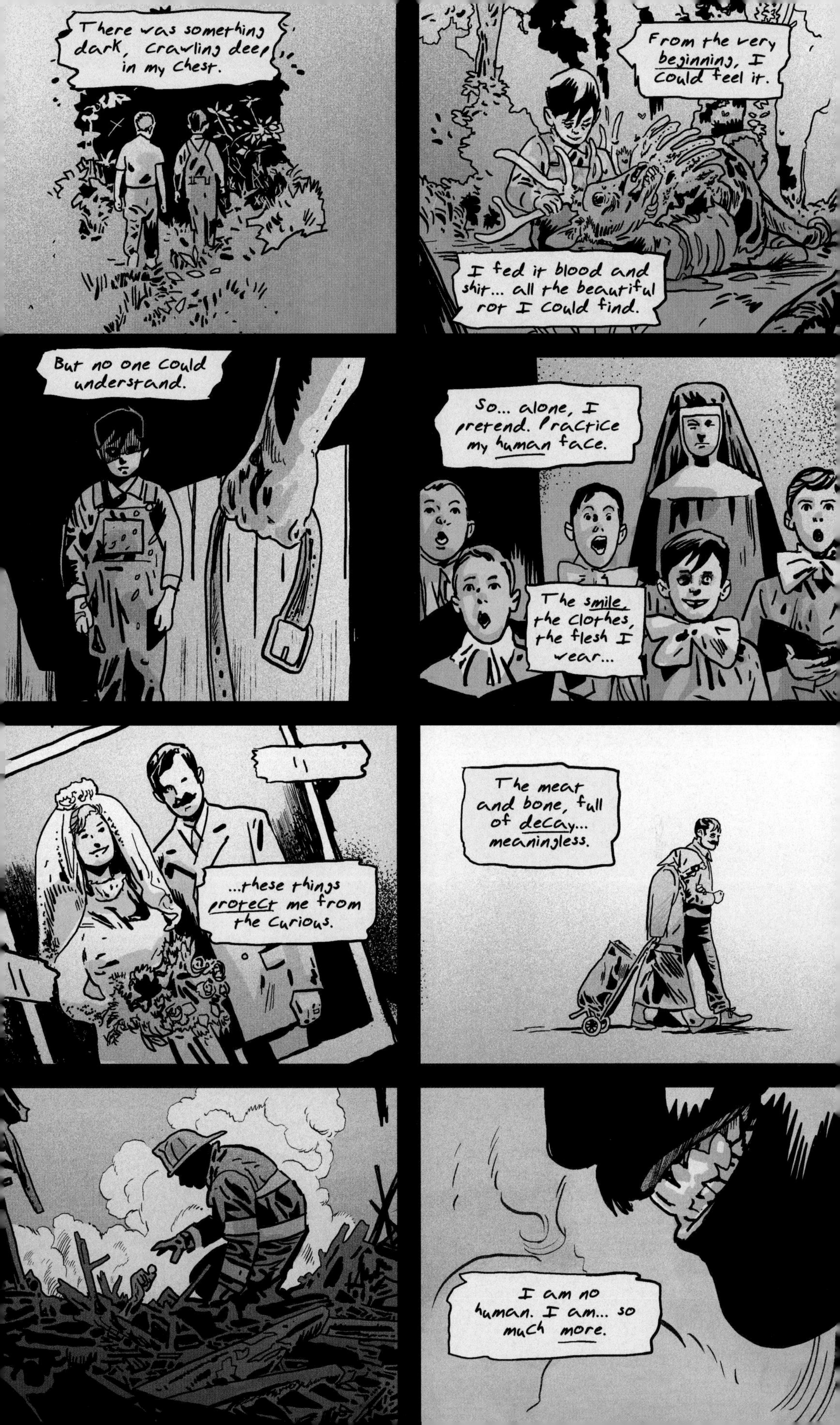
There was something dark, crawling deep in my chest.
From the very beginning, I could feel it.
I fed it blood and shit... all the beautiful rot I could find.
But no one could understand.
So... alone, I pretend. Practice my human face.
The smile, the clothes, the flesh I wear...
...these things protect me from the curious.
The meat and bone, full of decay... meaningless.
I am no human. I am... so much more.

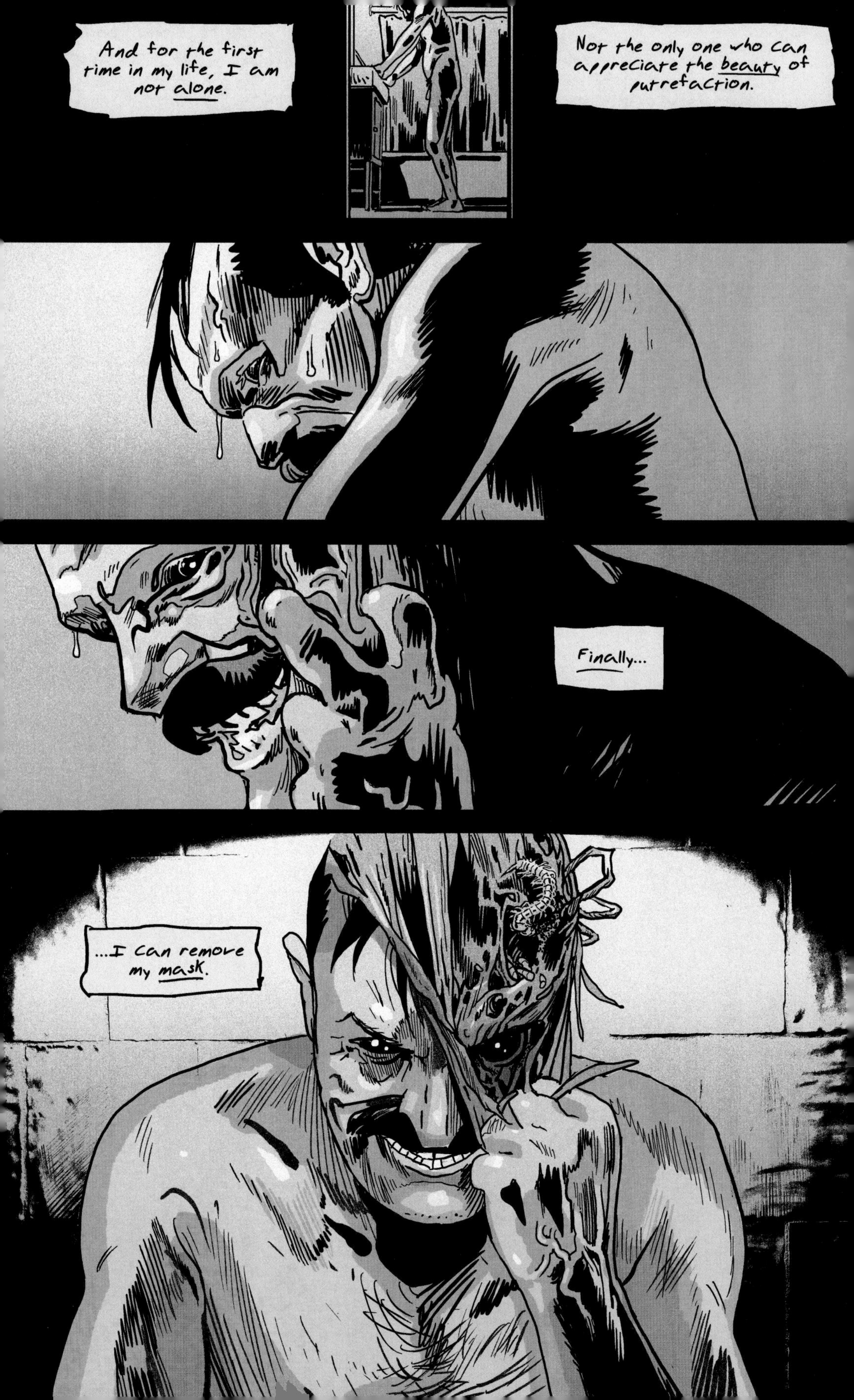
And for the first time in my life, I am not alone.
Not the only one who can appreciate the beauty of putrefaction.
Finally...
...I can remove my mask.

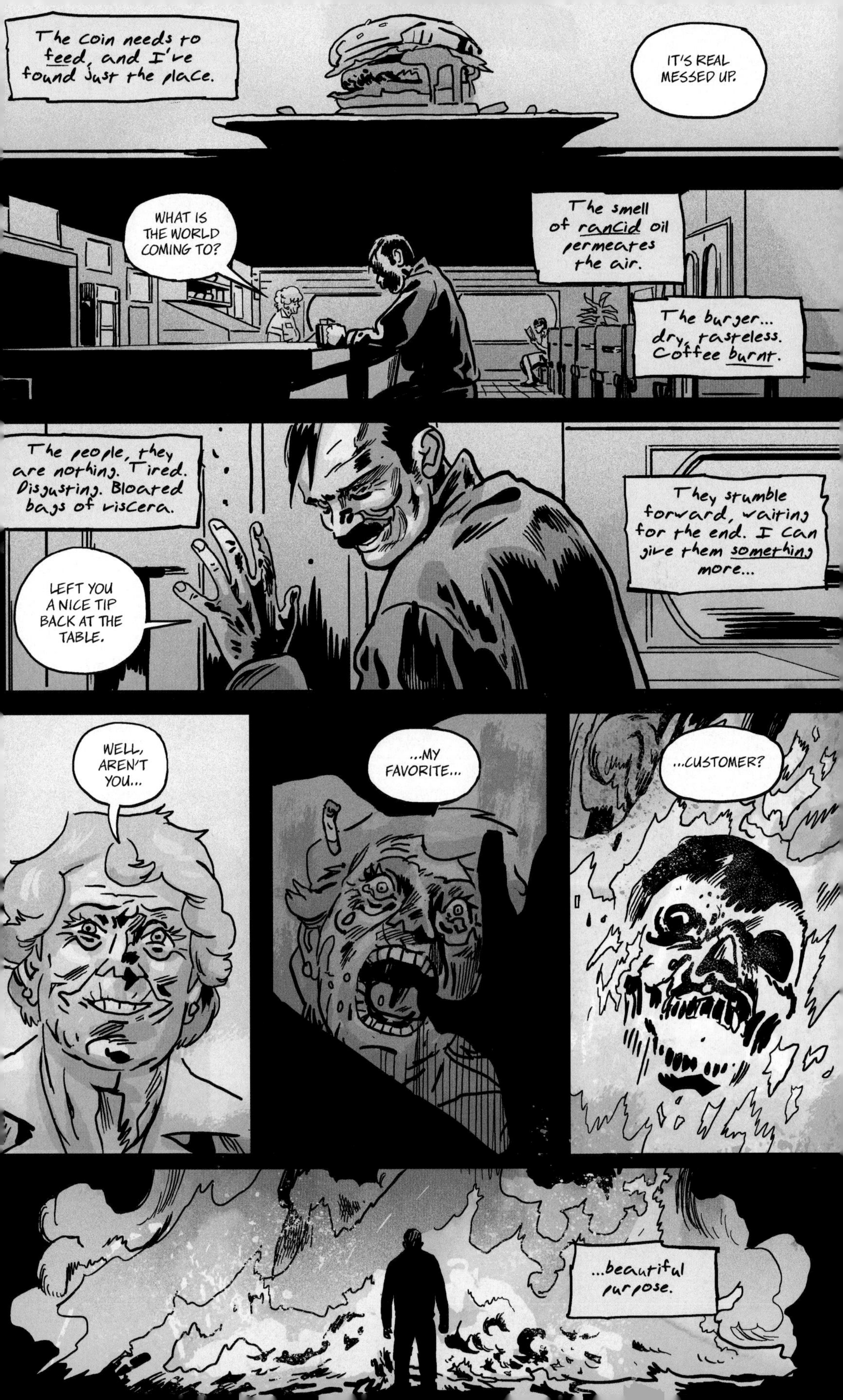
The coin needs to feed, and I've found just the place.
IT'S REAL MESSED UP.
WHAT IS THE WORLD COMING TO?
The smell of rancid oil permeates the air.
The burger... dry, tasteless. Coffee burnt.
The people, they are nothing. Tired. Disgusting. Bloated bags of viscera.
They stumble forward, waiting for the end. I can give them something more...
LEFT YOU A NICE TIP BACK AT THE TABLE.
WELL, AREN'T YOU...
...MY FAVORITE...
...CUSTOMER?
...beautiful purpose.

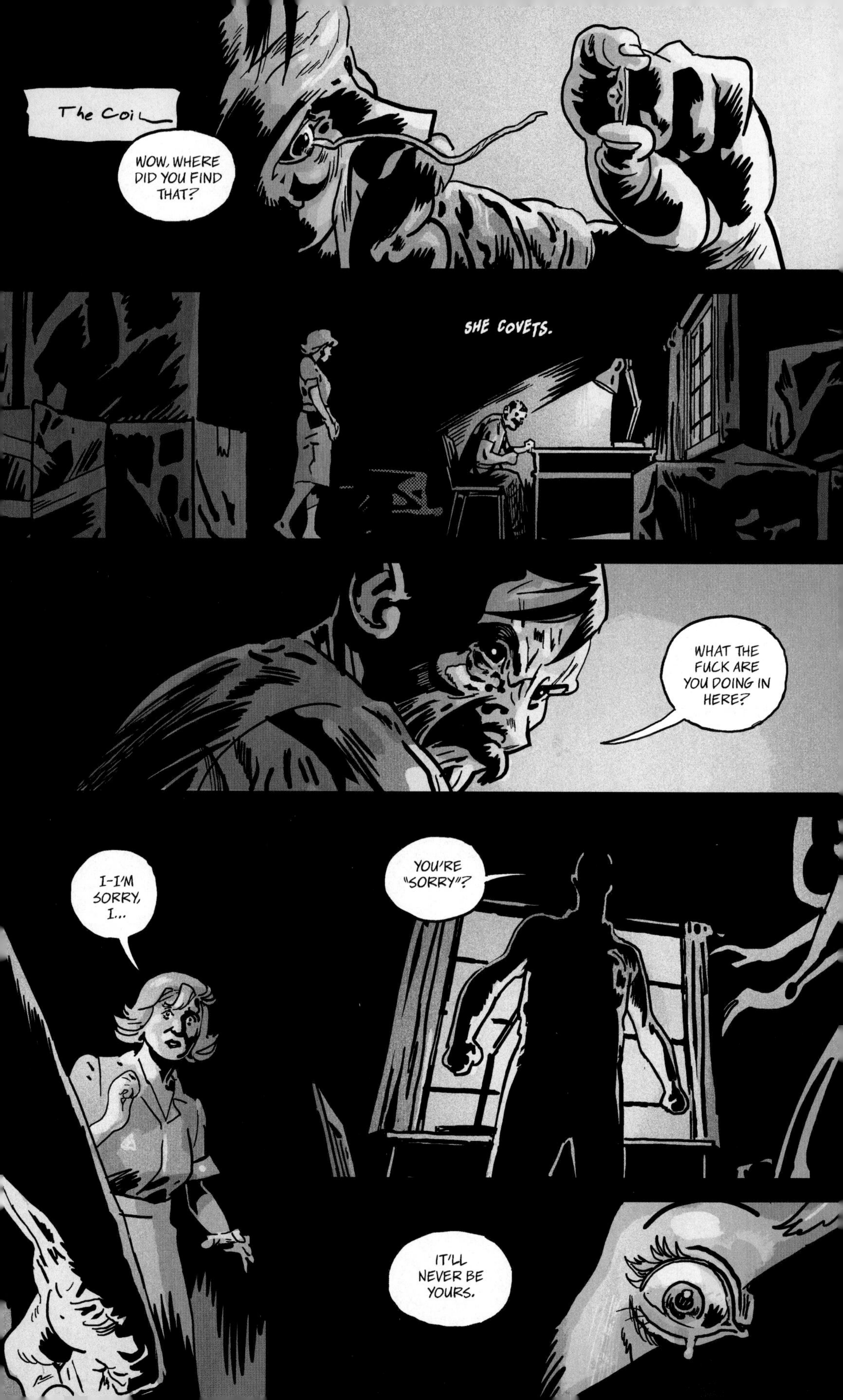
The Coil
WOW, WHERE DID YOU FIND THAT?
SHE COVETS.
WHAT THE FUCK ARE YOU DOING IN HERE?
I-I'M SORRY, I...
YOU'RE "SORRY"?
IT'LL NEVER BE YOURS.

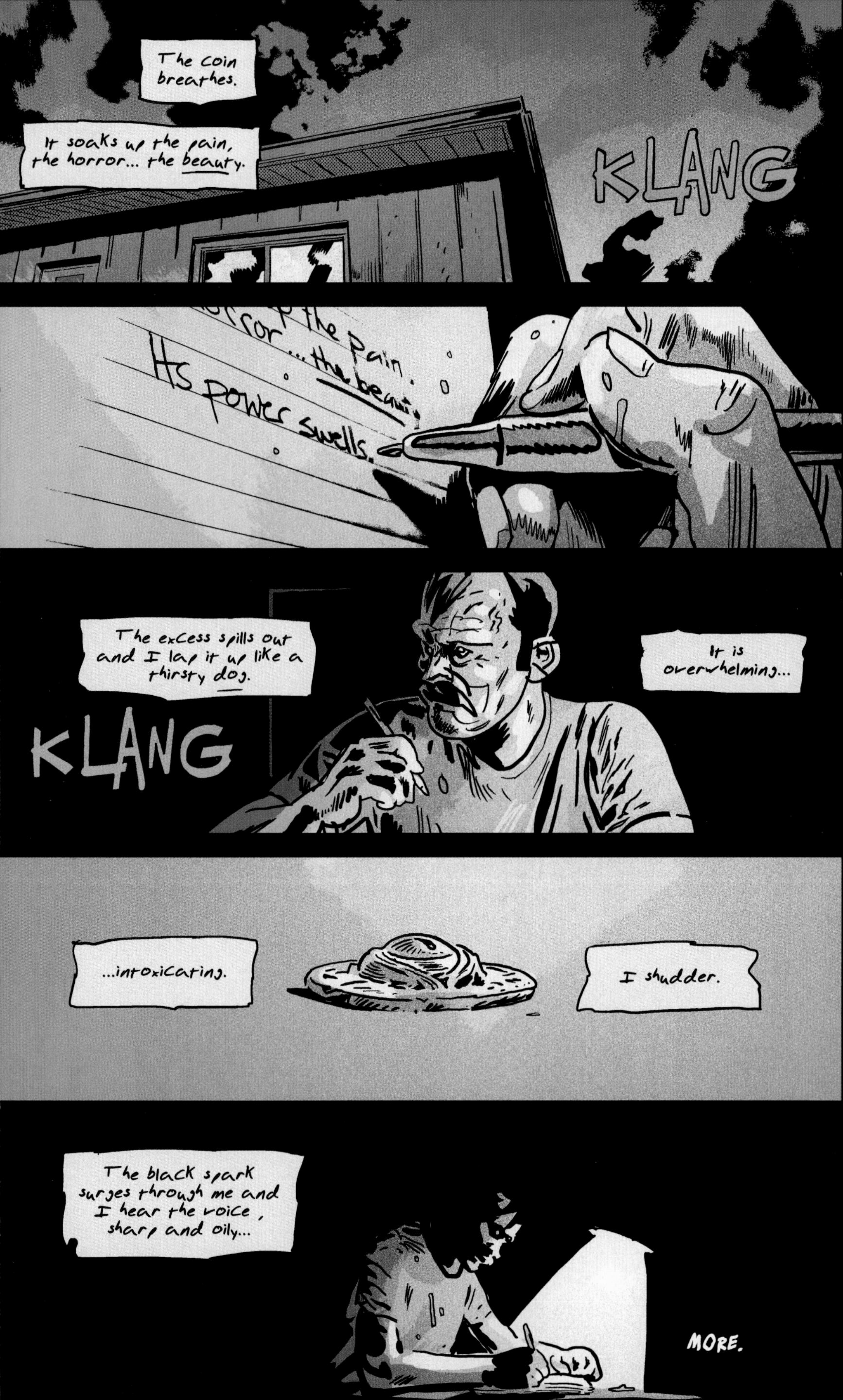

The coin breathes.
It soaks up the pain, the horror... the beauty.
KLANG
the pain. ...the beauty. Its power swells.
The excess spills out and I lap it up like a thirsty dog.
It is overwhelming...
KLANG
...intoxicating.
I shudder.
The black spark surges through me and I hear the voice, sharp and oily...
MORE.

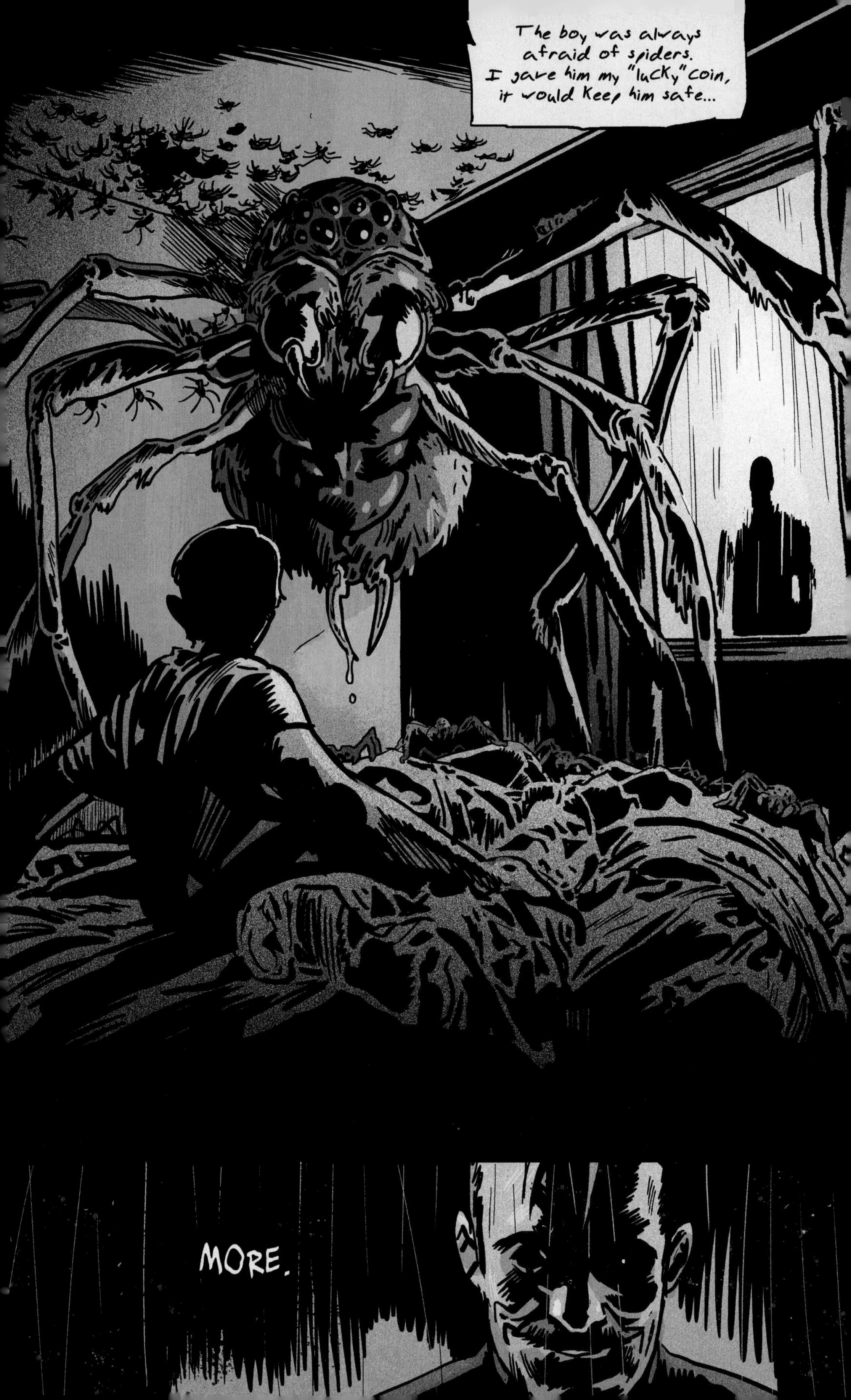
The boy was always afraid of spiders. I gave him my "lucky" coin, it would keep him safe...
MORE.

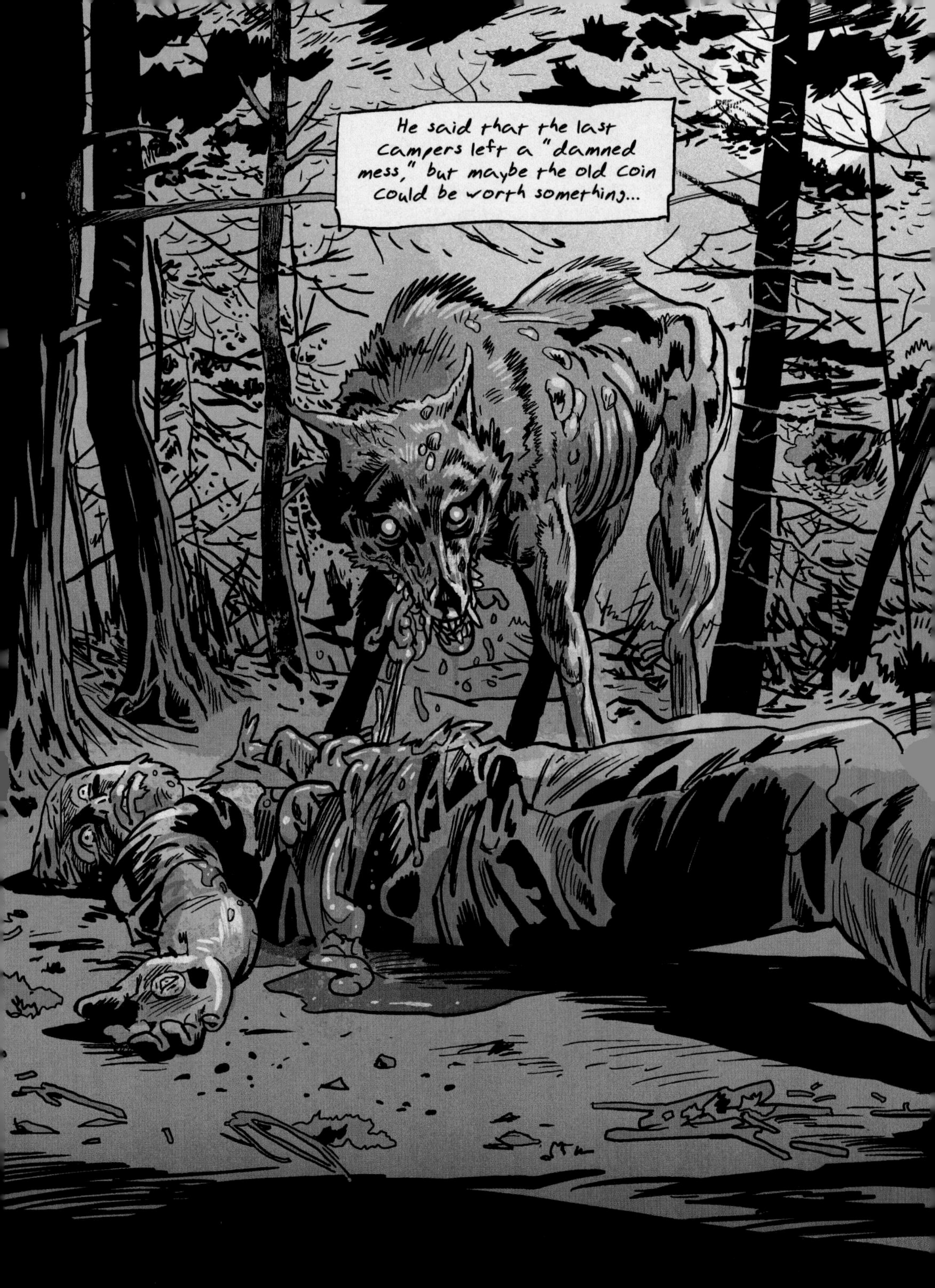
He said that the last campers left a "damned mess," but maybe the old coin could be worth something...

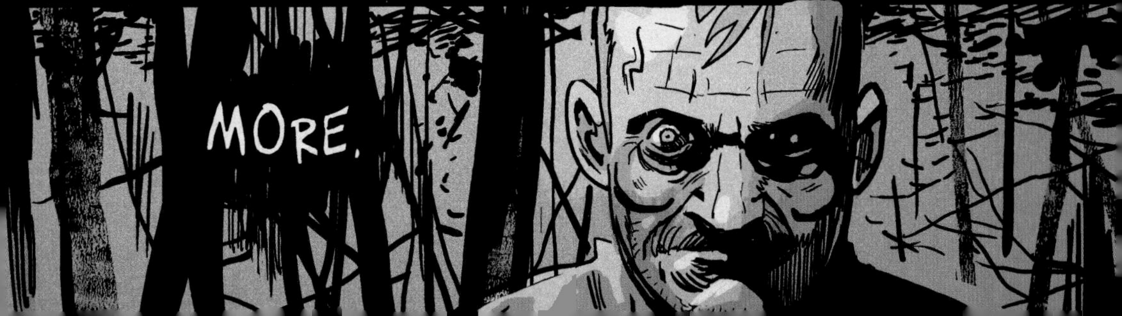
MORE.

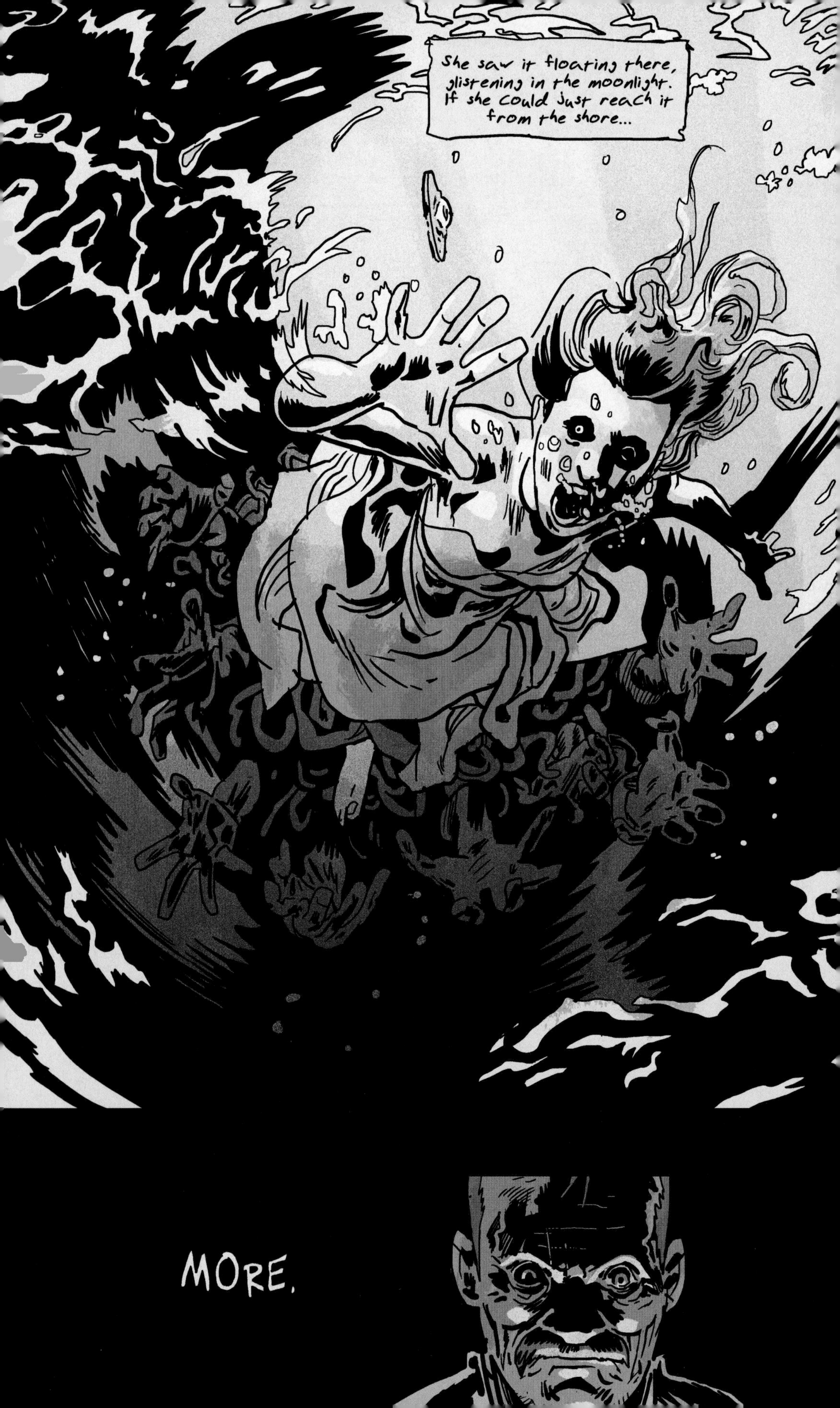
She saw it floating there, glistening in the moonlight. If she could just reach it from the shore...
MORE.

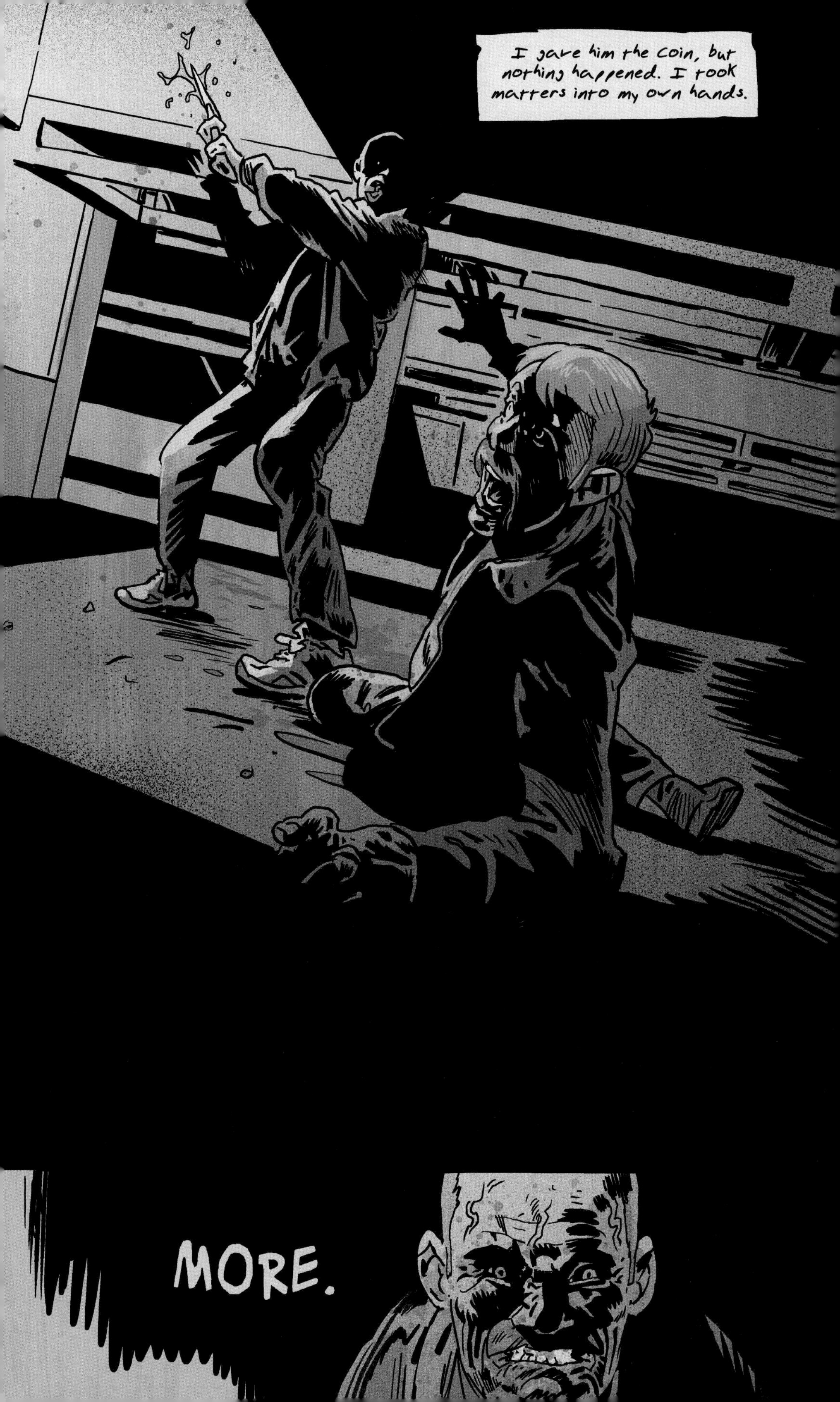
I gave him the coin, but nothing happened. I took matters into my own hands.
MORE.

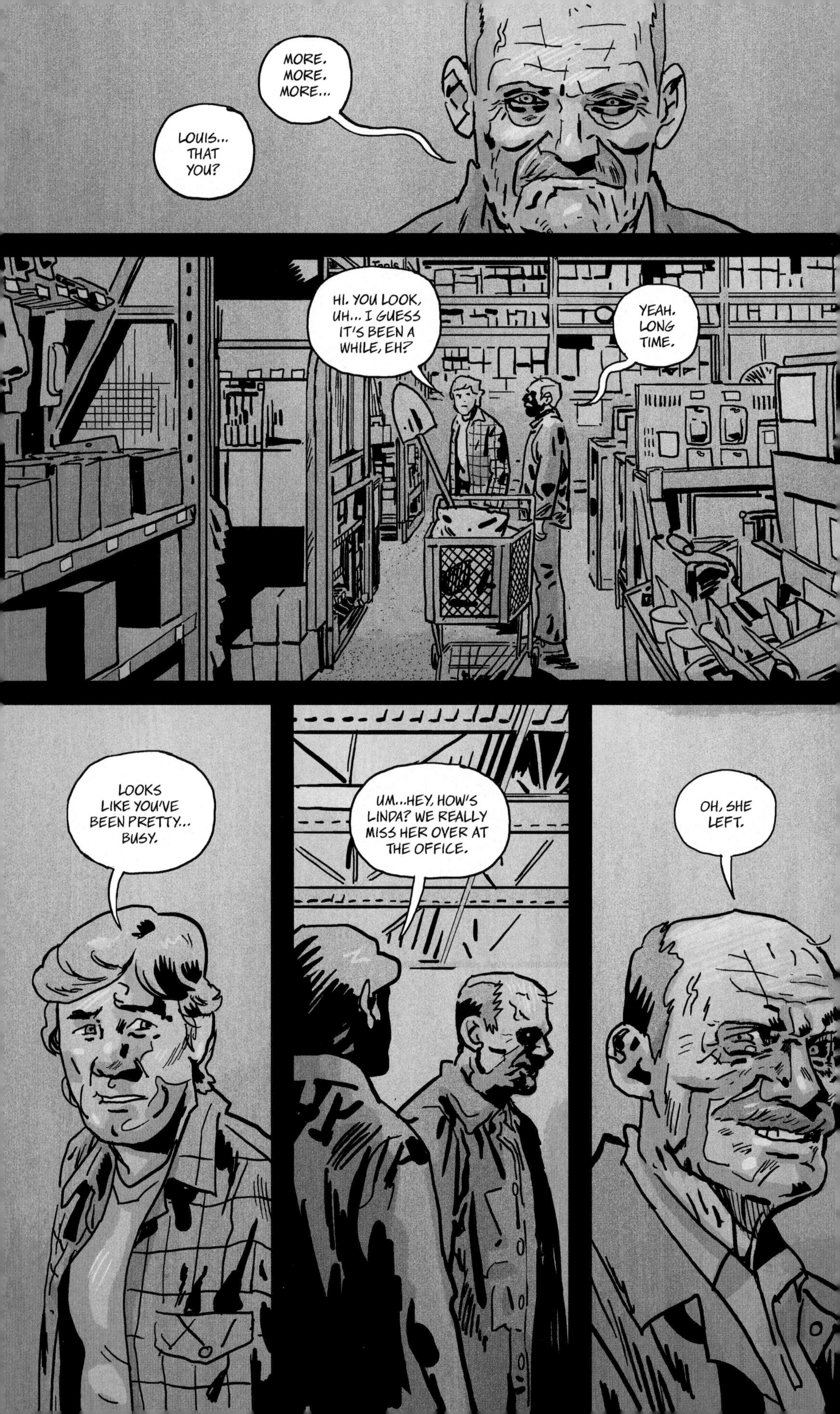
LOUIS... THAT YOU?
MORE. MORE. MORE...
HI. YOU LOOK, UH... I GUESS IT'S BEEN A WHILE, EH?
YEAH. LONG TIME.
LOOKS LIKE YOU'VE BEEN PRETTY... BUSY.
UM...HEY, HOW'S LINDA? WE REALLY MISS HER OVER AT THE OFFICE.
OH, SHE LEFT.

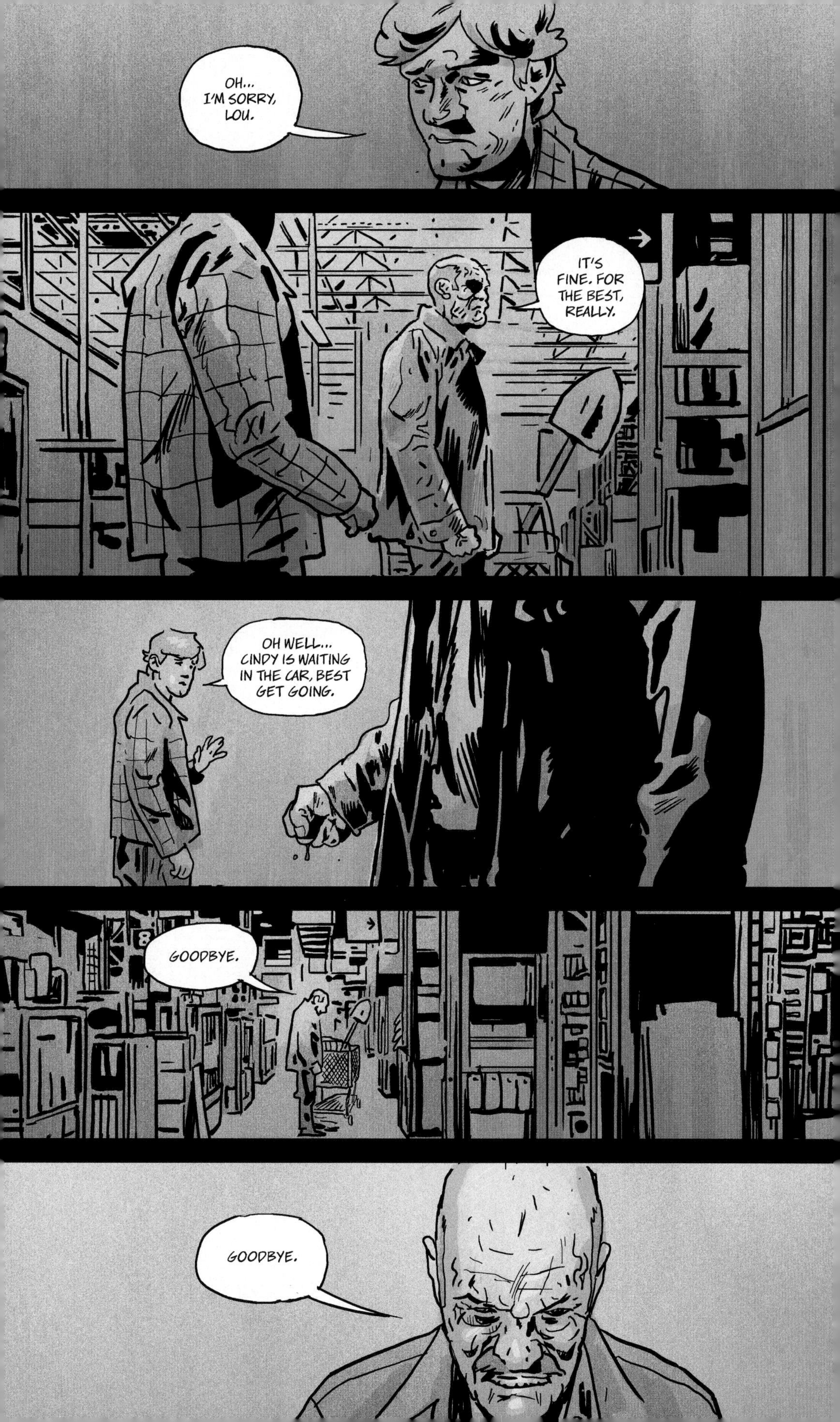
OH... I'M SORRY, LOU.
IT'S FINE. FOR THE BEST, REALLY.
OH WELL... CINDY IS WAITING IN THE CAR, BEST GET GOING.
GOODBYE.
GOODBYE.

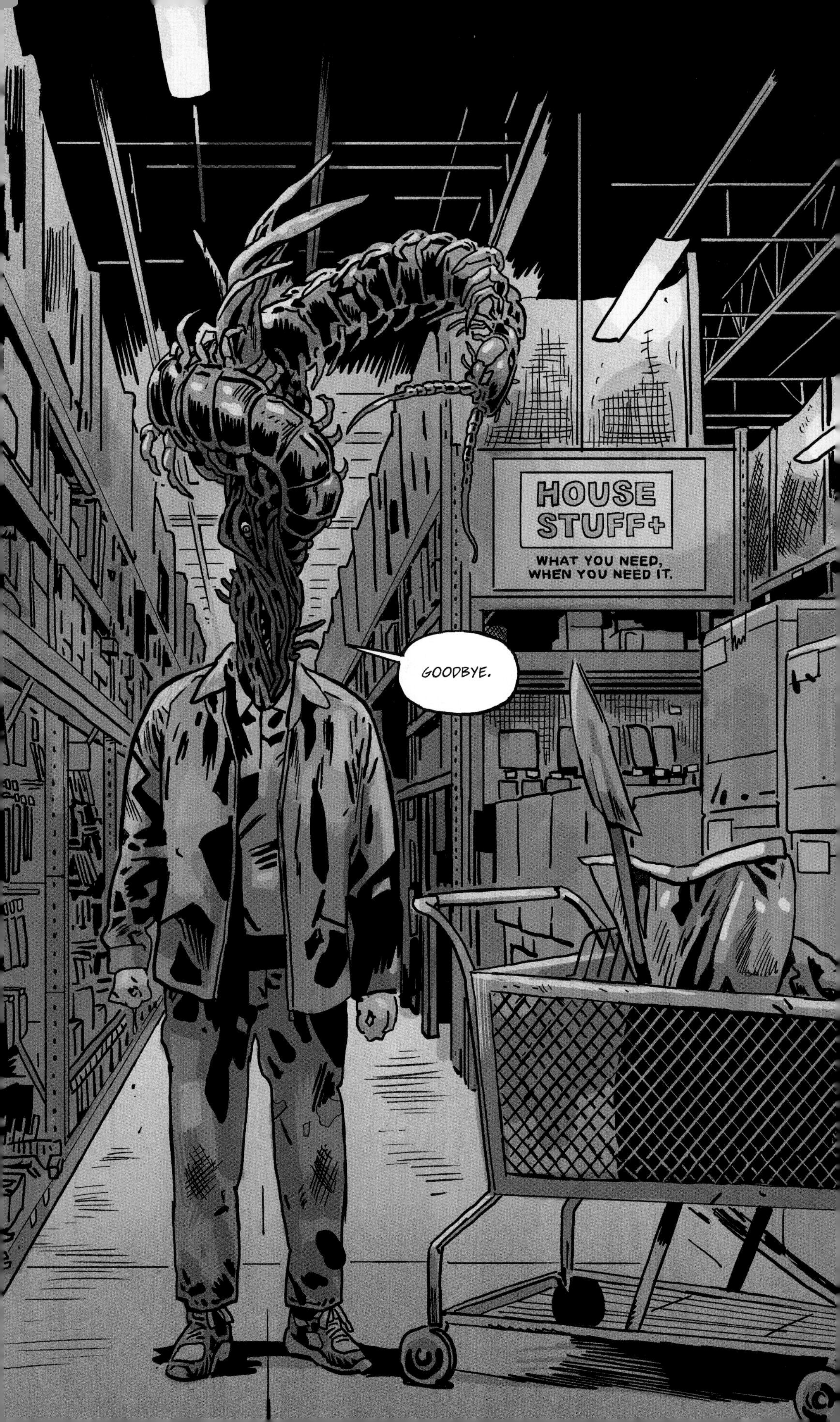
HOUSE STUFF+
WHAT YOU NEED, WHEN YOU NEED IT.
GOODBYE.

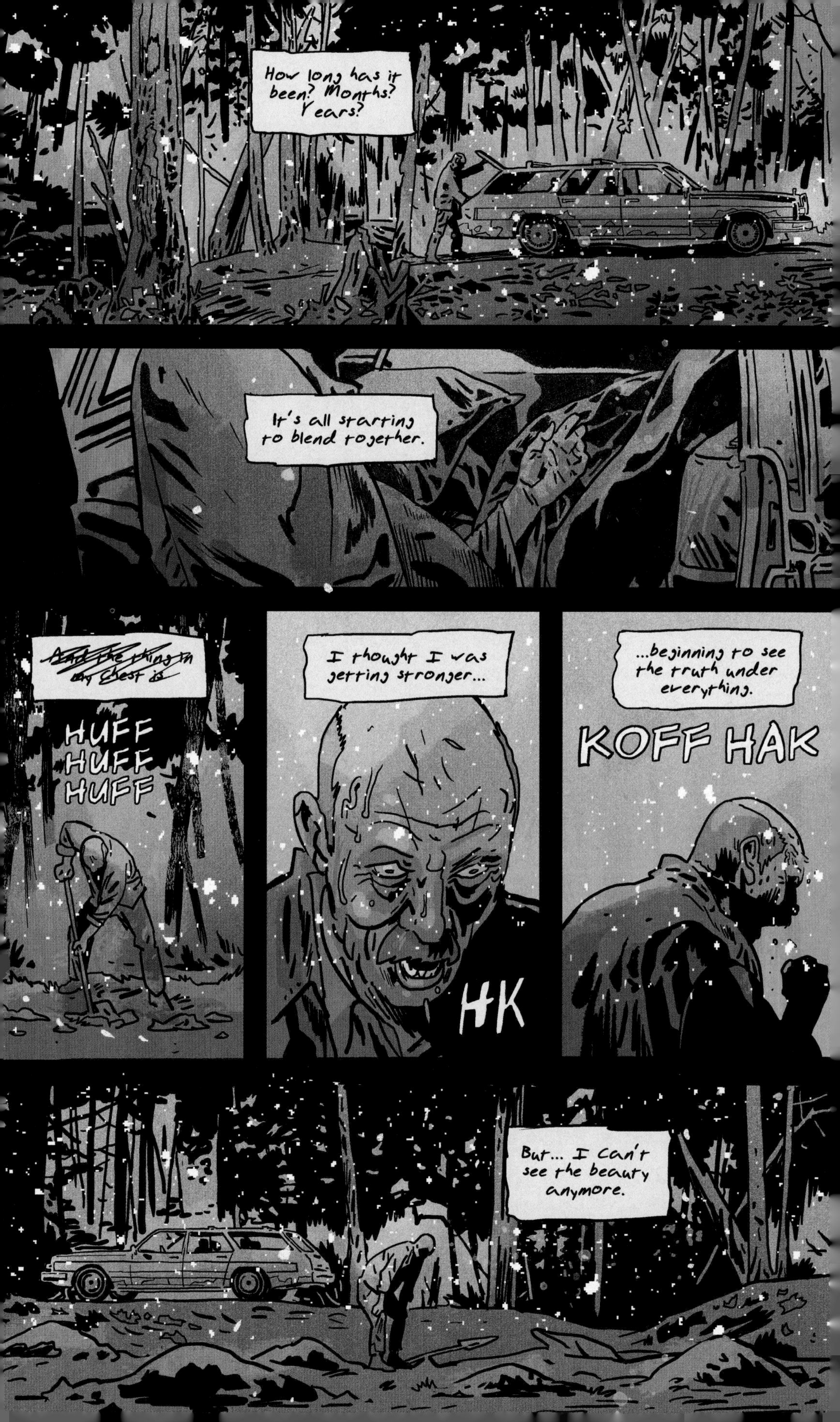
How long has it been? Months? Years?
It's all starting to blend together.
~~And the thing in my chest is~~
HUFF HUFF HUFF
I thought I was getting stronger...
HK
...beginning to see the truth under everything.
KOFF HAK
But... I can't see the beauty anymore.

OH, LOU.

has it all been a lie,

YOU HAVE WORKED **HEARTILY** FOR THE LORD AND IT HAS TAKEN A TOLL.

SHUT UP.

KLANG

NO NEED TO SPEAK SO HARSHLY, OLD FRIEND...

KLANG

SHUT THE FUCK UP!

I NEED TO SPEAK TO HIM.

WHY... WHY CAN'T I HEAR HIM ANYMORE?

POOR LOU, DID YOU THINK YOU WERE... SPECIAL?

YOU ARE NOT THE ONE TO BRING **REVELAT**... IT LOOMS IN THE DISTANCE... SO FAR AWAY STILL

KLANG

I DID **EVERYTHING** HE ASKED...

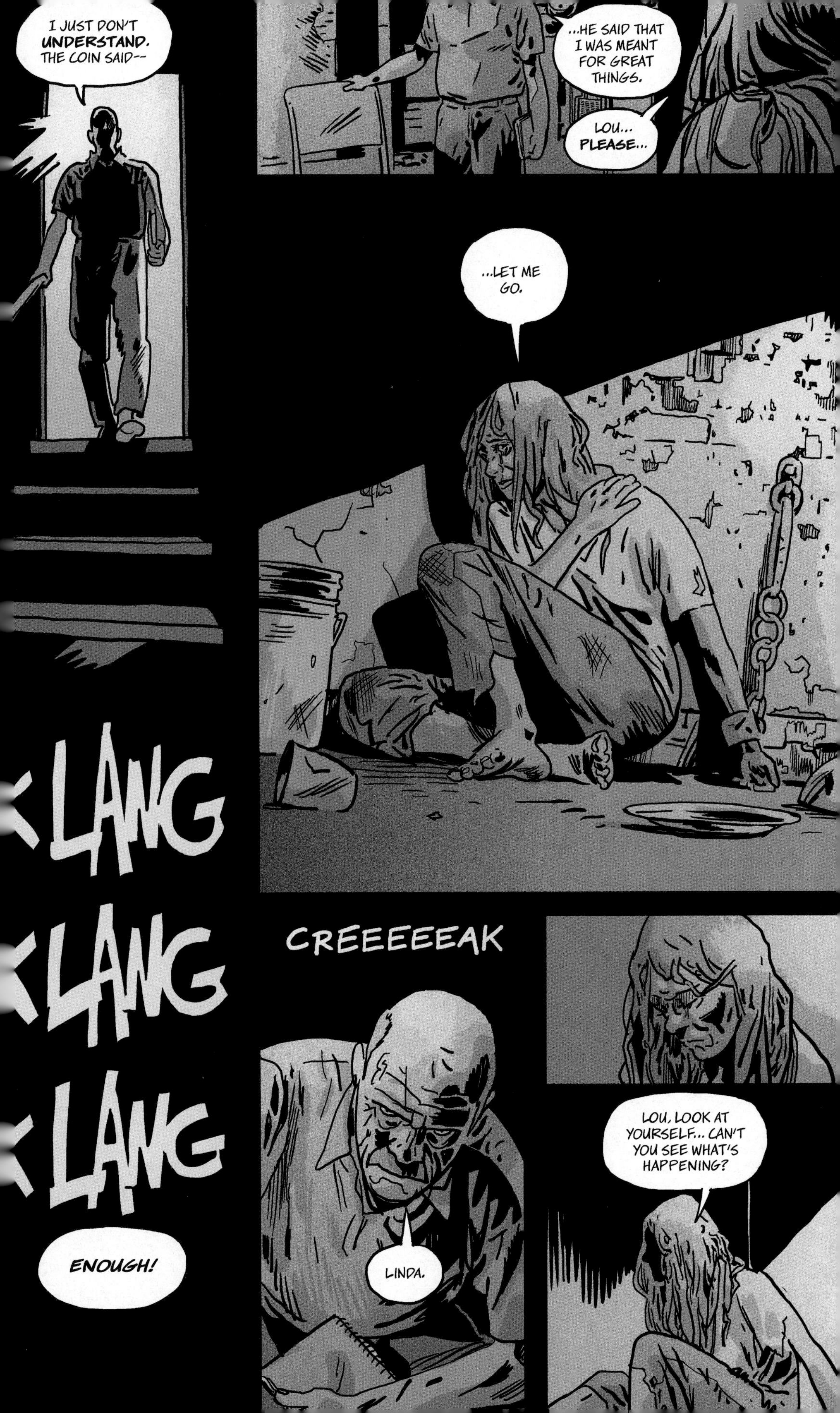
I JUST DON'T **UNDERSTAND.** THE COIN SAID--
...HE SAID THAT I WAS MEANT FOR GREAT THINGS.
LOU... **PLEASE...**
...LET ME GO.
KLANG
KLANG
KLANG
ENOUGH!
CREEEEEEAK
LINDA.
LOU, LOOK AT YOURSELF... CAN'T YOU SEE WHAT'S HAPPENING?

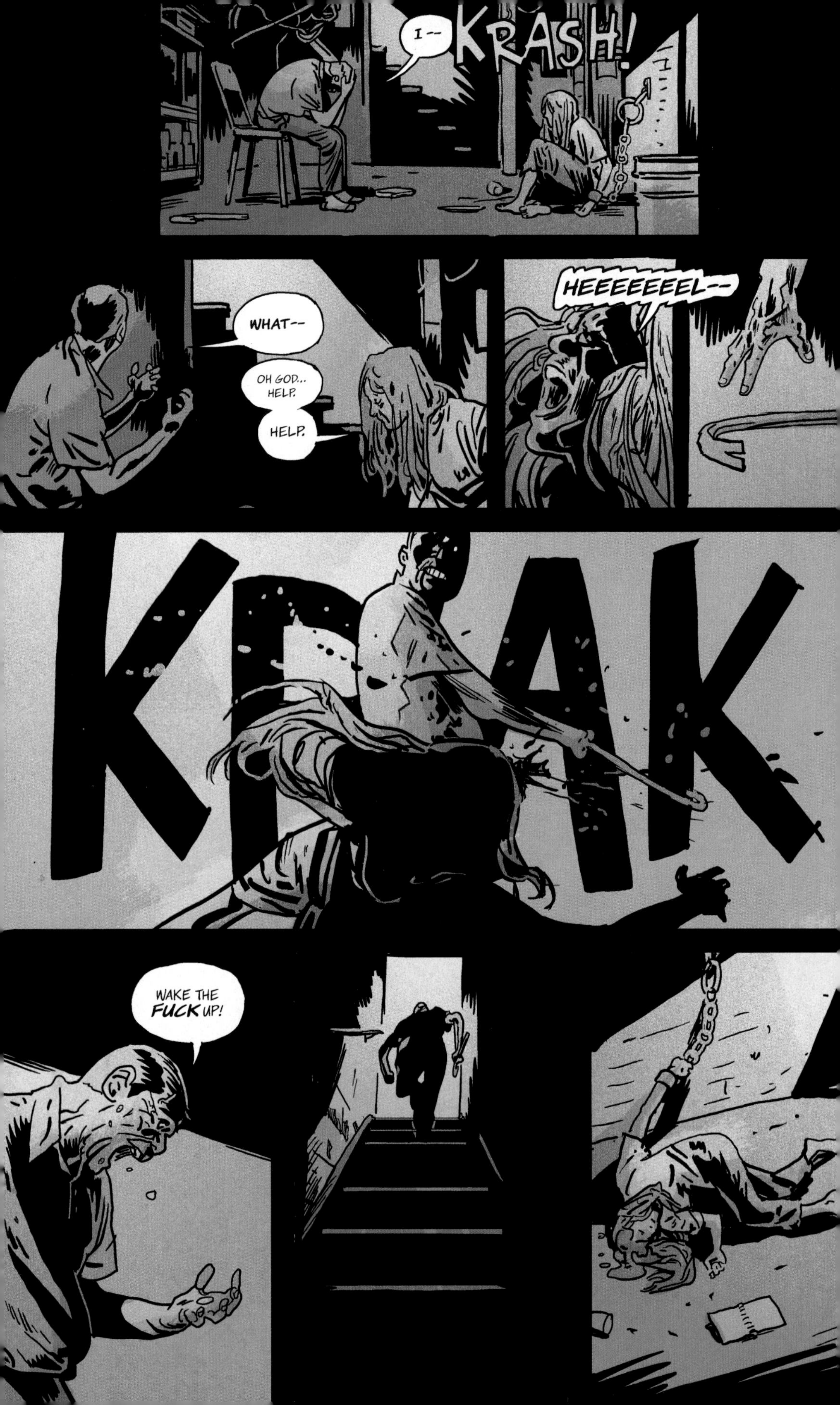

I--
KRASH!
WHAT--
OH GOD... HELP.
HELP.
HEEEEEEEL--
KRAK
WAKE THE FUCK UP!

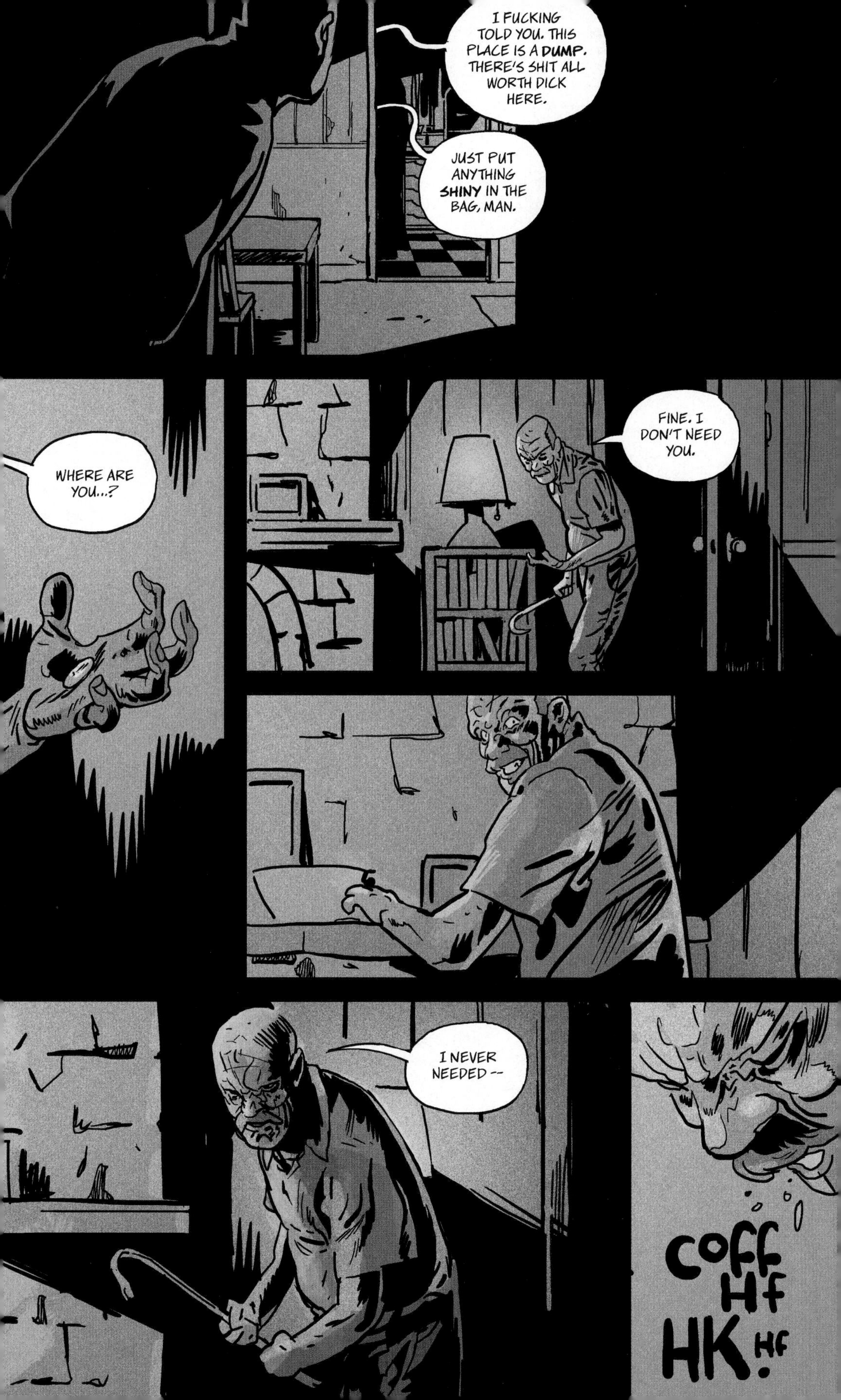
I FUCKING TOLD YOU. THIS PLACE IS A DUMP. THERE'S SHIT ALL WORTH DICK HERE.
JUST PUT ANYTHING SHINY IN THE BAG, MAN.
WHERE ARE YOU...?
FINE. I DON'T NEED YOU.
I NEVER NEEDED --
COFF
HF
HK!
HF

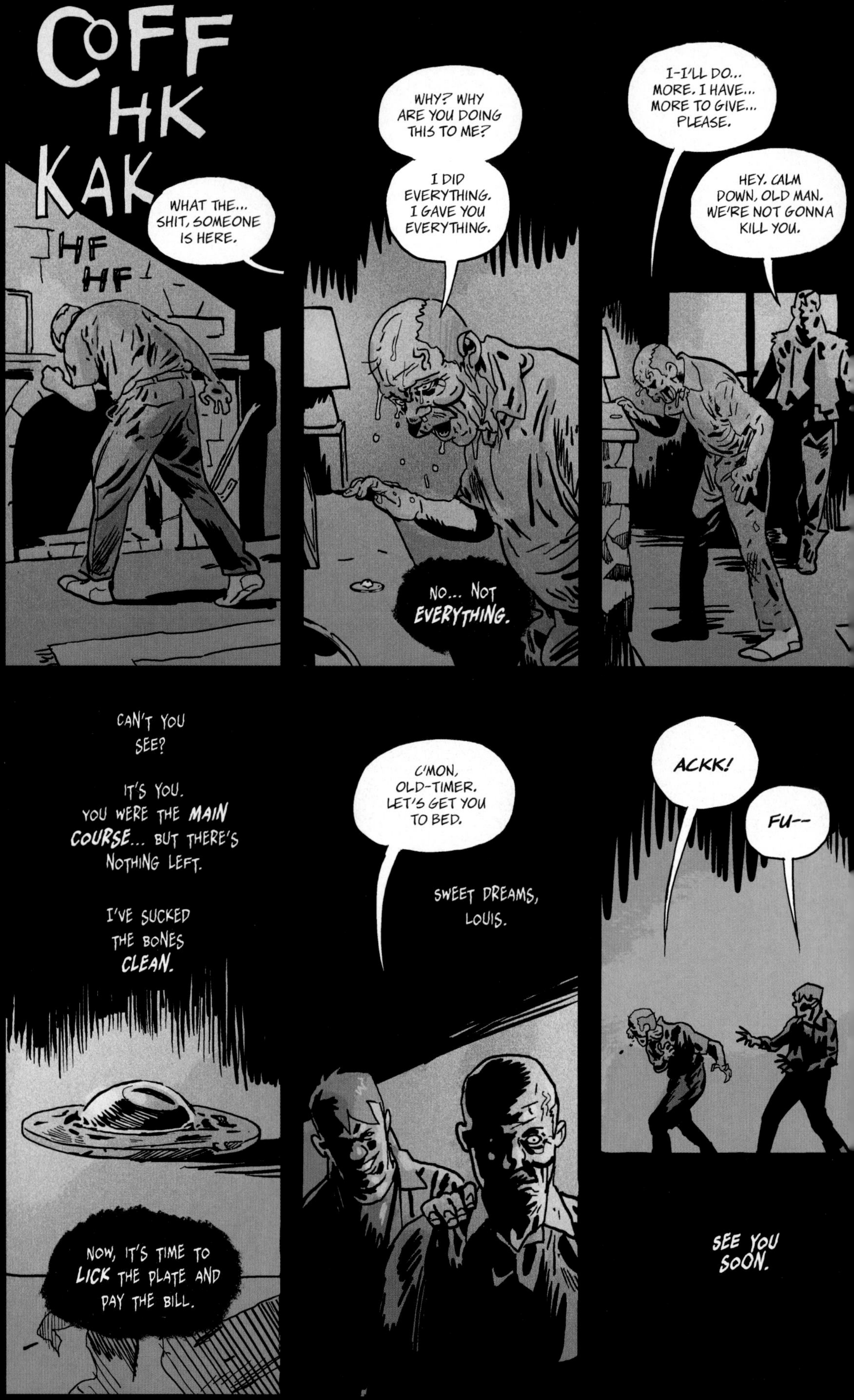
COFF
HK
KAK
WHAT THE... SHIT, SOMEONE IS HERE.
HF HF
WHY? WHY ARE YOU DOING THIS TO ME?
I DID EVERYTHING. I GAVE YOU EVERYTHING.
NO... NOT EVERYTHING.
I-I'LL DO... MORE. I HAVE... MORE TO GIVE... PLEASE.
HEY. CALM DOWN, OLD MAN. WE'RE NOT GONNA KILL YOU.
CAN'T YOU SEE?
IT'S YOU. YOU WERE THE MAIN COURSE... BUT THERE'S NOTHING LEFT.
I'VE SUCKED THE BONES CLEAN.
NOW, IT'S TIME TO LICK THE PLATE AND PAY THE BILL.
C'MON, OLD-TIMER. LET'S GET YOU TO BED.
SWEET DREAMS, LOUIS.
ACKK!
FU--
SEE YOU SOON.

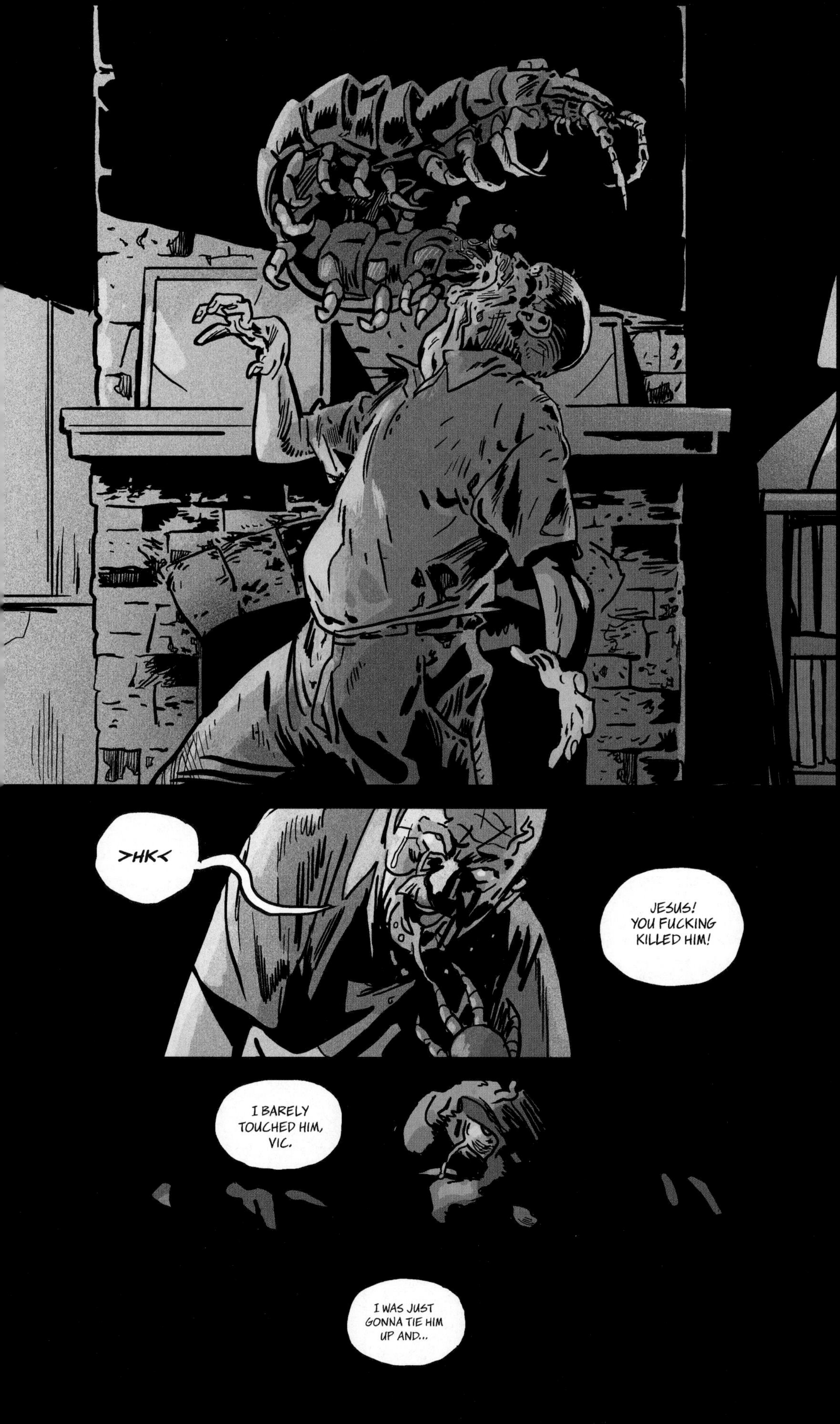
>HK<
JESUS! YOU FUCKING KILLED HIM!
I BARELY TOUCHED HIM, VIC.
I WAS JUST GONNA TIE HIM UP AND...

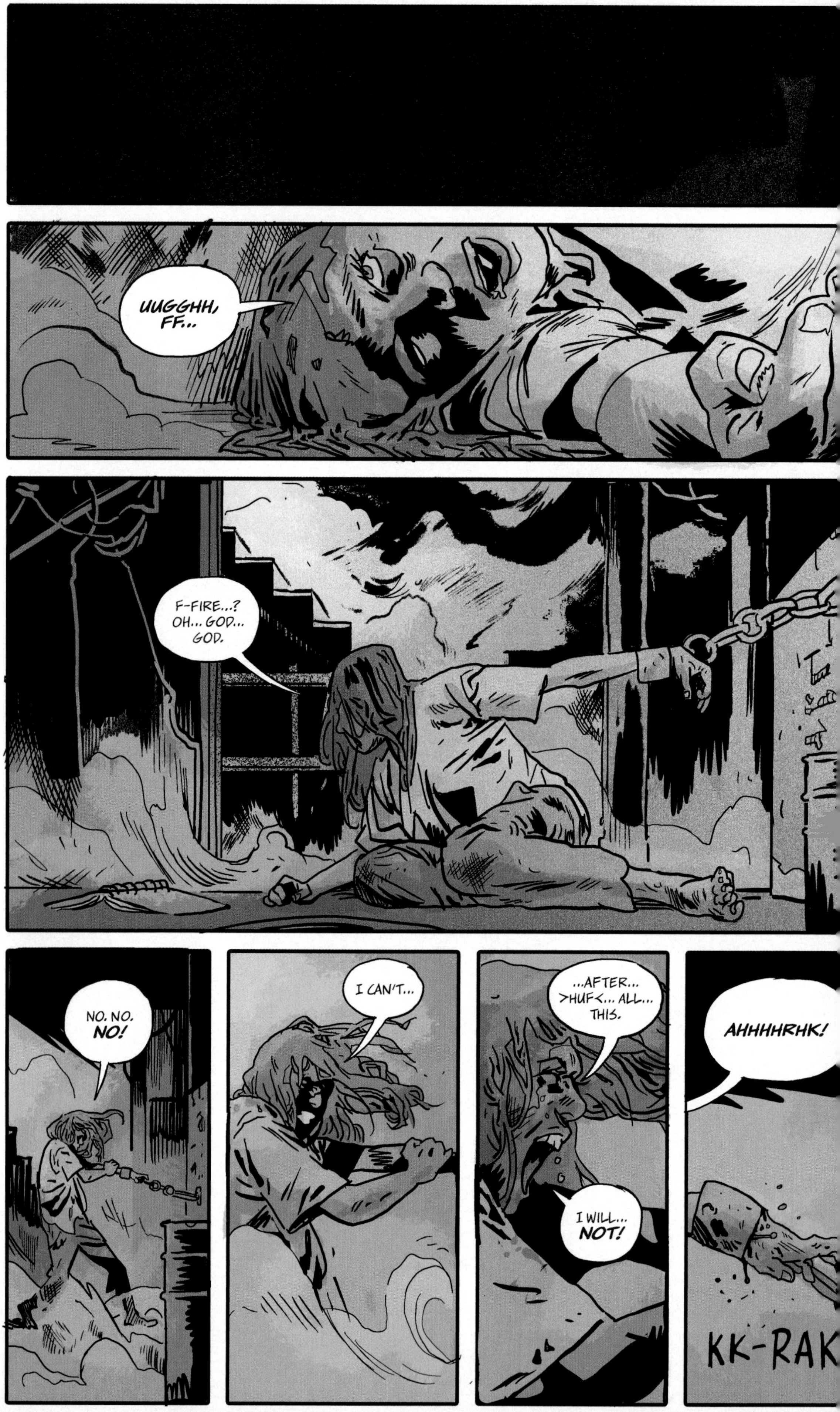
UUGGHH, FF...
F-FIRE...? OH... GOD... GOD.
NO. NO. NO!
I CAN'T...
...AFTER... >HUF<... ALL... THIS.
I WILL... NOT!
AHHHHRHK!
KK-RAK

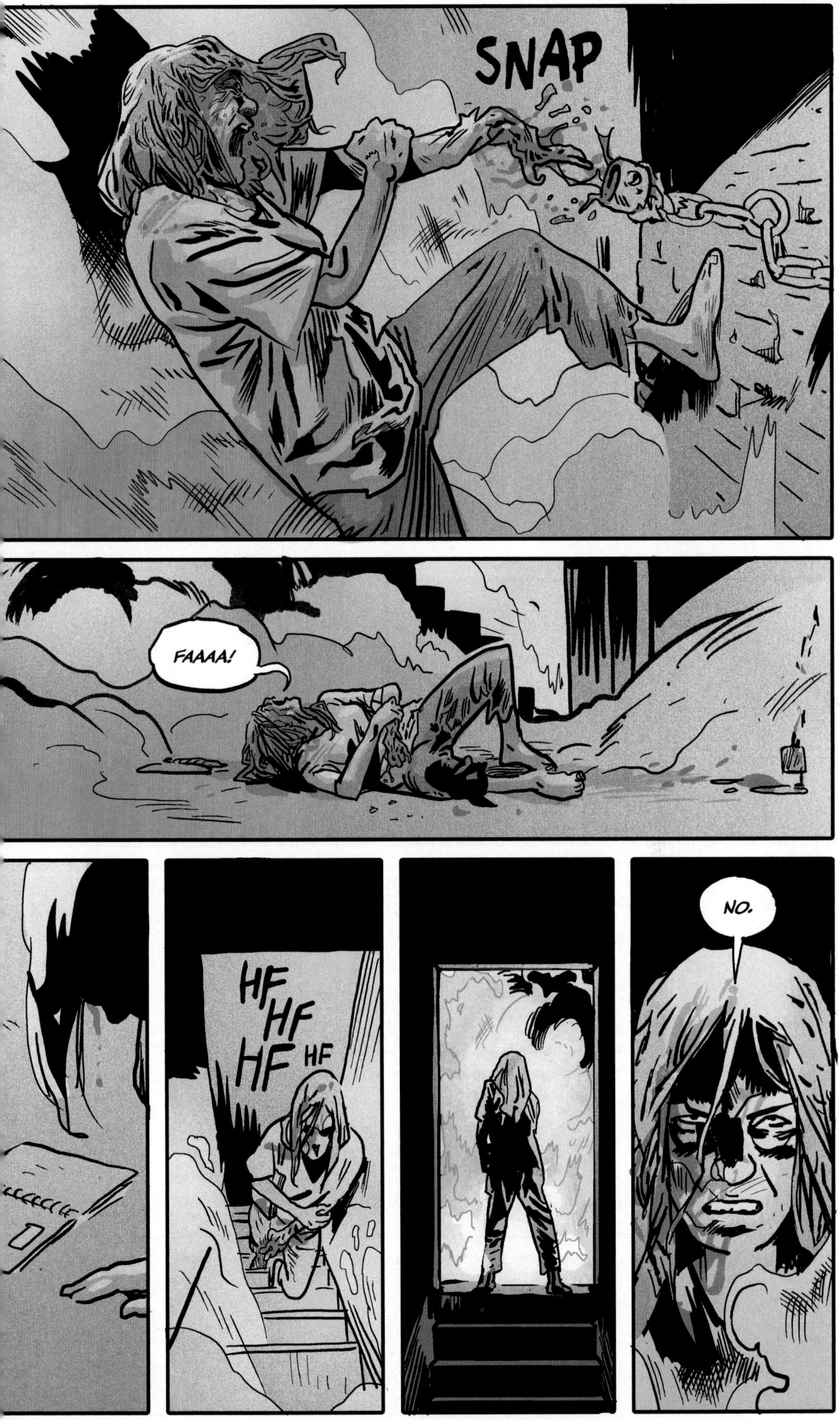
SNAP
FAAAA!
HF HF HF HF
NO.

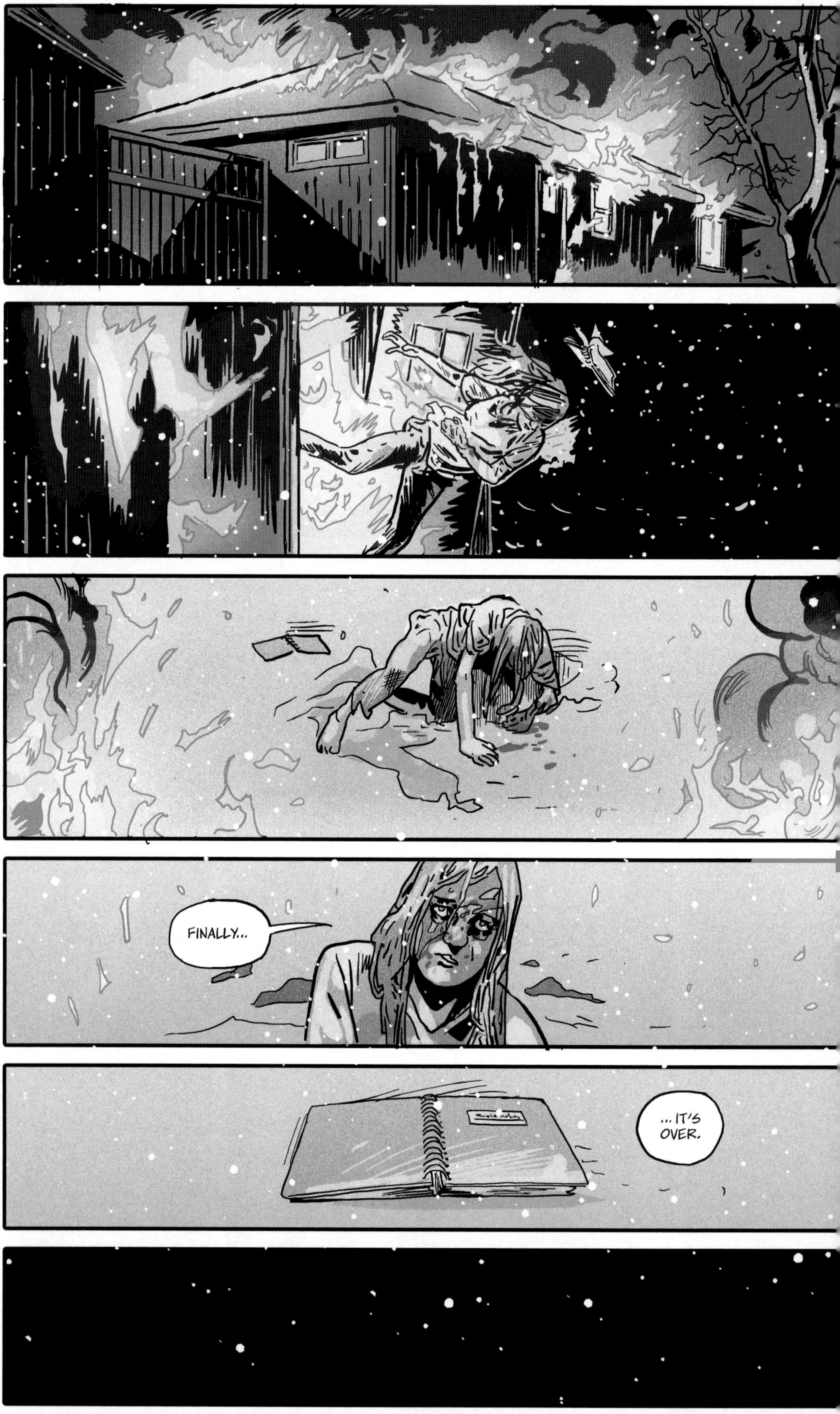
FINALLY...
...IT'S OVER.

Variant Cover Gallery

Issue 11 | Cover B | By Martin Simmonds

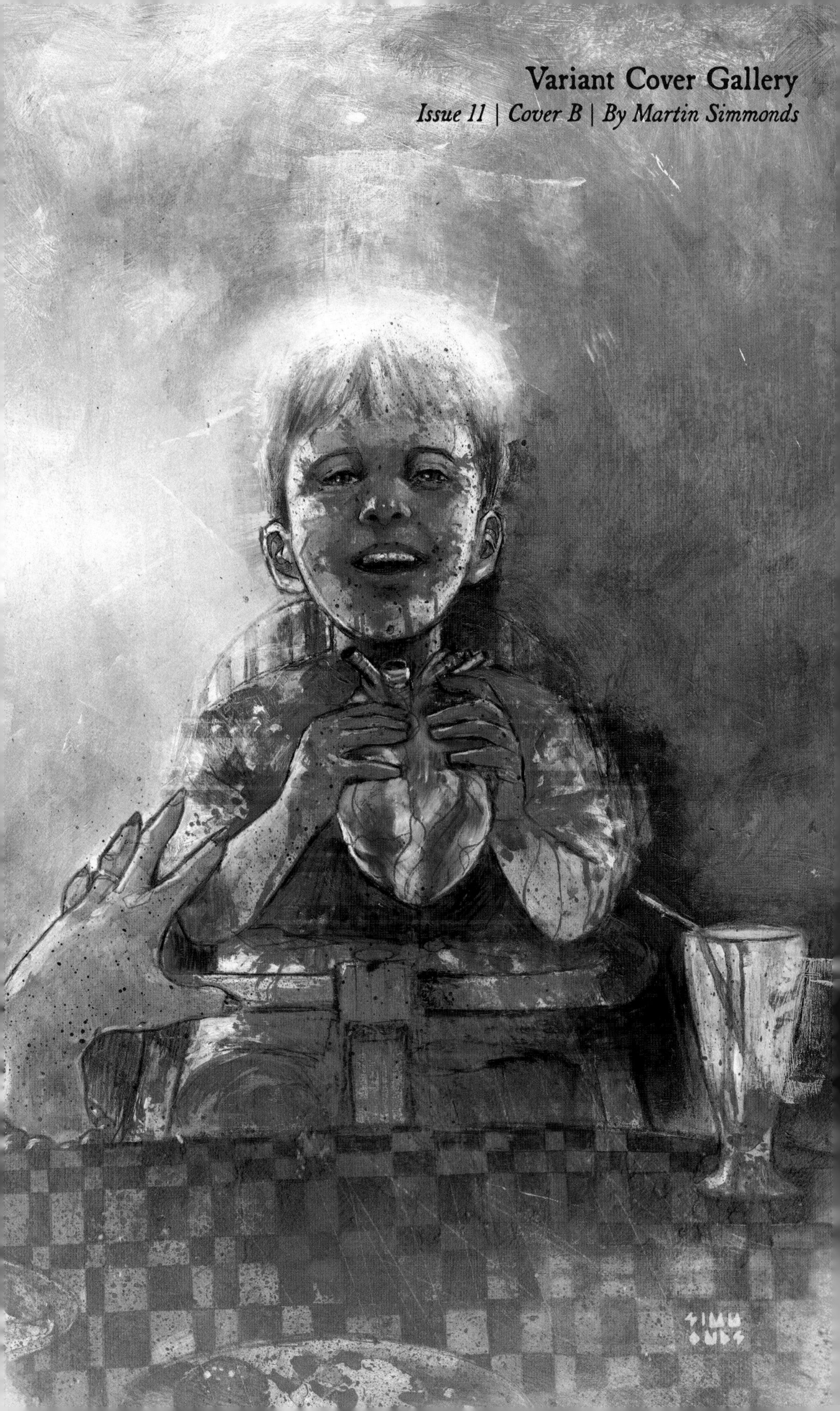

Issue 11 | Cover C | By Adam Gorham

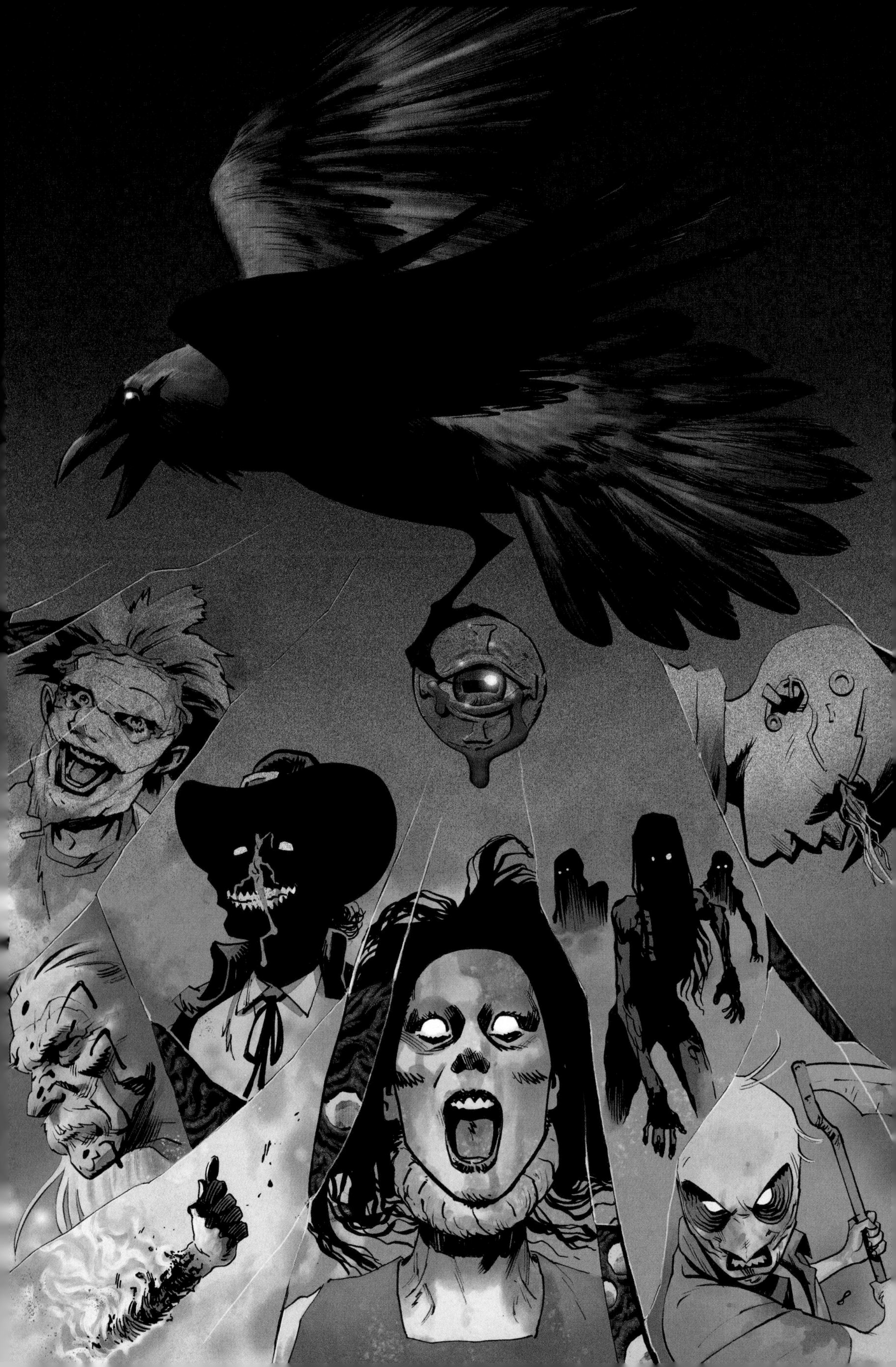

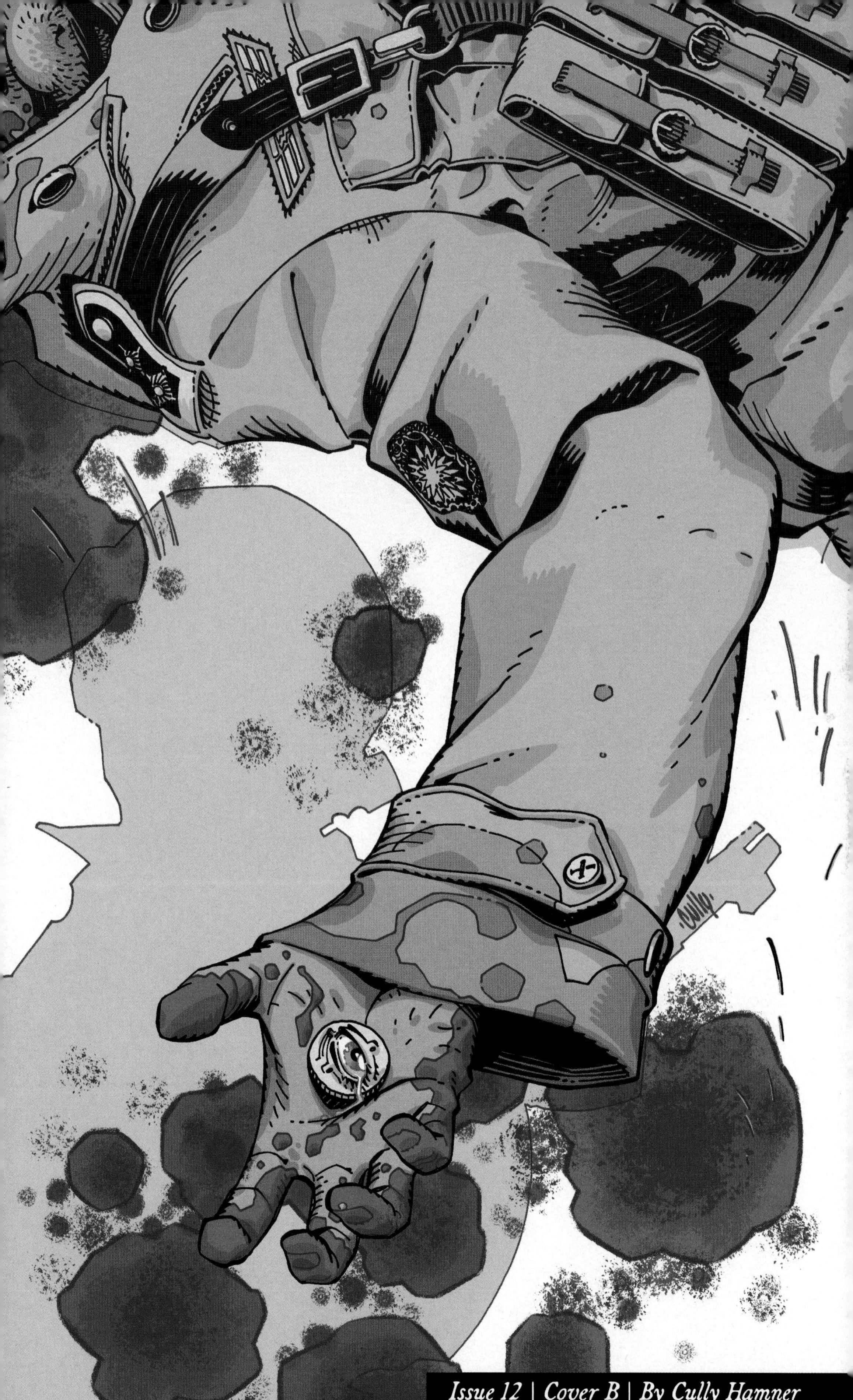

Issue 12 | Cover B | By Cully Hamner

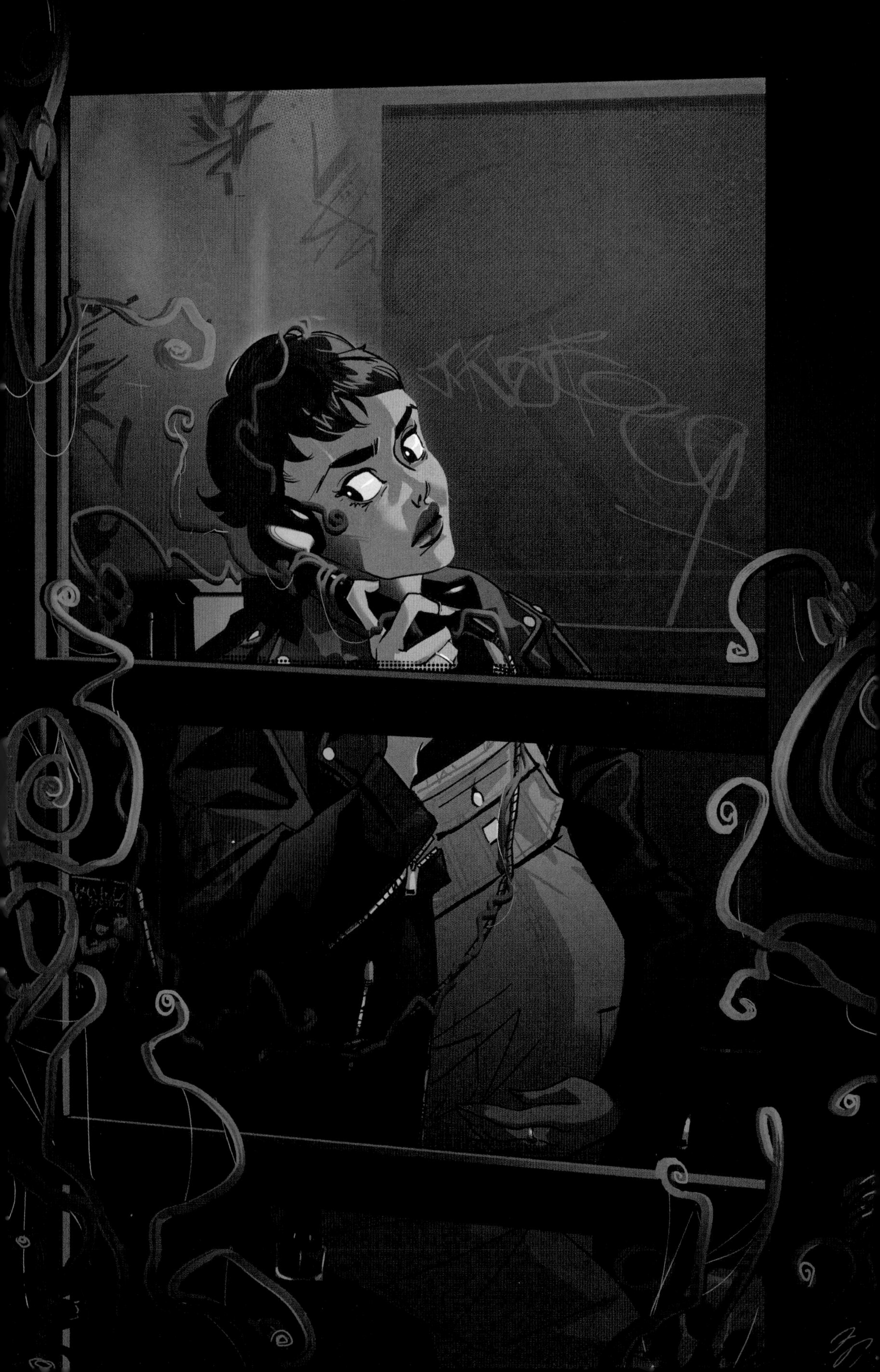

Issue 14 | Cover B | By Caspar Wijngaard

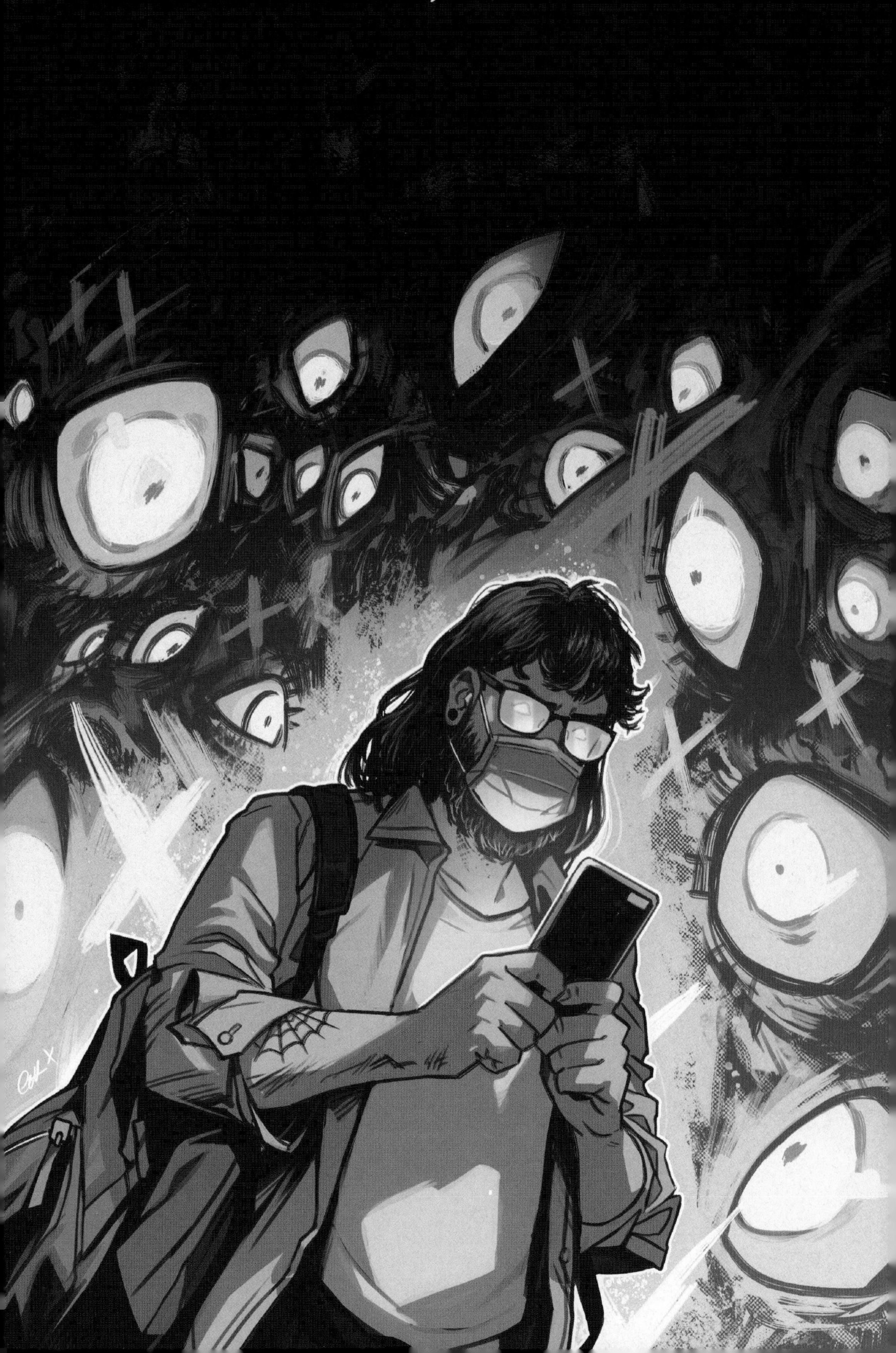

Issue 15 | Cover B | By Anwita Citriya

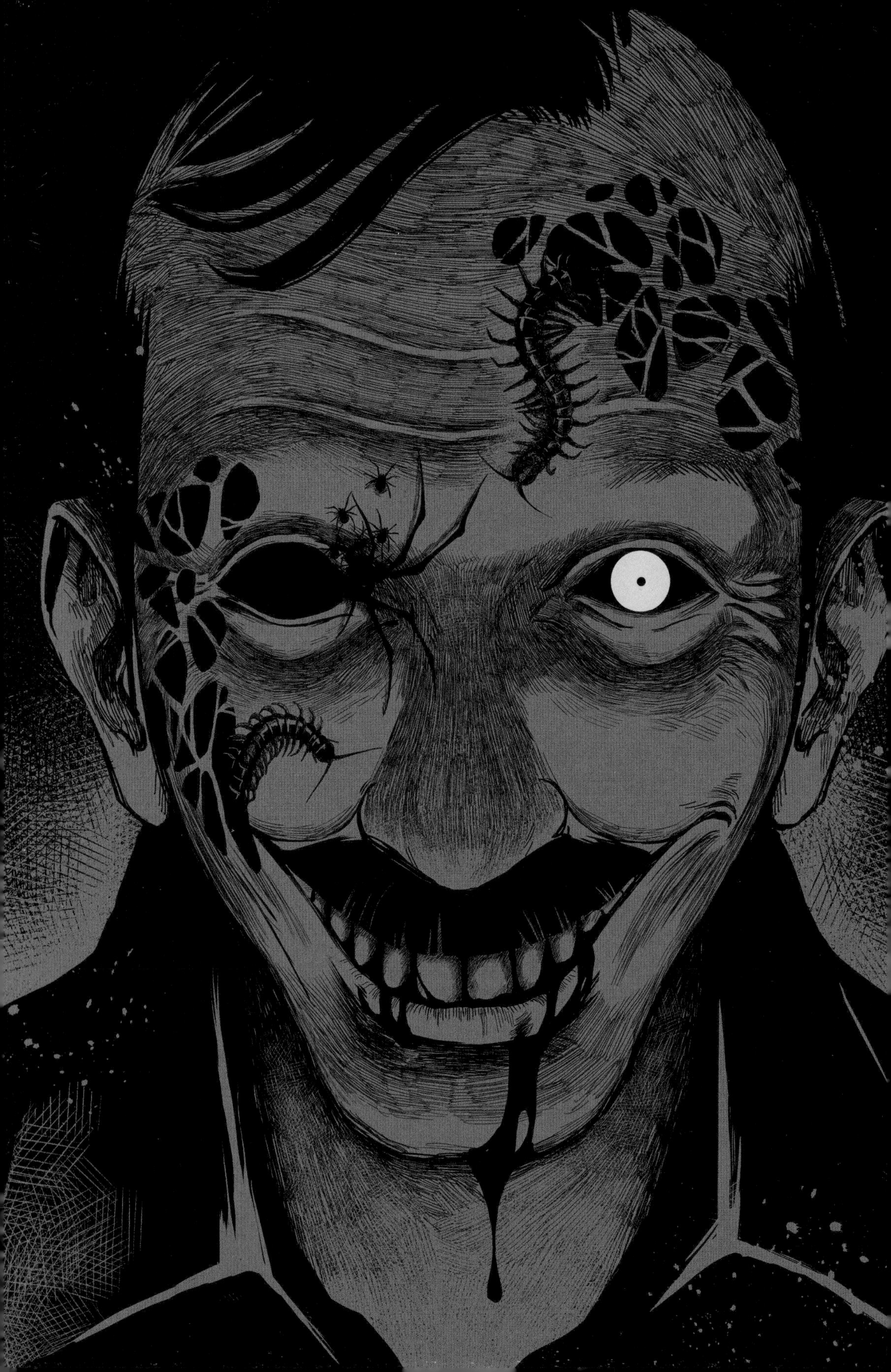